6/98

RACE DISCRIMINATION IN PUBLIC HIGHER EDUCATION

RACE DISCRIMINATION IN PUBLIC HIGHER EDUCATION

Interpreting Federal
Civil Rights Enforcement,
1964–1996

John B. Williams

PRAEGER

Westport, Connecticut
London

Library of Congress Cataloging-in-Publication Data

Williams, John B., 1944–
    Race discrimination in public higher education : interpreting
federal civil rights enforcement, 1964–1996 / John B. Williams.
        p.   cm.
    Includes bibliographical references and index.
    ISBN 0–275–95983–X (alk. paper). — ISBN 0–275–95984–8 (pbk. :
alk. paper)
    1. Discrimination in higher education—United States—
History—20th century. 2. Discrimination in education—Law and
legislation—United States—History—20th century. 3. Public
universities and colleges—United States—History—20th century.
4. Afro-Americans—Education (Higher)—History—20th century.
I. Title.
LC212.42.W55   1997
379.2'63—dc21   97–5595

British Library Cataloguing in Publication Data is available.

Library of Congress Catalog Card Number: 97-5595
ISBN: 0–275–95983–X
        0–275–95984–8 (pbk.)

First published in 1997

Praeger Publishers, 88 Post Road West, Westport, CT 06881
An imprint of Greenwood Publishing Group, Inc.

Printed in the United States of America

The paper used in this book complies with the
Permanent Paper Standard issued by the National
Information Standards Organization (Z39.48–1984).

10 9 8 7 6 5 4 3 2 1

Contents

Acknowledgments

A grant from the Spencer Foundation provided support for the work involved in conducting this study, although the conclusions and interpretations are those of the author. I also gratefully acknowledge the assistance and inspiration of the Collaborative on Systemwide Desegregation of Higher Education whose membership includes the following: Charles Abelmann, Harvard Graduate School of Education; James Anderson, University of Illinois–Champaign/Urbana; Jomills Braddock, University of Miami; Wendy Brown-Scott, Tulane Law School; Sylvia Hurtado, University of Michigan; Heather McCollum, Green Mountain College; Michael Nettles, University of Michigan; Gary Orfield, Harvard University; Ed St. John, University of Dayton; William Trent, University of Illinois–Champaign/Urbana; Marcia Wells-Lawson, Atlanta, Georgia; and David Wilson, Auburn University.

Introduction

Enforcement of federal civil rights laws and policies expanded into the nation's higher education community after the U.S. Supreme Court ruled in 1954 that equal, not separate but equal, education constitutes a right guaranteed under the constitution. New regulatory civil rights laws got passed in the 1960s for the first time, requiring the U.S. Department of Education (previously the Department of Health, Education, and Welfare [HEW]) and the U.S. Justice Department aggressively to monitor college and university systems, determining whether violations routinely were occurring. To liberal lawmakers of the time, legally and practically, it seemed necessary for the federal government to monitor and regulate, in addition to eliminating race segregation laws and processing formal complaints filed with the federal courts and the Office for Civil Rights at HEW by African-American and other aggrieved citizens. This was the case because, in the early 1960s, the practice of denying access to African-Americans and other racial groups was pervasive, insidious, and deeply embedded within the nation's K-12 and higher education communities. Eliminating race discrimination laws did not go far enough.

Thirty years ago, civil rights occupied a high place on the nation's public policy agenda. In addition to expanding the scope of regulatory laws and policies within higher education, federal officials adopted other strategies. Federal student financial aid laws constitute, for example, an incentive approach toward improving college access and choice for low-income and race minority youth, a goal not unrelated to expanding civil rights. However, it is the more aggressive federal regulatory civil rights laws, unlike those adopting incentive strategies, that today have become most unpopular. Beginning in the 1970s and continuing today, U.S. political culture assumed a more conservative, nonegalitarian character. Civil rights declined on the public agenda.

Within higher education, regulatory policies like Executive Order 11246, requiring colleges and universities to take "affirmative action" toward increased employment of race minorities, Title IX of the 1972 Higher Education Amendment, prohibiting discrimination against women, and Title VII of the 1964 Civil Rights Law, prohibiting racial discrimination in employment, almost always have provoked wide expression of deeply felt approval or disapproval. However, today's increasingly vocal and widely persuasive opponents of "affirmative action" or any other form of activist federal policymaking adopt a strident new strategy, threatening to end civil rights enforcement altogether. They suggest that the need for such laws is past: race and gender discrimination has ended, and federal civil rights laws convey unfair advantage to race minority and female students and employees. Some African-American, Asian, Latino, and female political leaders, educators, and intellectuals agree with this view. Milder opponents insist that civil rights regulatory policies do not work, in some instances producing dependence on the part of groups alleged to benefit from them. Government, in the view of many mild postmodern conservatives, inherently lacks capacity to promote many highly desired changes through regulatory policymaking. Adopting the correct incentives, in this way harnessing system dynamics generally associated with the private marketplace, should be employed more widely instead. Such proposals involve, for example, in Georgia in the 1980s, providing public funds to enable the state's relatively small private-sector colleges and universities to enroll race minority students and expanding the public two-year college sector, which allegedly can better provide remedial instruction that many race minority students require.

Some college leaders do not strongly and publicly support civil rights laws that adopt regulatory approaches for less ideological reasons. Many fear excessive government interference. Also, colleges and universities consider themselves "liberal" institutions, this aspect of their self-image having compelled voluntary desegregation prior or simultaneous to passage of federal civil rights laws. Federal civil rights enforcement after the new laws got passed seemed unnecessary and confounding of efforts that many college officials felt were already underway. Even in earlier times, when overwhelmingly liberal students and faculty actively approved federal civil rights policymaking, college and university leaders were circumspect in support for such laws. For those who support civil rights goals, it simply is easier to recruit race minority students and faculty quietly and voluntarily without promoting or sustaining a potentially disruptive civil rights campus dialogue.

Though civil rights regulatory laws and policies are, today, viewed with deepening skepticism, some aspects of them clearly and strongly affect important areas of college and university leadership, management, and decision making. Many have introduced permanent changes in higher education administration. For example, Executive Order 11242 requires colleges and universities to take affirmative action aimed at increasing employment of women and race minorities in areas of work where so-called underutilization occurs. Most stakeholders, however, incorrectly interpret this federal civil rights policy to mandate undertaking formal job searches whenever a major position becomes available. The subtle and inadvertent impact of the order involves making job searches a permanent aspect of the employment process within higher education. The unresearched but widely reported anecdotal impact of Executive Order 11242 is undeniable: What college or university decision maker does not today at least consider conducting a "search" to fill an important job vacancy? How many colleges and universities prior to passage of federal civil rights laws did not feel compelled to do so, particularly for faculty hiring? More compellingly, what admissions officer is today unaware of the March 18, 1996, *Texas v. Hopwood* (1996) court case, which prohibits the use of race as a factor in reaching college admissions decisions? Job searches and admissions criteria do not guarantee equal protection, but they do constitute a change in normal college and university operating procedures and, at one level, make it marginally more difficult for officials to engage in racially discriminatory practices.

However, some regulatory civil rights policies affecting higher education are not conducted in subtle ways. Reasons for overlooking their impact are different. Among the most broadly focused is Title VI of the 1964 Civil Rights Law. Title VI prohibits schools, colleges, and other institutions and agencies that discriminate on the basis of race from receiving federal funds. In addition to establishing constraints and providing a legal outlet for filing complaints, Title VI, coupled with Title IV of the 1964 law, empowers the U.S. Attorney General to investigate primary and secondary school districts and college and university systems, prosecuting those engaged in racial segregation. The effectiveness and scope of the school desegregation movement of the late 1960s and 1970s in large measure reflect the strong authority of these two statutes. This aspect of

Title VI enforcement, applied to public higher education, involves the Office for Civil Rights at the U.S. Office of Education and the U.S. Justice Department monitoring public college and university systems in states that, prior to 1954, operated separate but equal laws and policies.

Nineteen states fall into this category, rendering systemwide monitoring, as a form of federal civil rights enforcement, overwhelmingly complicated. Each of the 19 state systems is a complex, diffusely organized network of several relatively independent junior colleges, four-year institutions, and universities. Systemwide and campus-level governance differs from state to state, and civil rights problems assume different configurations from one institution to another within the same system and from one system to another. As later described, during the 1970s, systemwide Title VI compliance in an added bit of drama involved the Washington, D.C., federal district court monitoring HEW, making sure that the federal executive branch took seriously its responsibility to monitor several state higher education systems consisting of numerous four-year colleges, universities, and two-year colleges that enrolled over 63 percent of all African-American students at the time enrolled in higher education.

Stakeholders in states undergoing systemwide Title VI enforcement today strongly question the actual and potential effectiveness of civil rights policymaking because, simply stated, over the past 25 years, African-American enrollment and employment did not increase consistently or improve substantially in most of the 19 states regulated by federal officials. Changes in many important areas took place, but reverses also have taken place, no steady progress is apparent, and connections between government action and positive changes are uncertain. Moreover, civil rights discourse, informed by court decisions in the 1970s and 1980s, widely affirms that federal and state government officials have not properly conducted enforcement.

Such conclusions are widespread, though no national study of systemwide Title VI enforcement has been undertaken. The handful of studies and reports, in limited ways attempting to describe the impact of systemwide Title VI enforcement, virtually all support both conclusions of failure and of inadequate government conduct (U.S. Commission on Civil Rights, 1981; Williams, 1988; Committee on Education and Labor, U.S. House of Representatives, 1988; Committee on Government Operations, U.S. House of Representatives, 1987; Orfield, 1990; Blackwell, undated). It is tempting and convenient for some stakeholders to extend these judgments, concluding that government can never conduct civil rights enforcement properly and strongly enough to produce desired outcomes. To some critics, the planned outcome of federal enforcement, namely, "free student choice," is unattainable, because factors determining student choice cannot be controlled by government: "The federal government could be extremely active, and the states most cooperative, *yet policy success in eliminating racially identifiable campuses could still remain elusive because student choice is affected by so many factors that are not easily manipulated by federal and state officials*" (Ayres, 1984; p. 128).

This problem raises a broader issue of establishing the proper interpretation of federal and state civil rights enforcement aimed toward higher education. Although it may be reasonably certain that systemwide enforcement has, in many ways, failed, it is unclear why this outcome prevails. Is it the case, as Ayres has argued, that independent factors compromised federal attempts to accomplish free choice? Disagreeing with Ayres, in the court's judgment, state officials did not design remedies strongly suited to produce results and failed to implement weak remedies they designed, and federal officials did not compel state systems to design and implement decent remedies. Reaching the correct interpretive judgment about systemwide Title VI enforcement constitutes the purpose of this study.

This task is not as easy as it may seem. It is convincingly possible to interpret existing evidence in both ways — as proof of inevitable failure, along the lines of the Ayres statement, or of failed implementation, adopting the view of the courts. Formal research does not contribute an independent interpretation. Existing studies and personal testimony document the existence of traditional policy barriers to implementation, such as lack of sufficient support by African-American stakeholders, absence of clear goals, and weak monitoring. However, not included in these sources, absent from public record and, therefore, from the broader civil rights dialogue, are descriptions and interpretations of state and federal officials' actual responses to civil rights requirements that may or may not have been overriden by student choice factors, which, in the court's view, were misguided and poorly undertaken and, in the view of researchers, indicated absence of necessary policy resources.

Before expanding this observation, it should be acknowledged that, though few studies of systemwide civil rights enforcement as a federal and state government policy have been undertaken, volumes of studies document underrepresentation of race minorities within the nation's higher education community, including in states affected by Title VI monitoring. Also, many studies of this kind identify factors, such as poor high-school preparation, associated with low race minority student college access and retention. Failing to identify civil rights enforcement as a government policy, the large volume of studies, in general ways addressing the nation's race inequity problem in higher education, virtually ignore varying direct and background effects of regulatory civil rights laws. The unstated assumption may be that all forms of purposeful and inadvertent race discrimination underlying passage of such laws have been eliminated — therefore, they exert little impact. Recognizing the potential or real impact of such laws also acknowledges prior discrimination, but admitting prior discrimination sets the stage for federal intervention. A major, consistent finding of the accumulated body of policy research on higher education access and retention is that race, when other factors are controlled, does not substantially account for differences in student access and retention rates. This finding, bolstered by widely unstated, modernist assumptions about race assimilation, perhaps also accounts for researchers' failure to incorporate within study designs the sometimes subtle impact of government civil rights policymaking. At another level, regulatory civil rights policies, as suggested earlier, may operate subtly as a constraint upon higher education officials, a phenomenon difficult for researchers to conceptualize, observe, and measure.

Studies of civil rights enforcement involving government regulatory strategies will benefit from existing research on the broader phenomenon of race inequity in higher education. However, enforcement policy analysis first must contribute improved interpretations of government responses to civil rights regulatory responsibilities — goal interpretations, assumptions, implementation, leadership, and problems over the past 25 years. Current civil rights discourse narrowly seeks to determine whether numerical indicators — for example, increased African-American enrollment at traditionally white institutions, increased African-American employment, and increased assignment of new instructional programs at traditionally black institutions — suggest successful completion of planned remedies. If the indicators do not show progress, reasons get offered, leading to the kind of evidence described previously.

However, the complete story of enforcement involves both planned and informal, "unofficial" responses. Whether numerical enrollment goals got reached does not depend only upon faithfully and unfaithfully undertaking planned actions logically designed to accomplish them. Unplanned responses also help determine who gets what, when, and how. What planned and unplanned responses to civil rights enforcement contributed widely known results? What patterns did such responses take? Is it reasonable to expect that observable response patterns may have exerted a strong influence upon results obtained? Answers to such questions

provide a fuller portrayal of what took place to produce widely acknowledged outcomes.

Expanded knowledge about the dynamic aspects of failed Title VI
enforcement, based upon closer examination and more careful interpretation of stakeholder responses, is useful at the policy level, in this writer's
view, for improved planning, assessment, and problem solving. A fuller
portrayal of civil rights policymaking will challenge the spreading political judgment that federal policymaking of all types is inevitably unsuc-
cessful. Civil rights discourse today fails to offer such a challenge. A
recent speech by Republican presidential candidate Robert Dole exemplifies such widely accepted judgments: "It is time," he insisted, "to
unshackle the U.S. economy from the big government ball and chain and
go for the gold" (*Boston Globe*, 1996, p. 1). Dole campaigned for the pres-
idency in Boston during the time of the Atlanta Olympics, it is clear from
his speech. It should be noted that he and his contemporaries demonstrate
dissimilar affinity for regulating TV to prevent youth violence and similar
crusades. The problem then must involve when to regulate and whom
(Younis, 1990).

In general, neoconservative politicians like the former senator believe
that civil rights and other regulatory policies infringe upon the rights of
the regulated. According to U.S. House of Representatives Speaker Newt
Gingrich, "We should deal with each individual American in a unique
way. We should have affirmative action to help individuals based on individual need and individual accomplishment, but we should not have
genetic groupings" (Chafe, 1995). Interpreting Gingrich's view,

Of . . . interest is what Mr. Gingrich's logic implies about social change and the
government's responsibility to guarantee "equal protection." According to the
Speaker's reasoning, if discrimination based on membership in a racial group has
been the source of bias in the past, all one has to do is to pass a law banning such
discrimination. Immediately thereafter, presumably, people cease to be members
of the groups and instead become individuals, able to fend for themselves in a
competition based upon merit. By implication, the law makes their "group" identity evaporate overnight, along with all that once accompanied it. And since
members of the groups are now only individuals, government bears no particular
responsibility for protecting the group *per se*, or for insuring that its individual
members have an "equal start." . . . The problem is that life does not work that
way. (Chafe, 1995)

Displaying the way life actually works, and modestly challenging
Gingrich in the process, this study attempts to interpret more adequately

information about how systemwide civil rights enforcement has occurred within the higher education community. Do the details suggest a failed attempt because of inadequate effort or a good faith effort that leaves problems that African-American individuals must themselves resolve through equal competition with others? To accomplish this goal, the study incorporates a view missing from the current civil rights dialogue — that enforcement is a changing, interactive policy process begun when Congress passed the 1964 Civil Rights Law. The Title VI policy process entails important stakeholders taking actions and adopting "responses" to its passage and to responses by other stakeholders. Stakeholder responses do not all acknowledge goals and adopt action logically related to their accomplishment. Stakeholder responses outside the planned structure of formal enforcement affect the structure, in this way producing or influencing impacts. Unplanned stakeholder responses affect outcomes by influencing three important elements of the formally structured enforcement process — official interpretations of Title VI requirements, formulated remedies, and planned implementation.

Over the years, planned and unplanned civil rights responses have risen and fallen in intensity. As civil rights problems in higher education move up and down the nation's public policy agenda, formal federal and state enforcement responses fluctuate. The task at hand involves differentiating and interpreting informal stakeholder "responses" between 1969 and 1996 that occurred under circumstances of fluctuating formal enforcement.

The findings of this study do not challenge the overall judgment of failure surrounding Title VI in public higher education. On the contrary, the information provided suggests a fuller interpretation of failure. Deep understanding of past and current Title VI enforcement has not characterized Title VI policy dialogue over the past 30 years. Richer dialogue will not independently eliminate the problem of race minority underrepresentation, but effective policymaking, involving continuous and insightful dialogue, does constitute an important step in the right direction. It facilitates an important stage in the process of achieving compliance.

With this goal in mind, Chapter 1 chronicles important aspects of formal and informal federal — HEW and the Office for Civil Rights — responses, taking the form of interpretations of regulations and policy formulation and implementation during the period 1970–1990. It presents responses chronologically, establishing continuity. Relying upon enforcement documents — desegregation plans, compliance reports, and letters of finding — Chapter 2 describes, classifies, and analyzes state responses to federal enforcement. Because formal and informal stakeholder responses in all 19 states cannot be presented in a single volume, the second chapter portrays, classifies, and analyzes those of elected officials, government civil rights regulators, and public higher education leaders in the State of Georgia during the period 1981–1989. Adopting a similar outline, Chapter 3 describes recent Title VI enforcement in Mississippi during the period 1992–1996 after a key Supreme Court decision renewed systemwide federal intervention through the court system. The Mississippi plan and local responses to its development brought about through court litigation are portrayed, and patterns of policy planning and implementation are displayed. Chapter 4, looking at the present, analyzes and compares the Louisiana and Alabama court-ordered desegregation plans that were approved after the Supreme Court's *United States v. Fordice* (1992) ruling. The last chapter summarizes findings from the previous chapters, suggests how this information together expands understanding of enforcement, and recommends ways to expand and improve civil rights discourse using the new input.

The Appendix presents important demographic characteristics of the four state higher education systems included in this study, for example, student enrollment by race, number of institutions, and size and racial distribution of faculty. Background information of this kind is important for understanding the character, complexity, and scope of earlier analyzed civil rights enforcement. Table A.1 portrays demographic characteristics of the Alabama system, Table A.2 provides data describing the Georgia system, Table A.3 outlines important aspects of the Louisiana system, and Table A.4 presents characteristics of the Mississippi system. Data in Table A.4 supplement, but may also differ slightly from, similar Mississippi information in Chapter 3 because two different data sources were utilized.

Over the past 20 years, I have attended countless seminars, planning sessions, court sessions, and conferences on "higher education desegregation," "civil rights enforcement," "*Adams v. Richardson*" (1973)–related civil rights court cases, and "equal educational opportunity." I am usually, but at times needlessly, reminded that race inequity as a problem persists. I also leave convinced that little old or new information got communicated; that even supporters of civil rights policymaking continue to disagree with one another as a means of protecting their turf; that few present have seriously considered the risks involved in strongly addressing the problem; and that understanding of public policymaking ranges among participants from too deeply engrossed in details of bureaucratic structure to too loosely acquainted with how anything takes place in Washington and state capitals. My disillusionment dims in comparison to that of college leaders, government regulators, and students who directly encounter and earnestly confront race inequity problems in Title VI states on a day-to-day basis. The following study of civil rights enforcement grows out of their frustration.

REFERENCES

Adams v. Richardson, 356 F. Supp. 92 (D.D.C. 1973).

Ayres, Q. Whitfield. 1984. "Racial Desegregation in Higher Education." In *Implementation of Civil Rights Policy*, edited by Charles S. Bullock III and Charles M. Lamb, pp. 118–147. Monterey, Calif.: Brooks/Cole.

Blackwell, James. undated. "Desegregation of the Higher Education System in Georgia: A Critique." Workshop Paper, Southern Education Foundation, Atlanta, Ga. Mimeographed.

Boston Globe, August 8, 1996, p. 1.

Chafe, William H. 1995. "Providing Guarantees of Equal Opportunity." *Chronicle of Higher Education,* June 30, 1995, pp. B1–B2.

Committee on Education and Labor, U.S. House of Representatives. 1988. *A Report on the Investigation of the Civil Rights Enforcement Activities of the Office for Civil Rights*. Washington, D.C.: U.S. Government Printing Office.

Committee on Government Operations, U.S. House of Representatives. 1987. *Failure and Fraud in Civil Rights Enforcement by the Department of Education*. Washington D.C.: U.S. Government Printing Office.

Orfield, Gary. 1990. *The Reagan Administration's Abandonment of Civil Rights Enforcement in Higher Education*. Washington, D.C.: Joint Center for Political and Economic Studies.

Texas v. Hopwood, 78 F. 3D 932 (1996).

U.S. Commission on Civil Rights. 1981. *The Black/White Colleges: Dismantling the Dual System of Higher Education*. Washington, D.C.: U.S. Commission on Civil Rights.

United States v. Fordice, 112 S. Ct. 2727 (1992).

Williams, John B., ed. 1988. *Desegregating America's Colleges and Universities*. New York: Teachers College Press.

Younis, Talib, ed. 1990. *Implementing Public Policy*. Brookfield, Vt.: Government Publishing Co.

1

Federal Aspects of Civil Rights Enforcement in Higher Education, 1970–1990

Title VI of the 1964 Civil Rights Law, which prohibits discrimination on the basis of race, color, or national origin in any program or activity receiving federal financial assistance, empowered the U.S. Department of Health, Education, and Welfare and the Department of Justice, independent of the courts, to monitor, to negotiate, and to litigate against school districts engaged in segregation. Title VI enforcement within higher education translates into several different forms of policymaking and implementation. Most important, perhaps, the law provides legal avenues and mechanisms for individuals or groups of students, employees, and private citizens to file discrimination complaints against a college or university. Also important, Title VI requires systemwide auditing of public colleges and universities in states that, in the past, operated race segregation laws. The assistant secretary for civil rights and the director of the Office for Civil Rights (OCR) at the Department of Education hold major responsibility for enforcing Title VI through system monitoring. Federal enforcement, adopting systemwide regulatory approaches within public higher education in previously segregated states, has taken place over the past 30 years.

In an attempt to understand what has taken place, this chapter describes important aspects of the federal effort to desegregate public college and university systems between 1970 and 1990. Material in this chapter conveys, in a narrative format, interpretations of Title VI problems and compliance requirements and policy implementation by federal civil rights officials. In keeping with the overall theoretical approach of this study, interpretive and implementation "responses" characterize, from a broad federal perspective, Title VI enforcement over the past three decades.

EARLY STAGES OF ENFORCEMENT

Based upon reviews of demographic data and site visits, Leon Panetta, then OCR director, in 1969 and 1970 sent letters to the governors of ten states informing them that their public systems of higher education violated Title VI and, therefore, ran the risk of losing federal funds. The letters of finding described desegregation problems in the ten state systems and requested formal plans for addressing them (*Adams v. Richardson*, 1973).

At the time Panetta sent the first letters, case law on public K–12 school district desegregation was emerging and evolving, but federal executive branch officials interpreted and applied the new civil rights law within higher education for the first time. Judged by the information included in the OCR letters, the office's operant standards for judging the existence of segregation under Title VI were unsurprisingly uncomplicated but inconsistently applied. Some letters of findings emphasized persistently low black enrollments at traditionally white institutions (TWIs), and others cited disproportionately high African-American enrollments at traditionally African-American institutions, even though both problems existed in all ten states. Panetta's December 2, 1969, letter to then-Governor Mills E. Godwin of the Commonwealth of Virginia typifies the early OCR letters, describing some of the evidence leading to OCR's determination of unlawful segregation:

December 2, 1969

Honorable Mills E. Godwin
Governor of Virginia
Richmond, VA 23219

Dear Governor Godwin:

The Office for Civil Rights of the Department of Health, Education, and Welfare has required that all institutions of higher education receiving Federal financial assistance submit a compliance report indicating the racial enrollment at these institutions. Based on these reports, particular colleges are visited to determine their compliance with Title VI of the Civil Rights Acts of 1964. These visits, together with the reports received from the four-year State colleges and universities in Virginia, indicate that the State of Virginia is operating a non-unitary system of higher education.

Specifically, the predominantly white State institutions providing four or more years of higher education have an enrollment which is approximately 99 percent white. The predominantly black institutions have an enrollment which is predominantly black in similar proportions. In addition to this situation which prevails in individual institutions throughout the State, the two land grant colleges, Virginia Polytechnic Institute and Virginia State College, originally devised as separate agricultural and technical colleges, one for blacks and one for whites, remain structurally separate and predominantly of one race, the latter black and the former white. Another manifestation of the State's racially dual system of higher education is evident in the City of Norfolk in which are situated two large institutions, predominantly white Old Dominion University and predominantly black Norfolk State, the enrollment of which is 98 percent Negro.

Educational institutions which have previously been legally segregated have an affirmative duty to adopt measures to overcome the effect of the past segregation. To fulfill the purposes and intent of the Civil Rights Act of 1964, it is not sufficient that an institution maintain a nondiscriminatory admissions policy if the student population continues to reflect the formerly de jure racial identification of that institution.

This appears to be the situation at nearly all of the State institutions in Virginia, therefore, these institutions must discharge their affirmative duty by adopting measures that will result in desegregation as soon as administratively possible.

We are aware that the scope of authority of each individual institution is not broad enough to effect the necessary changes and achieve the desired objectives. However, this legal disability does not relieve responsible State officials of the duty to make whatever cooperative arrangements are needed to continue the eligibility of the institutions for Federal financial assistance. Accordingly, I am directing to you the request that a desegregation plan for the public institutions of higher education in Virginia which are under State control be submitted for comment to this office in outline form 120 days from receipt of this letter, and that a final desegregation plan be submitted for our approval no later than 90 days after you have received comments on the outline of the plan.

While I do not wish to stipulate the form which a desegregation plan should take, I would suggest that a system-wide plan of cooperation between institutions involving consolidation of degree offerings, faculty exchange, student exchange, and general institutional sharing of resources would seem to offer a constructive approach. The Southern Regional Education Board, established by the Governors of the Southern and Border States, has available the programs and the results of inter-institutional cooperation and no doubt the Board would be willing to work with you, members of your staff, the State college presidents, and other Virginia State education officials in order to formulate an appropriate plan. In addition, officials of the Bureau of Higher Education in Washington and the Regional Office of Education have had considerable experience in this area, and these officials would be available to assist appropriate State education officials.

Needless to say, our staff will be available to offer whatever services may be appropriate. Dr. Eloise Severinson, Regional Civil Rights Director, Office for Civil Rights, Department of Health, Education and Welfare, 220 Seventh Street, N.E. Charlottesville, Virginia 22901, would be the person to contact for any information and assistance.

We look forward to working with you to bring about a desegregated system of State higher education in Virginia.

Sincerely yours,
Leon E. Panetta
Director, Office for Civil Rights

Legal precedents from K–12 court cases apparent in Panetta's formulation of the problem and of responsibility for addressing it include requiring affirmative action beyond simply repealing segregation laws and policies. By 1969, it was clear to federal school desegregation enforcers that local school districts would simply repeal laws, ignoring strong evidence of continued de facto K–12 segregation if allowed to do so. However, the *Green v. County Board* (1968) case made clear school district responsibility to move beyond simply eliminating laws toward remedying the lingering effects of prior segregation. Panetta also emphasized the importance of both systemwide and college-by-college remedies, reflective of another problem the federal courts early encountered in desegregating K–12 systems.

Judged by the 1969–1970 letters, OCR's initial approach characterized the problem as the existence within each state of two separate sets of racially defined institutions. Exhibiting what today might be considered a naive approach, Panetta suggests remedial actions like "exchanges" and "coordinated efforts" to move faculty, students, and college resources reciprocally between white and African-American institutions. As indicated earlier, the 1969 letter puts the governor on notice that simply doing away with segregation laws without taking action to eliminate the racial identity of the various institutions is insufficient. (Interestingly, the state of Mississippi, the U.S. District Court of Northern Mississippi, and the Fifth Circuit Court more than 20 years later approved the argument that removing the laws was, alone, sufficient to meet Title VI and constitutional requirements.) The letter also acknowledges the problem of local college and university autonomy but specifies the need, nonetheless, for a systemwide plan that Virginia officials should design.

The second aspect of early enforcement involved states' submitting "desegregation plans" to OCR for approval. Mirroring the response of public school districts, state higher education officials' responses to Panetta's letters were not enthusiastic. However, Pennsylvania, Maryland, Georgia, and Arkansas joined Virginia in submitting plans that the Department of Health, Education, and Welfare (HEW) subsequently ruled unacceptable. Florida, Louisiana, Mississippi, North Carolina, and Oklahoma simply declined the opportunity to submit anything. In correspondence with OCR, state officials complained or strongly implied that federal expectations were unclear, that civil rights was not a clear state priority, and that federal authority was suspect (*Adams v. Califano*, 1977).

It is interesting that the letters got mailed in 1969 at the end of liberal federal leadership by Democratic party presidents that emphasized civil rights enforcement. Another set of letters emerged in 1979 at the end of another period of President Jimmy Carter's more liberal Democratic presidential leadership. Presidential campaigns and elections took place in both years, and Republican party candidates Richard Nixon and Ronald Reagan, the eventual winners, both campaigned strongly against school desegregation and other forms of civil rights enforcement. In 1970, when Nixon took office, perhaps not surprisingly, HEW stopped pressuring guilty states to submit new plans or to revise unacceptable ones (*Adams v. Richardson*, 1973). Upon election, President Nixon inaugurated a new policy of nonenforcement of federal civil rights laws and policies throughout government. Indicatively, action against primary and secondary school districts also declined. Between 1964 and 1970, HEW initiated about 600 compliance proceedings against local public school districts that refused to comply with Title VI desegregation requirements. About 100 enforcement proceedings materialized in 1968 and 1969, but during the first year of the Nixon administration, OCR initiated no enforcement proceedings (*Adams v. Richardson*, 1973).

The third important element of Title VI history consists of strong oppositional responses within the nation's civil rights community against Nixon's nonenforcement policy. Chief among this opposition, the

National Association for the Advancement of Colored People (NAACP) Legal Defense Fund (LDF) inaugurated a class action suit aimed at eliciting a change. LDF is famous for having successfully spearheaded primary and secondary school desegregation cases, including the *Brown v. Board of Education* (1954) decision, throughout the country. Like *Brown*, *Adams v. Richardson* (1973) delivered effects throughout education, forcing HEW officials, where higher education is concerned, to respond to the desegregation plans that had been received two to three years earlier, to institute enforcement proceedings where necessary, to monitor progress, and to conduct additional compliance reviews in other states.

Judge John Pratt of the U.S. District Court of the District of Columbia, ruling in favor of LDF's plaintiffs, held that "continuation of HEW financial assistance to the segregated systems of higher education in the ten states violated the rights of plaintiffs and others similarly situated and protected by Title VI of the Civil Rights Act of 1964" (*Adams v. Richardson*, 1973). He then ordered HEW within 120 days to begin enforcement proceedings against states that failed to comply. HEW appealed Pratt's decision, but the U.S. Second Circuit Court affirmed his ruling, allowing an additional 180 days after the submission of a state's desegregation plans for enforcement proceedings to begin (*Adams v. Richardson*, 1973).

Faced with a decisive 1973 Second Circuit Court ruling, Republican party officials cautiously renewed enforcement. HEW's OCR director organized the next important episode of the 1970s. He notified the ten states previously contacted in 1969 to submit new desegregation plans, and, by June 1974, eight of the ten had done so and obtained HEW approval. Louisiana again refused to submit a plan, and Mississippi's was deemed unacceptable. By adopting this approach, higher education in these two states effectively postponed federal intervention for several years. Both were referred to the Justice Department, which, in 1975, initiated litigation in federal district courts in Mississippi and Louisiana (*United States v. Louisiana*, 1981; *United States v. Finch*, 1981). Because a private desegregation suit was pending in Mississippi, the district courts asked the Justice Department to desist and join with Mississippi plaintiffs (*Adams v. Califano*, 1977). Through legal maneuvering and lack of sustained Justice Department attention, parties to litigation reached no final settlement in Louisiana until 1981 and none until 1992 in Mississippi. A more detailed description of litigation in Mississippi and Louisiana appears in Chapters 3 and 4.

FEDERAL DESEGREGATION GUIDELINES EMERGE

Combined outside pressure and OCR foot-dragging produced federal guidelines. Dissatisfied that federal officials moved deliberately enough, during 1974–1975, LDF, representing the original *Adams* plaintiffs, reviewed the eight state desegregation plans that HEW had approved and progress reports later submitted. Judging the plans to be inadequate and the reports to show little progress, LDF lawyers on behalf of the plaintiffs petitioned for further relief. The district court in *Adams v. Califano* (1977) granted plaintiffs' motion and, most important, ordered HEW to devise guidelines for desegregation and required the states to submit new plans. LDF and state defendants had long protested that federal Title VI guidelines were needed for planning and achieving compliance. Without such guidance from Washington, state systems could vaguely propose poor remedies and not be held accountable. From the state perspective, federal pressure was arbitrary. Panetta's 1969 letters resisted providing guidelines, deferring to the judgment of college and university officials, necessarily, perhaps, under timely assumptions of goodwill.

During the 1976 litigation, Maryland and Pennsylvania filed separate suits, removing them from *Adams v. Califano*. In a legal maneuver, Maryland sought relief from further regulation by HEW, arguing that the department had failed to adequately seek voluntary compliance before instituting enforcement proceedings (*Mandel v. HEW*, 1976). Subsequently, on August 9, 1977, the court ordered HEW to discontinue proceedings against Maryland until guidelines for the establishment of a new state desegregation plan were issued. Pennsylvania began negotiating a settlement with plaintiffs, reaching agreement seven years later, in 1983 (*Federal Register*, 1978).

HEW developed higher education Title VI desegregation guidelines by organizing a series of meetings and conferences with various stakeholders. According to the guidelines themselves, "The Department undertook an extensive consultation process within the Department and with interested outside parties. . . . [A] departmental taskforce was established to guide their development," including the general counsel, the director of OCR, the assistant secretary for education, the commissioner of education, and the assistant secretary for planning and evaluation. The task force consulted with various government and higher education officials in the six states affected by the court's most recent decision, with plaintiffs, with the National Association for Equal Opportunity in Higher Education, and with two panels of nationally recognized expert educators. The department issued its initial draft guidelines in July 1977 (*Federal*

Register, 1977), and obtained final court approval of them in February 1978 (*Federal Register*, 1978).

The *Adams* court record specifies major content areas for the guidelines. Court instructions include targeting both college and university systems and individual institutions (including students, faculty, staff, and board of trustees) and requiring detailed monitoring reports, including specific proposals, which HEW interpreted to mean goals and timetables. The version of the guidelines finally approved adopted what was considered, during their development, substantial approaches to compliance. Remaining in effect in 1996, they identify four major elements that must be reflected in a systemwide higher education desegregation plan: restructuring dual systems; increasing African-American enrollments at TWIs and increasing white enrollment at traditionally black institutions (TBIs); increasing "other race" faculty, administrators, nonprofessional staff, and trustees; and reporting and monitoring requirements.

In order to "disestablish the structure of the dual systems," OCR guidelines require in each state desegregation plan: "definitions of the mission of each state college and university on a basis other than race"; "specific steps to eliminate educationally unnecessary program duplication among traditionally black and traditionally white institutions in the same service arena"; "steps . . . to strengthen the role of traditionally black institutions in the state system"; and "prior consideration to placing . . . new . . . degree programs . . . at traditionally black institutions." The guidelines also suggest specific actions. These include reassigning duplicative instructional programs from one institution to another, mounting jointly conducted academic programs, adding new "high demand" programs at TBIs, and merging institutions or branches of colleges and universities (*Federal Register*, 1978).

The guidelines also require state systems to adopt strategies for increasing African-American student enrollment at TWIs. More specifically, the proportion of African-American high-school graduates in a state who enter the state college and university system should at least equal the percentage of whites who graduate and similarly matriculate. At each traditionally white, four-year institution and the system as a whole, specified annual increases in the proportion of African-American undergraduate enrollment should occur. By the 1982–1983 school year, such yearly increases should have resulted in a reduction by 50 percent of the disparity between the percentage of African-American and white high-school graduates entering public institutions, but no state need increase its current African-American student enrollment by more than 150 percent over the enrollment for the 1976–1977 school year.

Where graduate enrollment is concerned, the guidelines require goals for equalizing the proportion of white and African-American bachelor's degree recipients who enroll in graduate and professional programs in the state system. Separate annual and total goals must be established for each major field of study at the graduate and professional levels.

According to the guidelines, numerical goals for increasing the percentage of white students at TBIs should take place only when: increase in black student enrollment at TWIs is demonstrably improved; specific steps to enhance TBIs are successfully undertaken; competing instructional programs at geographically proximate African-American and white institutions within the same system are eliminated; and a complete assortment of new instructional programs has been assembled at TBIs. Goals for white enrollment at TBIs were required on September 1, 1979, assuming that the aforementioned changes had occurred.

The third substantive area addressed in the guidelines is the desegregation of faculty, administration, nonprofessional staff, and governing boards within the affected state systems. They call for an across-the-board increase in the number of African-Americans in all positions of employment and all fiduciary roles. More specifically:

1. The proportion of black faculty and of administrators at each institution and on the staff of each governing board or any other state higher education entity, in positions not requiring the doctoral degree, shall at least equal the proportion of black students graduating with master degrees from institutions within the state system, or the proportion of black individuals with the required credentials for such positions in the relevant labor market area, whichever is greater.

2. The proportion of black faculty and of administrators at each institution and on the staff of each governing board or any other state higher education entity, in positions requiring the doctoral degree, shall at least equal the proportion of black individuals with the credentials required for such positions in the relevant labor market area.

3. The proportion of black non-academic personnel (by job category) at each institution and on the staffs of each governing board or any other state higher educational entity, shall at least equal the proportion of black persons in the relevant labor market area.

4. Until the foregoing goals are met for the traditionally white institutions as a whole, the proportion of blacks hired to fill faculty and administrative vacancies shall not be less than the proportion of black individuals with the

credentials required for such positions in the relevant labor market area."
(*Federal Register*, 1978)

Where systemwide and institutional governing boards are concerned,
the racial composition of the state or area served must be reflected in their
composition. Timetables are required for accomplishing all the above
outcomes. The fourth area of the guidelines specifies requirements for the
submission of plans, deadlines, and timetables for monitoring progress.

ENFORCEMENT MILDLY ESCALATES

Using the new guidelines, Arkansas, Florida, Georgia, Oklahoma,
Virginia, and North Carolina in 1978 submitted new plans to HEW. After
negotiation and revision, five of the six were approved for the 1978–1979
school year. The University of North Carolina System's plan was rejected,
and sensing hopeless noncooperation, HEW inaugurated compliance
proceedings leading toward discontinued federal funding. Also, shortly
after President Reagan's inauguration in January 1981, HEW notified an
additional eight states of de jure segregation violations, requesting desegregation plans. The new states were Alabama, Delaware, Kentucky,
Missouri, South Carolina, Ohio, Texas, and West Virginia (Brown to
White, 1981; Dodds to Rockefeller, 1981; Mines to Rhodes, 1981;
Thomas to James, 1981; Dodds to Dupont, 1981; High to Bond, 1981;
Thomas to Riley, 1981; Thomas to Brown, 1981). With these additions,
Title VI systemwide enforcement included 19 previously segregated
states, though compliance was being monitored in some by district courts
and, in others, court findings of noncompliance had not been rendered.

Interestingly, few state officials publicly challenged HEW's findings of
lingering effects of past de jure segregation or of states' failure to institute
remedies. Only a few states actively and persistently resisted: Mississippi,
for example, argued that its community colleges founded after the *Brown*
decision never were legally segregated and, therefore, need not be
included in the state desegregation plan (*Adams v. Califano*, 1977).

The most highly publicized example of active controversy occurred
when HEW concluded that the 1978 University of North Carolina
System's desegregation plan, issued in accordance with the newly
released guidelines, "offered no realistic promise of desegregating the
University of North Carolina [System]" (*Adams v. Bell*, 1982). After the
department's first administrative steps toward terminating funding to the
university, University of North Carolina lawyers filed suit to block
enforcement of the guidelines at the Eastern District Court of North

Carolina, outside the jurisdiction of Judge Pratt in the Washington, D.C. district. The North Carolina lawyers sought to avoid Pratt's consistently favorable rulings. Judge Franklin T. Dupree in Raleigh denied HEW's petition to return jurisdiction to Pratt's court in Washington and ordered an administrative hearing in Washington to settle the issue. In a historical analysis of the North Carolina litigation, the issues to be adjudicated were summarized as follows: "As a result, the issues were framed between November 1979 and June 1980 as these: the history of OCR-UNC relations, 1965–1980; the nature of racial segregation in higher education; evidence of segregative acts and outcomes; states' rights; university governance and academic freedom; the Revised Criteria for Desegregation; and so forth" (Dentler, Baltzell, & Sullivan, 1983).

Clearly, a long hearing was in the making. Reflecting the Reagan administration's new priorities, a private attorney, Douglas F. Bennett, on behalf of then-U.S. Secretary of Education Terrell Bell, negotiated an agreement with the university. Dupree in Raleigh, later in 1981, ratified a consent decree between the two parties (*State of North Carolina v. U.S. Department of Education*, 1981). The decree remained in effect until December 30, 1988, after the U.S. Supreme Court refused in February 1984 to review it. Plaintiffs argued that the decree did not conform to the desegregation guidelines or require the University of North Carolina system to move far enough or fast enough to remedy the problem (*Chronicle of Higher Education*, 1982). Court action successfully removed Maryland from the *Adams* case but failed to relieve its state colleges and universities from compliance with the HEW guidelines. North Carolina's actions received more public attention and did completely remove the University of North Carolina System, not including its separate community college system, from HEW jurisdiction.

However, most states adopted face-saving postures: many plans avoided strongly acknowledging the problem, and others agreeably pushed further some of the remedies they had already initiated. The "Plan for the Further Desegregation of the University System of Georgia" begins, for example, with the following innocent assertion: "All materials submitted in this document are prefaced by the specific observation that the University System is neither now nor has been in recent years operated in a manner discriminatory toward any minority group. . . . [G]ood faith has been, and is being practiced, in all aspects of the operations of the University System of Georgia" (Georgia State Board of Regents, 1977, pp. 2–3).

Similarly, Florida's plan pleads earlier compliance with HEW requirements:

WHEREAS the State Board of Education, the State's system of universities and community colleges, and the Florida Legislature have taken positive actions to provide equality of education and equality of educational opportunities for all the citizens of Florida, and . . .

BE IT RESOLVED by the Board of Education, State of Florida that the Board adopts "Florida's Commitment to Equal Access and Equal Opportunity in Public Higher Education. (Florida State Department of Education, 1978, pp. i–ii)

Face-saving of this kind exemplified passive resistance, adopting a strategy of seeming to comply, of negotiating with federal officials, of submitting plans as required, of undertaking some commitments made in the plans, but on the whole doing little to accomplish desegregation. More detailed descriptions of state responses are presented in Chapter 2. It is important here, in conveying the federal role, to observe that, despite minimal state responses, the U.S. Department of Education (ED), established in 1980, and HEW in earlier years, for much of the first 20 years, cooperated with many states' strategy of passive resistance. On at least three separate occasions, plaintiffs successfully petitioned the courts for further relief. In each instance, the judge admonished state officials for poor effort and ED or HEW staff for approving plans that clearly did not meet the guidelines. The court also criticized ED and the Justice Department for failure to instigate compliance proceedings as required by statute (*Adams v. Weinberger*, 1975; *Adams v. Califano*, 1977; *Adams v. Bell*, 1983).

The last substantial and successful *Adams* petition occurred in 1982. Pratt reviewed state progress over a three or four year period, when ED-approved desegregation plans had been operational. His reading of approved plans and compliance reports was unequivocal. Where Arkansas, Georgia, Florida, Virginia, Oklahoma, and the community college system of North Carolina are concerned:

1. The "Revised Criteria Specifying the Ingredients of Acceptable Plans to Desegregate State Systems of Public Higher Education" (43 Fed. R. 6658, February 15, 1979) required each of the above states to desegregate its system of public higher education over a five-year period culminating in the 1982–1983 academic year.

2. In 1978 and 1979, HEW accepted plans to desegregate formerly de jure segregated public higher education systems from Arkansas, Florida, Georgia, Oklahoma, and Virginia and from North Carolina's community college system. The plans expired at the end of the 1982–1983 academic year.

3. Each of these states has defaulted in major respects on its plan commitments and on the desegregation requirements of the criteria of Title VI. Each state has not achieved the principal objectives in its plan because of the state's failure to implement concrete and specific measures adequate to ensure that the promised desegregation goals would be achieved by the end of the five-year desegregation period. (*Adams v. Bell*, 1982, p. 2)

He then required the above states to submit yet another plan by June 30, 1983, that promised actions leading to the goals established in their earlier plans, to choose strategies that would meet with success by the fall of 1985, and to submit a progress report by February 1, 1984. He also ordered the ED's OCR in an injunction to institute formal Title VI enforcement proceedings by September 5, 1983, if plans were not submitted and to evaluate the reports of progress in states with approved plans by April 1, 1984 (*Adams v. Bell*, 1983, pp. 3–4).

Noting that Pennsylvania had refused to submit a desegregation plan as ordered by OCR in 1981 that included remedies affecting so-called state-related institutions — Pennsylvania State University, the University of Pittsburgh, Temple University, Lincoln University, and the 13 community colleges in addition to the "state-owned" four-year institutions — the judge in another injunction ordered OCR to begin enforcement proceedings within 120 days unless a plan was submitted. Pennsylvania negotiated with OCR officials and eventually obtained approval for its desegregation plan, including the specifications acknowledged, within the alloted time period (*Adams v. Bell*, 1983, pp. 4–5).

ENFORCEMENT DECLINES DURING THE 1980s

The University of North Carolina and Maryland cases foreshadowed decreased federal enforcement. The North Carolina district court's decision to apply weaker sanctions than those included in the HEW guidelines suggests a course of action later adopted by another federal court, the U.S. Justice Department, and OCR. In *Grove City College v. Bell* (1982) the Supreme Court ruled that, under Title IX of the 1972 Higher Education Amendments, federal government can regulate only those programs or units of a college or university that are found guilty of sex discrimination, not the entire institution. Prior to that time, an isolated finding of discrimination provided the legal basis for examining all college or university units. In a speech at the American Affirmative Action Association conference in Atlanta on March 13, 1986, Louis Bryson of the Atlanta regional OCR office reported that, as a result of the *Grove City College* case, OCR's efforts to achieve compliance with Title VI in higher education had been slowed. He also reported that OCR was involved in a review of progress in all state systems affected by Title VI toward the goal of determining future policy. This court decision, though overturned legislatively by the 1987 Civil Rights Restoration Act, marked the beginning of a series of court rulings that, today, render systemwide enforcement more difficult.

Broader, more academic objections to the approach underlying the 1978 guidelines are summarized by Q. Whitfield Ayres in a 1983 article in *Public Interest*. He first asserts that OCR policy compels reduction and elimination of admissions, retention, and graduation standards claiming that

Since admissions officers at many white campuses consider an SAT score of approximately 750 to be the minimum acceptable for regular admission, the more selective white institutions would have to lower or eliminate traditional admissions standards to fulfill the OCR requirement. . . . Since students who score below 650 on the combined SAT frequently require substantial remedial work, institutional resources at more selective institutions would have to be diverted to remedial programs . . . failure rates on post-college tests and licensing examinations would increase. The recruitment of high quality faculty could prove more burdensome since one would expect to find few established scholars who desire to teach students who are severely deficient in basic skills. Finally the general reputation of more selective institutions would probably be tarnished, since a substantial component of a college's reputation rests on the selectivity of its admissions and the educational background of its students. (Ayres, 1982)

Ayres next asserts that the guidelines promote "leveling in programs and resources," in this way reducing quality. By requiring states to equalize resources between African-American and white institutions, the guidelines prevent states from deliberately concentrating resources in a limited number of flagship institutions, a traditional practice aimed at obtaining the highest quality education in a few places with limited financial resources. Ayres' third objection involves negatively narrowing undergraduate curricula, "which follows from the agency's (OCR's) effort to eliminate 'educationally unnecessary program duplication' among proximate black and white public institutions" (Ayres, 1982). By equalizing programs in this way, only a minimum number will be available at either institution. His fourth objection to the guidelines involves "increasing involvement of the federal government in higher education decision making" (Ayres, 1982). The guidelines "explicitly force college and university officials to include federal authorities in important curricular decisions, and they leave the door ajar for future prior-approval require-ments for higher education decisions should OCR's desegregation goals not be met" (Ayres, 1982).

The problem with such fears is that they inadequately reflect ways colleges and universities actually operate, and overlook the existence of race discrimination. Where admissions standards are concerned, it is by no means clear that admissions officers at white campuses consider a Scholastic Aptitude Test (SAT) score of 750 as a minimum acceptable standard. In fact, considerable disagreement exists among college admis-sions professionals, and many public institutions in previously segregated states, until the 1990s, operated on an open admissions basis requiring no SAT minimum score for any student, a relevant fact brought to bear strongly in Title VI litigation in the Louisiana federal court case. More-over, SAT officials argue strongly that SAT scores should be used along with other indicators for adequately projecting college perfor-mance. Using them to establish minimum standards involves using them incorrectly.

To suggest that educators associated with flagship institutions resisted building a broad range of attractive graduate and professional programs at small state institutions with no racial goals in mind amounts to obfusca-tion of historical fact. Similarly, asserting that, "Most states attempt to limit the development of excessive program duplication among proximate state campuses for economic efficiency" simply ignores the considerable evidence that officials in 19 states purposefully duplicated programs and institutions in the same geographical regions as means of implementing a policy of racial separation. Increased federal involvement in higher educa-tion decision making constitutes a consequence of violating civil rights laws. Involvement is justified by traditional canons of civil rights laws. What more could officials who engage in segregation practices expect in a modern democratic society?

Reflecting Reagan's ideological opposition to civil rights enforcement of any kind, his administration's less expansive interpretation of Title VI requirements in higher education are clearly revealed in a speech U.S. Assistant Attorney General Bradford Reynolds presented at the Southern Education Foundation on February 10, 1983:

The Civil Rights Division's enforcement activity is of a single purpose, and that is to achieve quality education in a desegregated environment.

At the primary and secondary levels, mandatory assignment programs requiring extensive dislocations of students have, in educational terms, seriously harmed school systems across this land, particularly in the larger metropolitan areas. Nor do you need me to tell you that the gradual erosion of public education that occurs at the preparatory grade levels has an equally distressing impact on our public institutions of higher education.

Our efforts in the Civil Rights Division have thus been to strive for a greater degree of sensitivity to the educational needs of particular communities that must respond to the constitutional and moral imperative of desegregation.

Not surprisingly, employing a similar philosophy to desegregate institutions of higher learning has met with considerably less resistance, principally because forced busing is not a viable option at this level.

The states of North Carolina, Louisiana, and most recently Virginia have entered into amiable settlements, and several other states are close to a final resolution of their higher education cases.

A principal reason for these positive results is this Administration's attitude toward black colleges and universities in this country.

Unlike our predecessors we believe the effort should be made to preserve and enhance predominantly black institutions, while promoting desegregation, rather than looking to merge them with white colleges or discontinue them altogether.

As with elementary and secondary education, at the centerpiece of our higher education desegregation program is the guiding hand of educational quality. An effective dismantling of dual systems of higher education depends upon eliminating all barriers which deny equal access to any public college or university in the state. . . . With respect to predominantly white institutions, we have employed a variety of techniques to increase other-race enrollments. Considerable emphasis has been placed on programs designed to inform students of available educational opportunities and to recruit other-race students. Developmental or remedial education programs have been utilized to reduce black attrition rates. Cooperative efforts between geographically proximate institutions have been required, including faculty and student exchanges and joint degree programs. These and other measures that we have adopted help to ensure equal access for all students, regardless of race, to a quality educational institution of their own choosing. (Reynolds, 1983, pp. 10–11)

In this statement, Reynolds confirms the new administration's policy of preserving the status quo. His assertions that no mergers will be sought and that agreements improving quality without race mixing would be negotiated relieved African-American college officials. However, his message also assured white college representatives that no substantial desegregation approaches would be undertaken at white campuses. In keeping with the administration's new policy of indirectly but strongly diminishing Title VI regulation, the Justice Department changed its role in several pending court proceedings affecting higher education, including the continuing *Adams* litigation. The Justice Department first asked Pratt to vacate his deadline for investigating civil rights complaints in higher education (Institute for Services to Education, 1982). LDF's 1985–1986 Annual Report summarizes Justice officials' added new mischief:

Recently the Justice Department challenged the standing of black parents and students to sue as plaintiffs, claiming that only the federal government has the right to bring suit under Title VI. The challenge came after LDF won two strong court orders in 1983 calling for definite time frames and immediate measurable progress. LDF has responded with a motion in the district court asserting that the black plaintiffs meet all of the judicial tests for standing, i.e. all are enrolled in schools covered by *Adams*, all suffer injury from racial discrimination in education, the injury is traceable to the Department of Education's inaction, and the relief sought is necessary to redress the plaintiff's injury.

A hearing on the standing and separation-of-powers issues was held in December 1985; a decision is pending. (NAACP Legal Defense and Education Fund, 1986, p. 14)

Justice's challenge was successful. Judge Pratt, in a reversal of politics if not of law, ruled lack of standing, and LDF's judicial vehicle for applying pressure to the several states unceremoniously disappeared in 1986.

Other elements of the nation's official civil rights policymaking apparatus also declined, beginning with Reagan's election. For example, the U.S. Commission on Civil Rights, a bipartisan, semi-independent federal commission established by Congress during the early 1960s to monitor and report on the nation's civil rights problems, in April 1981 issued a report, "The Black/White Colleges: Dismantling the Dual System of Higher Education," demonstrating the existence of Title VI violations in higher education and illustrating government's failure to honestly confront the problem. However, shortly after Reagan got elected, his newly appointed members of the commission changed the agency's direction, reducing its mission. Illustrating its new, more conservative mission, commission members voted not to publish a 1983 report demonstrating the negative effect of reduced federal student aid funding upon African-American institutions. This vote characterized the commission performance beginning in the early 1980s, initiating and maintaining little policy discourse supportive of civil rights enforcement in higher education or anywhere else.

Two congressional committees attempted to provoke a national dialogue on diminishing civil rights enforcement. The U.S. House of Representatives' Committee on Government Operations conducted public hearings and issued a report on "Failure and Fraud in the Civil Rights Enforcement By The Department of Education" on October 2, 1987, and the House of Representatives' Committee on Education and Labor conducted an "Investigation of the Civil Rights Enforcement Activities of the Office for Civil Rights at the U.S. Department of Education," reporting findings in December 1988. Both reports strongly denounce poor enforcement, not only of Title VI in public higher education but also in all civil rights arenas. However, both strongly worded reports gained little attention in Congress and the news media and failed to compel a response by OCR officials beyond enduring strident cross-examination during the hearings and issuing rebuttal statements that affirmed taking no new action. Lack of public and congressional interest in civil rights hearings of this kind demonstrate that no aspect of the previous "liberal Democratic establishment's" national civil rights policy dialogue went unsilenced by the "Republican revolution" of the 1980s.

BEGINNING OF THE END OF OFFICE FOR CIVIL RIGHTS ENFORCEMENT IN HIGHER EDUCATION

Unexpectedly, OCR wasted little time after the 1986 court decision in letting the *Adams* states off the hook. Desegregation plans expired for several of them in 1985 and 1986. Having reviewed the "final reports" submitted by the ten states, OCR submitted letters of finding to the governors of the states on February 9, 1988. Arkansas, North Carolina's Community College System, South Carolina, and West Virginia were ruled in complete compliance. OCR asked Delaware, Florida, Georgia, Missouri, Oklahoma, and Virginia to adopt additional remedies by December 31, 1988, or to risk termination proceedings. Where long-term actions were needed, the OCR asked for assurance by the deadline specified and a schedule for completing needed remedies. All states responded, and Florida and Georgia have since been ruled in compliance. The others on the above list still await a final OCR ruling.

Review of the 1988 letters reveals that OCR employed process, not impact, criteria for judging final compliance. Each letter first contains a summary of the revised criteria followed by a section entitled "standards of review," which states that:

In determining whether (a state) is not in compliance with Title VI, OCR assessed whether the state and institutions covered by the (desegregation) Plan substantially implemented the affirmative measures contained therein.

In cases where a measure specified in an approved desegregation plan has not been implemented, OCR may determine that a state is in substantial compliance with such plan if all of the facts show that significant actions were taken to achieve the objective(s) intended to be carried out by such measure. In making this determination, OCR may consider some of the following factors: (i) whether OCR previously approved a change in the approved plan permitting such measures to be eliminated and/or replaced with another comparable measure; (2) whether the state or an institution, as the case may be, at its own initiative undertook another comparable activity; or (ii) whether the failure to implement a measure in a given area was not significant in light of all other measures undertaken in that area." (Daniels, 1988)

These instructions clearly establish extent of implementation of approved remedies, rather than results obtained as the agency's operating standard. Following this same route, the letters next note that failure to achieve numerical goals and timetables do not by definition indicate failure to comply:

Although the *Revised Criteria* referred to numerical goals and timetables, which in turn were to be incorporated into an approved desegregation plan, these goals and timetables were established as indices to measure progress. They were expressly not intended as measures of compliance with Title VI. Thus, OCR will not presume illegal discrimination solely because a state fails to achieve one or more numerical goals. Conversely the achievement of numerical goals would not necessarily relieve the state of its legal obligation under Title VI to comply substantially with the terms of an approved desegregation plan. (Daniels, 1988)

Reflecting this strategy, the letters unsurprisingly provide almost no information about goals and timetables. Empirical measures are used only to demonstate achieved resource parity between traditionally African-American institutions and traditionally white ones that exhibit a similar mission and demographic profile. Judgments refer narrowly to substantial implementation of planned activities, not empirical outcomes. OCR uses the majority of space in the letters to summarize the state's accomplishments in the form of reporting activities undertaken "substantially." This approach also is clear in those letters that convey deficiencies to states that have not yet achieved compliance. The letters to Florida, Georgia, Missouri, Oklahoma, and Virginia specify promised "activities" that were insufficiently implemented.

Florida's deficiencies involved:

(1)   failure to complete renovation of four buildings at FAMU;

(2)   failure to implement satisfactorily planned programs to increase African-American enrollment in selected instructional programs at Broward, Central Florida, Chipola, St. Johns River, Pasco Hernando Community Colleges;

(3)   failure to implement satisfactorily staff employment and promotion programs at Central Florida, Florida Keys, and Edison Community Colleges, and at Florida Atlantic University. (Daniels to Martinez, 1988, p. 4)

Georgia failed:

(1)   to construct and renovate physical facilities at the State's three TBI's;

(2)   to develop a jointly administered agricultural extension program between University of Georgia, a TWI, and Fort Valley, a TBI;

(3)   to adopt measures aimed at increasing transfers from Albany Jr. College, a TWI, and Albany State College, a TBI. (Daniels to Harris, 1988, p. 6)

Missouri's shortcomings included:

(1)   at the University of Missouri-Columbia, failure to establish a system of tranferring library science credits from Lincoln University, a TBI; to develop a social work consortium aimed at increasing African-American graduate enrollment in social work; and to establish graduate recruitment programs for African-Americans. (Daniels to Ashcroft, 1988, p. 5)

The Oklahoma system did not satisfactorily:

(1)   provide funds for instructional equipment at Langston University, a TBI;

(2)   document whether program duplication exists between Langston and Northeastern Oklahoma University in Tulsa, and take appropriate action. (Daniels to Bellmon, 1988, p. 6)

The Commonwealth of Virginia did not satisfactorily:

(1)   at Virginia State, a TBI, increase faculty salaries, improve the library, meet business school and engineering technology accreditation standards, develop a replacement for the discontinued nursing program, establish a new undergraduate computer science program, or complete repairs of physical facilities;

(2) at Norfolk State, another TBI, undertake building construction and repairs, and meet standards to accredit the business school and the computer science program;

(3) at Longwood College, establish a center for minority affairs and develop a recruitment brochure to attract African-Americans from the 16 community colleges. (Daniels to Baliles, 1988; p. 6)

The perspective reflected in specifying these shortcomings is narrowly focused upon inauguration and completion of planned actions or activities. The overall outcome of increased enrollment or employment or TBI enhancement goes unaddressed. As long as Virginia's Longwood College officials, for example, develop a brochure and distribute it, they will be ruled in compliance. The letters also adopt Reynolds' emphasis upon enhancing TBIs and ignoring TWI problems.

The states involved reputedly designed, took action, and attempted to produce results over a period of at least 15 years. Over this extended period, it is unlikely that OCR staff were unaware of the potential inadequacy of both the implementation and the impact of the state plans. This is the case, because, over the years, Pratt, on several occasions, found negative evidence of both kinds. He ruled that several states, including most of the ones contacted in 1988, had "not achieved the principal objectives in [their] plan[s] because of (their) failure to implement concrete and specific measures adequate to ensure that the promised desegregation goals would be achieved" (*Adams v. Bell*, 1982, p. 2).

Moreover, earlier letters of finding issued by the same OCR staff members indicated the important distinction between implementing programs and attaining goals. For example, the January 1983 evaluation letter to the governor of Florida indicated that:

This is the third evaluation letter we have sent to you assessing progress in implementing Florida's *Plan* and seeking improvements in *Plan* performance. Although the *Plan* does not expire until the end of academic year 1982–83, it seems certain that important *Plan* goals and objectives will not be achieved by that time. As noted above, there has been virtually no improvement in reducing the gap between the enrollment of blacks and whites at the undergraduate level. On the graduate and professional level, the black/white enrollment gap is increasing. In contrast to the community colleges' success in achieving their employment goals for blacks, the State universities' lack of measurable progress is a serious problem and affects Florida's ability to achieve the goals of its *Plan*. The inability of the State to fulfill its commitments to FAMU, as shown in the lack of progress in implementing new programs, and declines in student enrollment (both black and white), have thwarted the enhancement process that was projected in the *Plan*. In some instances, it appears that failure to achieve these goals is due to lack of vigorous and complete *Plan* implementation. In others, it appears that the *Plan* did not contain sufficient measures to achieve the goals. (Thomas, 1983, p. 5)

The findings related in this letter aim in two equal directions: Florida unsuccessfully took some steps aimed at remedying prior segregation, and other steps simply were not taken. To earlier Washington regulators, both problems constitute an indication of continued noncompliance.

Clearly, Title VI regulation declined during the 1980s at the federal level. Evidence of the true meaning of Assistant Attorney General Reynolds' 1983 speech emerged, among other places, in the Tennessee case. According to the 1986 NAACP LDF *Annual Report*:

As reported last year, we had achieved a comprehensive settlement in Geier v. Tennessee in a case to desegregate the state's public higher education systems. . . . Although the State of Tennessee agreed to the settlement, the Justice Department — an intervenor in the case since 1968 — opposed it on the ground that it established too many numerical goals and was not based upon proof that any specific black student is being discriminated against today.

The district court rejected the Justice Department's objections. The Department of Justice appealed; LDF is requesting the Sixth Circuit affirm the district Court order. A decision is pending. (NAACP Legal Defense and Education Fund, 1986, p. 14)

The sixth circuit court affirmed the Tennessee court order. However, the Reagan and Bush administrations clearly had moved in the direction of diluting remedies, de-emphasizing the importance of goals and timetables, prohibiting complaints, and requiring higher standards of proof of discrimination. This strategy applied to all civil rights enforcement, not just higher education. The strategy also included reduced funding and assigning priority within OCR to the elementary and secondary arena (*Chronicle of Higher Education*, 1982, p. 22; 1983, p. 17). Diminished agency capacity produced fewer compliance proceedings, not atypically ordered by the courts, in response to long delays at the state level and slow processing of compliance data, including failure for several years to issue letters of finding in response to annual state compliance reports; by 1986, only three years of data had been processed and analyzed, though several states began submitting required surveys and narrative reports in 1976.

Though President Bill Clinton's election promised to increase civil rights enforcement, strong policymaking has not emerged. In 1994, OCR under new leadership published a notice in the *Federal Register*, headed

"Notice of Application of Supreme Court Decision." In it, Norma Cantu, the new OCR director and former director of a nationally known civil rights advocacy agency, the Mexican-American Legal Defense Fund, explains federal responsibility for Title VI compliance and provides reassurance that the decision is consistent with the OCR's 1978 "Revised Criteria." The criteria "specify a broad range of factors, which include those addressed in *U.S. v. Fordice* (a 1992 Supreme Court finding of continued non-compliance in Mississippi's higher education system) that must be included in a statewide higher education desegregation plan to be acceptable." The statement reaffirms that all states "with a history of de jure segregated systems of higher eduction have an affirmative duty to ensure that no vestiges of the de jure system are having a discriminatory effect on the basis of race" (*Federal Register*, 1994).

Cantu promises to respond to new complaints against state systems and, moreover, to apply the new Supreme Court standard in reviewing expired statewide desegregation plans in Florida, Kentucky, Maryland, Pennsylvania, Texas, and Virginia. In doing so, OCR will avoid burdening black students and faculty: "The Department will strictly scrutinize State proposals to close or merge traditionally or historically black institutions, and any other burdens on black students, faculty or administrators or diminish the unique roles of those institutions" (*Federal Register*, 1994).

Despite reassuring pronouncements of this kind, the Clinton administration's record of civil rights activity in education is controversial. An early 1995 300-page report by the Citizens' Commission on Civil Rights, a monitoring group composed of experienced former civil rights officials and other private citizens, provides convincing evidence of slow action by the Clinton White House: no one at the White House is designated to oversee civil rights policy; considerable conflict preceeded the late appointment of the assistant attorney general for civil rights at the Justice Department; there exists no school desegregation policy agenda at OCR; and federal college scholarship programs have declined (Schmidt, 1995).

The Clinton administration has taken few prominent stands on civil rights discrimination in higher education. Unflatteringly, Michael Williams, U.S. assistant secretary for civil rights under President Bush, observed that "the ball has not been advanced one year, under this (the Clinton) Administration, further than it was with ours" (Schmidt, 1995, pp. 1 and 15). Cantu and Isabelle Pinzler, deputy assistant attorney general for civil rights at the Justice Department, counter that: active involvement in school desegregation cases like the one in Kansas City has increased; current action is prohibited by case backlogs, diminished budgets, and discouraged staff from the Bush and Reagan administrations;

new guidelines have been issued for handling racial harassment cases; fewer education problems can be addressed today through the Constitution, because legal barriers have been eliminated and because potential defendants have assumed greater sophistication at avoiding prosecution; and the number of complaints in fiscal year 1994 at OCR increased by 35 percent showing increased confidence in federal commitment (Schmidt, 1995, p. 15).

A later report by the U.S. Civil Rights Commission is decidedly more critical of the Clinton administration's civil rights effort. This study analyzes the work of civil rights divisions in the departments of Justice, Education, Health and Human Services, Housing and Urban Development, and the Equal Employment Opportunity Commission and U.S. Labor Department's Office of Federal Contract Compliance Programs. It reports that, between 1981 and 1994, the number of employees working on civil rights enforcement declined by 19 percent, and the Clinton administration's budget for fiscal year 1996 increases the number by only 6.4 percent. Republican members of the commission disapproved of the report, suggesting its findings were questionable and that it was improperly approved (*Atlanta Journal-Constitution*, 1995).

Without clear signals from top leadership, Title VI enforcement in higher education under Clinton heads simultaneously in two related but separate directions. In fall 1995, OCR inaugurated what it termed a new approach to civil rights enforcement in higher education. Florida Governor Lawton Chiles accepted the U.S. secretary of education's invitation to engage in negotiations among Florida "stakeholders" to produce a higher education desegregation plan. OCR recently ruled Florida in compliance based upon a review of its 1988 final report and work it accomplished between 1976 and 1988. The purpose of the negotiations is to avoid future contentious litigation and to provide a strategy for voluntarily advancing desegregation within the state college and university system. According to Raymond Pierce, deputy assistant secretary for civil rights at ED, "Whereas before we were federal officials telling them what to do, and in some cases finding them guilty, we now want to try to work as partners" (Burd, 1995). In Florida, special panels of federal and state officials conducted hearings of private citizens, college officials, and other stakeholders and devised desegregation proposals and presented them to the governor for possible inclusion in the state budget. OCR has promised to try out this approach in other states but to adopt old strategies through the courts if the new approach fails (Healy, 1995).

After two years, according to Healy (1997a), several proposals will be approved by the Florida panel. These include increasing state need-based financial aid, continuing race-based financial aid programs, continuing alternative admissions criteria for minority students, and hiring retention specialists to assist minority students at public universities. There still existed some disagreement over enhancement of Florida A&M the state's only TBI. OCR proposed spending $14 million and $8 million in consecutive years for building projects, $2.5 million for core academic programs, $3 million for land-grant programs, and $1.5 million for scholarships for architectural students at Florida A&M. Nancy McKee, representing the governor of Florida on the negotiating panel, responded that "OCR's interest in FAMU was probably a little greater than what we had originally anticipated" (p. A32).

Around the same time of the new compliance strategy in Florida, the Justice Department referred Ohio back to OCR for further investigation. OCR referred Ohio to the Justice Department ten years ago when it failed to reach agreement with state officials upon an acceptable desegregation plan. After ten years, Justice referred the case back to OCR in January 1996 for reinvestigation. OCR's 1981 finding of underfunding at Central State University, the state's only historically African-American institution, is currently under review by OCR and Ohio state officials. Central State faces a budget deficit of $6 million, which the university board plans to address through downsizing strategies. Both the vice-chancellor of the Ohio State Board of Regents and the assistant secretary for civil rights at ED describe renewed enforcement as a "partnership," language not unreflective of the new Florida strategy, but undertaking a compliance review reverts to old OCR practices (Hawkins, 1996). It is also the case that Ohio never prepared a satisfactory plan and, thus, requires an approach similar to that undertaken in the past. Florida did operate an approved plan over the years. Further monitoring after compliance in Florida adopts the new approach described by the current assistant secretary.

In Ohio, based upon review of preliminary proposals, Pierce requested a desegregation plan focusing upon enhancement of Central State University by the end of June 1996. Pierce noted that "the draft proposals that we reviewed do not include any specific commitments by the State to make positive change at Central State" (Healy, 1996). More specifically, the deputy secretary requested a proposed mission statement that insures Central State University's academic distinctiveness, measures to assist Central State University's financial problems, and new degree programs. The plan developed by consultants proposed new management systems, facilities, and academic programs but made no specific financial commitments. A governor-appointed state management team later took over governance of the university, and Governor George Voinovich asked the Central State board of trustees to resign. The management team closed several dormitories, requiring some students to relocate at other local universities (Hawkins, 1996).

In March 1997, ED threatened to cut off funding to Ohio's public higher education system. Pierce indicated that the OCR broke off negotiations with Ohio state officials, out of frustration, because state lawmakers failed to introduce legislation to improve Central State University. They were, instead, discussing closing the institution or merging it with another university. Ohio lawmakers responded by claiming they would not be coerced into spending additional money on Central State unless they were sure the institution was well managed. Eugene Watts, a Republican state senator, warned that OCR threats would fuel the drive to close Central State University (Healy, 1997b).

SUMMARY AND ANALYSIS

In broad outline, federal Title VI policymaking between 1964 and 1990 involved a pattern of: OCR issuing an interpretation of requirements, federal civil rights officials approving plans and compliance records, LDF petitioning the federal court for future action by responsible agents, rulings by the court that plans were inadequate and incompletely implemented, and renewed requests for plans from OCR to the states. This response pattern got repeated over a 20-year period, ending when conservative federal civil rights leaders claimed successfully that LDF's plaintiffs lacked court standing.

The observed pattern by no means constitutes strong federal civil rights policymaking. Actions were reluctant and required court orders. No strong leadership voices emerged, and no substantial and sustained policy dialogue developed. The only overarching and substantive policy document prepared over the first 20 years was the guidelines that the court ordered in 1976. In a barely disguised effort to reduce civil rights enforcement during the Reagan and Bush administrations, government civil rights officials in the 1980s responded by issuing policy interpretations that reduced emphasis upon many strong aspects of enforcement incorporated in the guidelines. No Supreme Court or other definitive legal rulings occurred until 1992. Court litigation in the D.C. District Court focused upon proving that OCR had not required the states to engage in potentially effective compliance policymaking or to carry out the limited plans that college and university systems presented. Unlike school desegregation enforcement, continuing court oversight, except in a few states, aimed narrowly at the executive branch of federal government. In most instances, the courts did not become intimately involved in the details of remedy design or implementation except to the extent of examining OCR irresponsibility when called upon by plaintiffs.

LDF's work constituted a persistent informal policy resource that could not alone strongly guarantee enforcement. LDF's work is incompletely and narrowly portrayed here as a litigation strategy, when, in fact, LDF organized national, state, and local forums to facilitate policy dialogue, monitored desegregation plans and implementation reports, published reports on progress, and lobbied federal and state officials. However, playing multiple roles — legal advocate, community organizer, policy specialist — also somehow created unsurmounted obstacles. In any case, Pratt's 1986 ruling ended the progressive and active role that LDF officials played.

The role that mid-level regulators played also illustrates the observed fluctuating and weak federal enforcement response pattern. Responding to diverse and changing pressures from federal civil rights leaders, many apparently pretended to enforce the law. Pretending to enforce the law involved more than simply approving plans and reports that, by reasonable standards, did not meet legal requirements. It also involves constructing rationales for approving limited compliance. This finding does not indict all federal civil rights officials. Many worked hard over the years to enforce Title VI. However, strong evidence exists, alone in the 1988 letters ruling compliance, of pernicious decision making, a response apparently supported by conservative federal agency leadership of the previous decade.

A mountain of research today emphasizes the important semi-independent role that mid-level government officials play within policy implementation in large bureaucratic organizations. A major finding of such studies is that so-called street- and mid-level bureaucrats strongly affect policy outcomes, simultaneously interpreting decisions reached by decision makers and taking into account other factors, like their own self-interests. The role that mid-level federal regulators played in Title VI implementation particularizes and extends this general finding. Civil rights officials who approved poor state desegregation plans and devised reasons to justify such actions established a unique accommodation to three sets of pressures — their supervisors' requirements, their need to keep their jobs, and sustaining college and university systems under regulation. Changes in federal leaders' interpretations of Title VI are noted previously. Variation provides one occasion for mid-level officials to seek accommodation. Clearly, maintaining employment constituted a primary self-interest issue, because funding for civil rights enforcement declined over the years, and positions in OCR and other civil rights offices disappeared at high rates. Assuming some prior connection between federal officials and regulated state college and university systems — regional OCR regulators attended or may have worked at some of these regional institutions — or other sympathetic attention, mid-level officials' civil rights enforcement duties clearly constituted a challenge to past and existing organization and control. Title VI at one level seeks to change who gets what, why, and how within regulated higher education communities.

Because federal officials' interpretations of Title VI requirements probably set the tone for later responses within the sequence of repeated enforcement events — for ED approving plans, for court judgments, for LDF intervention, and for reinterpretations — the several interpretations deserve expanded attention. Title VI enforcement exhibited in the 1969 letters involved a "dual system" interpretation of the nation's civil rights problem in de facto segregated higher education systems — vestiges of prior laws adversely affecting African-American enrollment and employment. This early view briefly got expanded into a "systemwide racial imbalance" response expressed in the 1978 *Revised Criteria* (*Federal Register*, 1978, p. 6658). However, in the 1980s, a more vague, less expansive Reagan-Bush administration policy of "quality education in a desegregated environment" emerged.

The 1969–1970 OCR letters warn that states were operating "nonunitary systems." The problem was that white institutions predominantly enroll and employ whites, and African-American institutions predominantly enroll and employ African-Americans. Little additional information is provided about what might constitute an agreeable remedy; remedies were left to the college and university systems to devise. The letters also emphasized that systemwide approaches were necessary, and that repealing official discriminatory polices and practices was insufficient.

The 1978 guidelines, reflecting K–12 desegregation court cases (for example, *Green v. County Board of New Kent County*, 1968, and *Swann v. Charlotte-Mecklenberg Board of Education*, 1971), constituted a response to the controversy faced by the *Adams* court: "It is important to note that we are not here discussing discriminatory admissions policies of individual institutions. To the extent that such practices are discovered, immediate corrective action is required, but we do not understand HEW to dispute that point. This controversy concerns the more complex problem of systemwide racial imbalance" (*Adams v. Richardson*, 1973, pp. 1164–1165).

The early OCR letters emphasized the dual system problem, but the guidelines request plans "designed [not only] for the dismantling of a dual system of higher education, [but also] for the desegregation of a statewide system, for the removal of the vestiges of racial segregation, and for the correction of 'systemwide racial imbalance'" (*Federal Register*, 1978, p. 6659).

In this way, they endorse the earlier dual-system approach but add a new twist, perhaps designed to expand remedies toward a slightly different set of goals. Plans must assure "that the system as a whole and each institution within the system provide an *equal educational opportunity* [author's emphasis], are open and accessible to all students, and operate . . . in a manner that promises realistically to overcome the effects of past discrimination and to dissestablish the dual system." (*Federal Register*, 1978, p. 6660). Emphasis in the guidelines upon numerical goals and timetables constitutes an essential element of the race imbalance approach that the federal courts came to endorse in primary- and secondary-school desegregation cases. Numerical goals specify the numbers and percentages of "other-race" students to be enrolled or staff to be hired at the various institutions, taking into account some standard like the percentage of African-American high-school graduates in the state or the number of individuals receiving a master's degree within the state system.

Movement from the "dual system" view toward a more substantial "racial imbalance" or "equal educational opportunity" problem-solving and remedial policymaking perspective probably occurred as knowledge accumulated within the nation's civil rights community about how more successfully to conduct compliance. Starting with the letters, moving toward production of the guidelines, and extending into the 1980s, when slightly more specific desegregation plans and reports emerged, OCR and other civil rights advocates, veterans of K–12 court battles, and many committed government officials applied knowledge gained from experience.

This evolution is not inconsistent with the nation's experience of desegregating K–12 school districts. Acknowledging unanticipated difficulties encountered in accomplishing public school desegregation, several court cases, exemplifed by *Swann*, affirmed the need for increased specificity in the direction of prescribing goals and timetables. Also, an earlier district court decision in *Adams v. Richardson* (1973) concluded that previous state plans lacked specific commitments for change, and in *Geier v. Blanton* (1997, p. 646), the court expressed dissatisfaction with state higher education desegregation plans that "lack specificity, in that there is no showing of funds to be expended, no statement of the number of students to be involved, and most importantly, no time schedules for either the implementation of the projects or the achievement of any goals."

Further evolution in the opposite direction during the 1980s consisted of Reagan and Bush administration officials seeking "quality education in a desegregated environment" (Reynolds, 1983, p. 10). Although few within the civil rights and higher education communities were fooled into thinking that this approach constituted an honest and credible attempt to interpret and enforce the law, policymaking during this time appears to have defined the problem as one of overextended government intrusiveness. In this view, civil rights policymaking, perversely unaided by Title VI implementation, failed during the 1970s because overly zealous government intervention resulted in local opposition. Despite the fact that local citizens were the ones guilty of passing and sustaining the effects of segregation laws, their opposition to federal attempts to provide remedies should be primarily taken into account. Indeed, they constitute sufficient cause to reduce federal enforcement. Such reasoning also underlay President Andrew Johnson's compromise of 1877, which resulted in the withdrawal of federal troops from the South and passage of segregation laws after the Civil War. Under many circumstances in recent times, conservative Republicans have winningly employed a strategy of pitting cherished local control against public responsibility to remedy state-ordered violations of civil rights.

Masking primary concern for local whites' opposition, insensitivity to local community needs and aspirations in its most virulent form, according to the Reagan interpretation, involved threatening to close or merge traditionally African-American colleges and universities for purposes of achieving racial balance. The new policy alternative for the 1980s involved both enhancing and preserving African-American institutions and de-emphasizing student and faculty transfers between African-American and white institutions. Policies encouraging such transfers, tried during the 1970s, were ruled disruptive and insensitive to local needs, not dissimilar to forced busing to achieve K–12 desegregation. Another aspect of overextended federal involvement consisted of LDF clients' official legal "standing" within the Washington, D.C., district court. Relying upon Supreme Court decisions that curb the emergence of class action cases like *Adams*, the Reagan administration legal challenge successfully ended the *Adams* case, an essential policy resource for education desegregation during the 1970s.

What remained at the end of the decade of the 1980s was a standing disagreement between two branches of federal government. The D.C. federal district court's finding of nonstanding in the *Adams* case ended its enforcement role, which, for years, involved issuing orders for increased OCR and Justice enforcement. However, its 1986 decision did not overturn previous interpretations of evidence that led to consistent findings that OCR and ED were inadequately monitoring and implementing Title VI. At the end of the 1980s, the district court's earlier view of continuing state noncompliance contrasted sharply with OCR's judgment of compliance, regardless of its leaders' changing interpretations of requirements. The 1992 *Fordice* decision confirmed the view of the judiciary, at least for a time.

REFERENCES

Adams v. Bell, D.C. Civil Action No. 70-3095 (March 24, 1983).

Adams v. Califano, 430 F. Supp. 118, 121 (D.D.C. 1977).

Adams v. Richardson, 356 F. Supp. 92 (D.D.C. 1973).

Adams v. Weinberger, 391 F. Supp. 269 (D.D.C. 1975).

Ayres, Q. Whitfield. 1982. "Desegregating or Debilitating Higher Education." *Public Interest*, Fall 1982, pp. 100–116.

Brown, Cynthia G., Assistant Secretary for Civil Rights, USED to Mark White, Attorney General, State of Texas, January 15, 1981.

Brown v. Board of Education, 347 U.S. 483 (1954).

Burd, Stephen. 1995. "Exemptions for Black Colleges in Dole Bill Elicit Both Praise and Concern." *Chronicle of Higher Education*, September 22, 1995, p. A48.

Chronicle of Higher Education, June 21, 1996, p. A22; September 22, 1995, p. A48; October 27, 1995, p. A32; Vol. 28, No. 1, February 29, 1984, p. 11; Vol. 25, No. 16, December 15, 1982, p. 22; Vol. 26, No. 10, May 4, 1983, p. 17.

Daniels, Legree S., Assistant Secretary for Civil Rights, USED to Honorable William Clinton, Little Rock, Ark.; Honorable Michael Castle, Dover, Del.; Honorable Bob Martinez, Tallahassee, Fla.; Honorable Joe Frank Harris, Atlanta, Ga.; Honorable John Ashcroft, Jefferson City, Mo.; Honorable James Martin, Raleigh, N.C.; Honorable Henry Bellmon, Oklahoma City, Okla.; Carroll Campbell, Columbia, S.C.; Honorable Gerald L. Baliles, Richmond, Va.; Honorable Arch Moore, Charleston, W.Va., February 9, 1988.

Dentler, Robert A., Baltzell, D. Catherine, and Sullivan, Daniel J. 1983. *University on Trial*, p. 6. Cambridge, Mass.: Abt Associates.

"Disputed Report Rips Civil Rights Enforcement." *Atlanta Journal and Constitution*, June 24, 1995, p. A11.

Dodds, Dewey E., Regional Civil Rights Director, Region III, Department of Education, letters to Honorable John D. Rockefeller IV, Governor of West Virginia and Honorable Pierre S. Dupont IV, Governor of Delaware, January 7, 1981.

Federal Register, 1994, Vol. 59, No. 20, p. 4272.

Federal Register, 1978, Vol. 43, No. 32, pp. 6658–6664.

Federal Register, 1977, Vol. 42, No. 155, pp. 40780–40785.

Florida State Department of Education. 1978. *Florida's Commitment to Equal Access and Equal Opportunity in Public Higher Education.* Tallahassee: Florida State Department of Education.

Geier v. Blanton, 427 F. Supp. 644 (M.D. Tenn. 1997).

Georgia State Board of Regents. 1977. *A Plan for the Further Desegregation of the University System of Georgia.* Atlanta: Georgia State Board of Regents.

Green v. County Board of New Kent County, 391 U.S. 430 (1968).

Grove City College v. Bell, 687 F. 2nd 684 (C.A. 3 1982).

Hawkins, Denise. 1996. "U.S. Gives Ohio Time to Improve Central State U." *Black Issues in Higher Education*, February 22, 1996, p. 8.

Healy, Patrick. 1997a. "States Consider Desegregation Plans Amid Uncertainty over Federal Goals." *Chronicle of Higher Education*, February 21, 1997, pp. A31–A32.

Healy, Patrick. 1997b. "U.S. Tells Ohio It Must Improve Central State U. or Lose Funds." *Chronicle of Higher Education*, April 4, 1997, p. A30.

Healy, Patrick. 1996. "Ohio Told to Provide Details on Plan to Improve Central State." *Chronicle of Higher Education*, June 21, 1996, p. A22.

Healy, Patrick. 1995. "Citizens with a Stake in College are Asked to Help Desegregate Them." *Chronicle of Higher Education*, October 27, 1995, p. A32.

High, Jesse, Director, Office for Civil Rights, Region VII, USED to Honorable Christopher Bond, Governor of Missouri, January 15, 1981.

Institute for Services to Education. *The Adams Report: A Desegregation Update.* Washington, D.C.: Institute for Services to Education, 1982.

Mandel v. HEW, 411 F. Supp. 542 (D.-Md. 1976).

Mines, Kenneth, Office for Civil Rights, Region V Director, letter to Honorable James Rhodes, Governor of Ohio, May 12, 1981.

NAACP Legal Defense and Education Fund. 1986. *Annual Report, 1985–86.* New York: Legal Defense Fund.

Panetta, Leon, Director of the Office for Civil Rights, U.S. Department of Health, Education, and Welfare, letter to Honorable Mills E. Godwin, Governor of the Commonwealth of Virginia, December 2, 1969.

Reynolds, William B. 1983. "The Administration's Approach to Desegregation of Public Higher Education." *American Education*, 19 (1983): 9–11.

Schmidt, Peter. 1995. "Clinton Civil Rights Agenda Cloudy, Advocates Say." *Education Week*, January 25, 1995, pp. 1, 15.

State of North Carolina v. U.S. Department of Education, Eastern North Carolina Civil Action No. 79-217-CIV-5, *Consent Decree*, July 17, 1981.

Swann v. Charlotte-Mecklenberg Board of Education, 402 U.S.1 (1971).

Thomas, William H., Office for Civil Rights, Region IV Director, letter to Honorable Bob Graham, Governor of Florida, January 28, 1983; Honorable John Y. Brown, Jr., Governor of Kentucky, January 15, 1981; Honorable Fob James, Governor of Alabama, and Honorable Richard W. Riley, Governor of South Carolina, January 7, 1981.

United States v. Finch, Civil Action, No. 75-9 K (N.D. Miss. 1981).

United States v. Fordice, 112 S. Ct. (1992).

United States v. Louisiana, Civ. No. 74-68 (M.D. La.), Consent Decree (September 7, 1981).

University System of Georgia. "Annual Progress Report: Implementation of a Plan for the Further Desegregation of Georgia." October 14, 1983. Mimeographed.

2

Formal and Informal State Title VI Enforcement Patterns, 1970–1990 — Case Study of the Georgia State University System

Chapter 1 usefully portrays important federal responses to passage of Title VI — federal officials' findings of race inequity in state systems, changing interpretations of Title VI, reactions to litigation led by the Legal Defense Fund (LDF). However, Title VI policymaking only begins in Washington. Federal courts, the Office for Civil Rights (OCR), and the Justice Department ultimately must coax or coerce state higher education systems into taking action. Of course, 19 state systems are involved, each one diverse and complex, with a wide range of institutional missions, governance structures, physical plants, and instructional programs. Manifestations of the race inequity problem also differ from one state system to another, and in view of all the important differences, state and local responses to federal enforcement not unexpectedly, but independently, vary over time in important ways.

Chapter 1 provided a variety of evidence that federal aspects of enforcement were demonstrably weak during the period 1970–1990. The federal district court in Washington, D.C., ruled on at least three occasions that OCR officials approved unpromising state plans and failed to monitor implementation adequately. However, Chapter 1 provided few details about state responses — the content of unsatisfactory plans and compliance reports. Reaching accurate interpretive judgments about the evidence of Title VI compliance constitutes the work of government with which this study is concerned — resolving the standoff between stakeholders who claim that compliance has failed because it inevitably will and others who claim that failure results from poor effort.

The federal district court's interpretation of failed compliance, bolstered by wide-ranging personal testimony, is deeply acknowledged within the nation's civil rights and higher education communities. However, how either interpretation gets reached is not widely understood and debated. It is only through detailed examination of what actually took place, an analysis to date not undertaken, that deeper understanding of civil rights policymaking in public higher education will emerge. Improving the civil rights dialogue, a need established in Chapter 1, will depend upon a more detailed account of the federal court's findings and of detractors' observations, a task expanded in this chapter, which looks in greater detail at the state and campus levels of the compliance process.

The following portrayal and analysis focuses upon state and local campus responses to federal compliance requirements and interaction, often taking the form of written dialogue between federal regulators and state compliance officials. How did state officials respond to federal interpretations of Title VI requirements? What kinds of plans and implementation strategies did states enact with federal approval? What strategies led to federal and state agreements that the court ruled inadequate? What forces facilitate uncorrected, insufficient enforcement, whatever forms it took? Do reasons for failed compliance — insufficient effort versus uncontrollable negative factors — emerge from existing plans and reports?

To portray and analyze state level enforcement, this chapter relies upon written dialogue from official compliance documents. Desegregation plans and compliance reports convey state interpretations of desegregation problems, state interpretations of federal requirements, and critical conflict by state officials. The tone, style, and quality of written plans and reports, as well as their content, convey a sense of state response and other intangible aspects of what actually was taking place. Undisputedly, analyzing official documents does not convey an unbiased or definitive portrayal of all aspects of state-level civil rights enforcement. True and total organizational and human reactions to federal policymaking are not always publicly stated or satisfactorily interpreted from formal statements and published reports — though unexpressed true opinions in this context likely are those supportive of civil rights enforcement. Similarly, it is impossible within reasonable page limits to portray state and local responses and interactions with federal officials in all 19 states over a 20-year period.

The shortcut established in this chapter involves looking in depth at a single state, providing a case study of enforcement in the state of Georgia over the time period 1981–1989. A case study approach seems appropriate because the goal of the chapter involves portraying state-level civil rights compliance as a dynamic set of policy responses. Through such a portrayal, Chapter 2 attempts to probe, but not necessarily bolster, evidence about the failure of Title VI enforcement. Portraying state and federal interaction using written reports and plans in a single state reasonably illustrates a new response-centered perspective for discussing and understanding systemwide civil rights compliance in public higher education.

With this modest goal in mind, it was necessary to choose a case study state in which sufficient enforcement took place. Many states (as indicated in Chapter 1) simply did not "respond" very often, and in many states, federal and state officials did not correspond with each other very often. Enforcement in Georgia displayed a comparatively energetic character. Considerable correspondence and dialogue took place, beginning with issuance of the 1978 federal desegregation guidelines. As Chapter 1 suggested, the guidelines signaled the beginning of a brief but heightened period of enforcement that concluded, for several states, including Georgia, around 1989–1990. Federal responses to Title VI responsibilities were less clearly reported for the earlier period, 1969–1978. The time period of the following case study, 1978–1989, covers two discernible periods of federal enforcement: first, the guidelines occurred during the Carter administration and symbolized a stronger federal compliance strategy, and second, the watered-down Reagan administration's "quality with desegregation" enforcement policy by 1989 resulted in an OCR ruling of compliance in Georgia through adequate effort.

A mountain of correspondence took place between Georgia state officials and OCR during the period 1978–1989. A 1985 letter of finding from regional OCR director William Thomas to Georgia Governor Joe Frank Harris (Thomas to Harris, 1985) itemizes 27 major documents that OCR, at that time, considered official components of the state's desegregation plan. Items listed included the 1974, 1978, and 1983 official desegregation plans, along with amendments taking the form of letters, reports, and supplemental data clarifying, extending, documenting, or revising materials orginally submitted. In addition to these documents, the state annually submitted compliance reports (typically consisting of a narrative overview of action taken and progress achieved for the system as a whole and each college and university in the system) and an "OCR Survey" (containing a wide range of monitoring data on enrollment and employment). In response to the 1982 court order, OCR began systematically analyzing these data and issuing annual letters of finding that identify areas for improvement and acknowledge clear accomplishments. Proper OCR monitoring concerned itself with whether reasonable plans were offered, whether implementation took place, and whether results were obtained.

Analysis of these materials and others unmentioned also ranges beyond the scope of this inquiry. It may remain forever impossible to convey the wide range of purposefully limited enforcement amid the mountain of OCR desegregation plans and reports for the period under study. Happily, for present purposes, it will not be necessary to do so. Summary and analysis of "data" contained in the following key documents illustrate the dynamic character of enforcement between 1978 and 1989 adequately for this study: the 1978 statewide desegregation plan; the 1983 Addendum, or revised plan; a 1985 progress report from the University of Georgia; and the 1987 OCR "Factual Report."

Comparatively energetic interaction between state and federal enforcement officials took place in Georgia, resulting in volumes of reports, for a variety of reasons. First of all, Georgia operates three traditionally African-American institutions (traditionally black institutions [TBIs]). North Carolina operates five TBIs, but all other Title VI states operate only one or two. Treatment of these institutions constitutes one of the most controversial and complicated aspects of Title VI enforcement. Simply stated, Georgia's civil rights problem, more thoroughly than that of most other states, embodies enhancing or closing three TBIs. Federal civil rights enforcement is more visibly controversial in a state with three African-American institutions because, on the one hand, enhancement remedies are expensive but, on the other, they also are risky, potentially resulting in one form of closure or another. For example, if too many white students enroll, the African-American identity of an institution changes. Thus, enhancement strategies are monitored closely by all stakeholders. Stakeholders in Georgia include members of an extensive and internationally known private African-American higher education community centered in Atlanta.

Also, federal enforcement after 1980 focused upon the TBI enhancement aspect of the guidelines. Foreshadowing this emphasis, reflecting the more elaborate and closely watched problem of dealing with three public African-American colleges, Georgia officials, urged by OCR during the Carter administration, undertook a very controversial civil rights remedy that involved exchanging academic departments between a white and an African-American college in Savannah. The business administration faculty at Armstrong State, a traditionally white college, were reassigned to the campus of Savannah State, one of the state's three African-American institutions, located a few miles across town; the education faculty from Savannah State were relocated to the campus of Armstrong State. A similar exchange, it is reported, took place in Tallahassee, Florida, between Florida A&M, an African-American institution, and Florida State. However, the academic programs involved in the Florida exchange were less central to the mission of the two institutions, and less sustained conflict seems to have been involved. Perhaps the most substantial and ceaselessly controversial desegregation restructuring took place in Nashville, Tennessee, where a federal court ordered traditionally African-American Tennessee State University to assume ownership and governance of the Nashville campus of the University of Tennessee, the state's flagship institution. The Tennessee merger resulted from a district court decision, and the Savannah program exchange resulted from OCR monitoring. They are, nevertheless, viewed as the most widely known and controversial early Title VI enforcement episodes and provided the occasion for considerable contact between state and federal civil rights and higher education officials.

The overall pace of enforcement, demonstrated in Chapter 1, increased somewhat during the Carter administration. The fact that Jimmy Carter, a moderate Democrat and former governor of the state, got elected president of the country in 1975 after several years of the Nixon administration's policy of limited civil rights enforcement, may have centered federal attention upon Georgia. Federal officials perhaps increased compliance pressures in Georgia to enhance Carter's civil rights record in the eyes of prominent African-Americans, whom he needed to strongly support his administration.

The Georgia higher education system is unique in that its longstanding board of regents exercises a great deal of strong central authority over all the public colleges and universities in the state. An increasingly active board during the 1980s meant that many important central decisions, assumed inconsequential to federal Title VI enforcers, later proved otherwise. Court cases attempting to end the state's new board of regents' test of basic skills as a graduation requirement focused public attention throughout the state for a period upon federal civil rights enforcement within the higher education community. The board inaugurated the Regents Testing Program in 1972, requiring public college students to achieve a passing score before receiving degrees in 1973. This new policy coincided with a federal court decision in a case, brought by H. W. Berry of Fort Valley State College, alleging that Fort Valley was "academically inferior" to traditionally white institutions (TWIs) in the state system. The court in *Hunnicutt v. Burge* (1973) ruled in favor of the petitioner, basing its decision in part upon data comparing pass rates of students at Fort Valley with those of white students at other institutions. (Berry also filed a complaint with OCR, but the OCR determined no violation of Title VI in February 1977 [a decision it backed away from later, in July, claiming that OCR officials had used the wrong legal standard in reaching their determination].) Similarly, OCR in 1980 affirmed a complaint submitted by Eleanor A. Johnson, the mother of an African-American student at Armstrong State, that argued that the Regents Testing Program discriminated against African-American students.

Activist board policymaking provoked related incidents in November 1983. The regents placed on probation 39 teacher education programs in 12 Georgia institutions because of low scores that students achieved on a new state-mandated teacher certification test. Five programs at Albany State and five at Fort Valley State were among those placed on probation. Afterward, local college officials and the regents' staff agreed to eliminate ten teacher education programs at two TBIs (Albany State and Fort Valley) and at one TWI (Armstrong State). (Recall that the teacher education programs eliminated at Armstrong orginally were located, prior to the Savannah merger, at Savannah State, a TBI). Georgia's public African-American colleges, like most in the nation, started out as teacher-training institutions. Many Georgia citizens who consider themselves stakeholders in Savannah State, Albany State, and Fort Valley, or African-American higher education in general, along with Albany State and Fort Valley State students, faculty, administrators, and alumni, protested the program closings. At the very least, the teacher education program closings, the federal judge's finding in the Fort Valley case, and OCR's finding in the Johnson complaint, at the time of their occurrence in Georgia, focused wide public attention, perhaps more than in other states, upon Title VI enforcement.

CASE STUDY OF TITLE VI
ENFORCEMENT IN GEORGIA

The U.S. Department of Health, Education, and Welfare officially acknowledged Georgia's segregation problem in 1970 when OCR Region IV director Paul Rilling notified the Georgia chancellor that the university system violated Title VI, continuing "to operate a dual system of higher education based on race" (Rilling to Simpson, 1970). OCR accepted the university system's initial desegregation plan on June 21, 1974, but following a district court order (*Adams v. Bell*, 1982), David Tatel, Carter administration OCR director, informed the governor of Georgia that a new plan had to be submitted because the state system had made insufficient progress. Using the 1977 federal Criteria Specifying the Ingredients of Acceptable Plans to Desegregate State Systems of Public Higher Education, Georgia officials submitted a second plan, which Tatel provisionally approved on March 14, 1978, and finally approved on March 2, 1979.

OCR approved Georgia's plan despite protests by LDF. Undaunted by OCR willingness to accept what its staff considered poor planning and bolstered by later evidence of poor performance, LDF in 1981 successfully petitioned Judge John Pratt in the Washington, D.C., District Court for further relief under the umbrella of the *Adams* case. Pratt agreed that Georgia, and five other states, "defaulted in major respects on (their) plan commitments. . . . [Georgia] has not achieved its principal objectives because of . . . failure to implement concrete and specific measures adequate to ensure that the promised desegregation goals would be achieved" (*Adams v. Bell*, 1982, p. 2).

In this ruling, the judge disapproved the state's planned and actual responses, ruling them inadequate in design and incompletely implemented. He then ordered Georgia to submit another plan by June 30, 1983. OCR Regional Director William Thomas notified the governor on January 31, 1983, that vestiges of segregation remained and that further planned policymaking would be necessary. A third plan, the 1983 Addendum, got assembled with a projected completion and expiration date of December 31, 1985.

On September 23, 1985, U.S. Department of Education (ED) Assistant Secretary for Civil Rights Harry Singleton notified Joe Harris, the governor of Georgia, that OCR would conduct on-site compliance reviews at the colleges and universities covered by the 1983 plan toward completing a final evaluation of progress. The decision to be reached involved either asking for continued compliance activities — a new plan — or ruling compliance with Title VI. Singleton invited but did not require the governor to submit a final report. H. Dean Propst, chancellor of the Georgia system, declined the opportunity to submit additional report documents. In a December 31, 1985, letter to Lamar Clements, acting director of the OCR Region IV office, Propst reported that,

We very carefully considered the preparation of such a report but ultimately determined that its contents would unnecessarily duplicate previous reports. . . . Our August, 1985, Annual Progress Report is designed to be particularly comprehensive in nature. . . . We are (however) submitting supplementary information for OCR review. . . . An analysis of some of the "External Factors Which Constrain Achievement of Desegregation Goals in the University System of Georgia" . . . (and) representative narrative reports prepared by University system presidents (at Georgia State, University of Georgia, Kennesaw College, Georgia Southern, Clayton Junior College and Bainbridge Junior College) in July 1985, designed to provide an overview of desegregation activities at their institutions. (Propst to Clements, 1985)

After conducting site visits and reviewing compliance reports, OCR issued a Georgia Higher Education Desegregation Plan Factual Report (GFR) on March 27, 1987. The GFR set the stage for a decision about further Title VI enforcement in Georgia higher education. On February 9, 1988, OCR issued a final letter of finding to the governor of Georgia that a ruling of compliance would be forthcoming if three improvements involving the state's three African-American institutions were completed. These involved:

(1) constructing and renovating physical facilities at the three institutions;
(2) developing a jointly administered agricultural extension program between the University of Georgia and Fort Valley State; and
(3) adopting measures to increase student transfers from Albany Junior College to Albany State. (Daniels to Harris, 1988)

OCR ruled compliance in Georgia in 1989.

The 1978–1979 Georgia Desegregation Plan

This study's initial view of state responses emerges from a summary (which follows) of the 1978 Georgia systemwide desegregation plan. Several aspects of the state's Title VI noncompliance finding were to be dealt with in the plan in keeping with the new federal guidelines. Unequal operating and capital funding, program duplication between TWIs and TBIs, and inadequate mission designations and ranges of instructional programs were the three important areas of focus specified in the guide-lines concerning unequal treatment of TBIs. Low total and percentage enrollment of African-Americans systemwide and at TWIs, low total and percentage enrollment of whites at TBIs, differential retention, and differential high-school-college matriculation constitute elements of unequal enrollment to be dealt with, specifying goals and timetables. Low employment of African-Americans at white institutions and low employ-ment of whites at African-American institutions, unreflective of the racial characteristics of local and state employment pools, had to be dealt with through desegregation planning, including goals and timetables, in Georgia in the 1978–1979 plan.

Concerning the first problem area, the 1977 Georgia desegregation plan (Georgia State Board of Regents, 1977) includes the following data and other content:

It promises to establish institutional missions on a basis other than race.

It agrees to implement and, later in the plan, discusses recommendations of a joint Savannah State–Armstrong State academic program review committee.

It promises to further desegregate Fort Valley State College (a TBI).

It establishes a joint study committee for Albany State (a TBI) and Albany Junior College, charging the committee with responsibility to plan jointly run AA-BA programs with accompanying student recruitment and advisement to facilitate increased mobility and enrollment in the planned programs.

The state's three African-American institutions received 10 of 42 academic programs (70 were proposed) approved by the regents between 1974 and 1976, indicating that systemwide, dramatic program approval decreases took place after 1974: 68 were approved in 1974, 26 in 1975, and 17 in 1976. Moreover, at the time of the plan, the regents were considering a new BA degree program in political science at Albany State, a new BA in social science and one in computer science at Fort Valley State, and a BA program in science education degree program at Savannah State.

Expense and general allocations for senior colleges as a whole between 1977 and 1979 and the state's three TBIs were about the same even though on a full-time–equivalent basis, the TBIs were receiving more money, because enrollments at TBIs had declined, beginning in 1972.

The state will allocate $11–22 million capital funds (whatever final amounts get approved by the governor and the legislature) on a "systemwide priority basis . . . apply(ing) available capital resources to obtain maximum plant quality" at the three TBIs.

Already, at Albany State, a $1 million business administration building was under design, and land had been acquired to "reorient the School's entrance"; at Fort Valley State, a $200,000 animal technician facility was under construction and a $1.1 million library renovation was under design and landscaping surrounding the school at a cost of $300,000 was "being considered"; at Savannah State, $960,000 construction of a dormitory, $680,000 renovation of the library, and purchasing of land around the campus also was underway.

Acknowledging need for improvement, 38.7 percent of four separate state student aid programs reportedly went to African-American students in 1976, with an average award of $1,124, and an average for whites of $1,127.

In response to referring to academic program duplication between Armstrong State (a TWI) and Savannah State, several actions were planned or underway: the vice-chancellor initiated development of guidelines providing for cooperation and joint programs in 1975–1976; an appointed duplication committee made recommendations for jointly run and other instructional programs, mainly to attract African-American students to Armstrong State; a recruitment committee began recruiting African-Americans at local high schools in the areas; and department heads examined the duplication problem, producing a list of unduplicated and duplicated, and proposed a new jointly run undergraduate degree program and jointly run graduate program.

In the future, new instructional programs will be placed at the three TBIs to attract whites.

The impact upon desegregation of recent and planned changes in the higher education system will be assessed.

Concerning the enrollment problem:

Though "minority" enrollment grew from 30,686 students in 1960 to 125,269 in 1976, a decrease is likely from 26.2 percent in 1970 to 21 percent in 1982; regardless, the regents will review campus recruitment, requiring each institution to develop a plan within six months for identifying "academically prepared" African-American students.

A 16 percent disparity for first-time African-American freshman enrollment exists at four-year TWIs, but a planned increase involves 1,579 additional first-year African-Americans at TWIs and 82 additional whites at TBIs by 1982–1983.

Reflecting reports that African-American and white public college graduates enter graduate and professional schools within the Georgia system at equal rates but that African-Americans are concentrated in education, business, and social science programs, the regents during 1978–1979 will develop a detailed commitment to identify promising "disadvantaged" students and provide opportunities to develop their skills for graduate enrollment.

African-American student attrition in Georgia's four-year colleges was one-third greater than attrition of whites in 1976, requiring the system to establish unspecified programs aimed at remedying this problem.

Based upon specified analysis, mobility between two- and four-year institutions does not constitute a barrier to desegregation, it is reported, because a systemwide uniform core curriculum exists.

Concerning the third area, staff and faculty hiring:

Without reporting details of the system's employment problem, the regents will require an affirmative action plan of each institution to be submitted to Washington by July 1978 after review by the vice-chancellor, and will establish an applicant clearinghouse for administrative and faculty positions, requiring departments and administrative offices by January 1972 to post vacant positions and to search for black applicants.

Assuredly, recent appointments to governance boards are more representative of the state's racial composition, a practice that will continue.

Discussion and Analysis

Viewed closely, the 1978–1979 plan identifies ten discrete actions, each constituting a response to federal 1978 guidelines. Four aim at enhancing TBIs; one directly involves increasing white enrollment at TBIs; four involve increasing African-American student enrollment; and two involve hiring African-Americans at TWIs. When the plan got submitted, some actions were underway, others were completed, and others were being planned. The ten essential actions were:

1. unspecified future capital allocations for the three TBIs and $1 million to Albany State, $1.6 million to Fort Valley State, and $1.5 million to Savannah State for planned, "considered," currently underway, or completed campus improvements;

2. promised race neutral insitutional missions throughout the system;

3. a promise to consider assigning new instructional programs at the TBIs, including joint programs between Albany State and Albany Junior College, ten new instructional programs already having been assigned between 1975 and 1976;

4. a promise to assess duplication and, if necessary, to eliminate duplicated programs between Savannah State and Armstrong State;

5. a promise of 82 additional first-time-in-college whites at TBIs by 1982–1983;

6. a promise that each college and university will establish an African-American student recruitment plan despite a projected "minority" student enrollment decline;

7. promised 1,579 added first-time-in-college African-Americans at TWIs;

8. promised programs to identify and train promising "disadvantaged" graduate students;

9. promised college and university affirmative action hiring plans by July 1978; and

10.   promises of an applicant clearinghouse.

These elements of the plan, taken together, reflect the state's response to its interpretation of federal Title VI requirements. To place the ten plan elements into perspective, it is useful to compare them with the 1978 guidelines. It is also useful to ascertain whether they derive from a sufficiently clear description of a specific civil rights problem (that is, evidence of financial aid shortages leading to underenrollment of African-American high-school graduates); whether they incoprorate specific details of planned action (that is, goals and timetables); whether believably valid program theory underlies and accompanies remedies proposed (that is, a theory that increasing college recruitment visits to majority African-American high schools will increase application and admissions rates); and whether apparent obfuscation of problems, remedies, or outcomes is present (that is, presenting "minority" instead of African-American student enrollment trends).

The actions clearly contain little information of the kind the guidelines call for. The plan does not, for example, portray or set goals for African-American student enrollment as required. The guidelines thoroughly request several enrollment and enrollment goal iterations, in this way strongly assessing progress — total system, individual institution, first-time freshmen, retention, percent of high-school graduates. Information about only two attendance measures — adding African-American and white first-time-in-college students — and systemwide enrollment get included in the plan. Many other flaws in reporting and goal setting along this line are clear.

The planned actions also lack specificity, for example, it is unclear what programs will be planned to identify and prepare additional African-American graduate students. Brief details about planned remedies are insufficient for predicting their potential ineffectiveness. Many lack substance and promise little success in the sense that no plausible underlying program theory exists. Armstrong State is unlikely, for example, to produce increased African-American student applicants and enrollees by simply letting African-American high-school students know that they are welcome to apply. Insufficient specificity and thoroughness and failure to provide information requested, at one level, characterize Georgia's responses as incomplete, however, at another level, such problems also suggest little concern for the equity goals of Title VI enforcement.

Judged by their scope, the ten actions by no stretch of the imagination constitute a substantial desegregation remedy. It is highly unlikely, for example, that adding ten new instructional programs and spending $4.1

million constructing facilities will "enhance" three college campuses. Similarly, no thoughtful person would agree that adding 82 white and 1,579 African-American students to a system with total enrollment of roughly 61,000 constitutes reasonable progress. Formulation of the ten plan elements purposefully or incompetently misleads; for example, reporting "minority student" enrollment and proposing recruitment of "disadvantaged" students for graduate school. Allocating capital funds on a "systemwide priority basis" also falls into this category. Past systemwide priorities are what resulted in federal Title VI enforcement. The regents' decision-making approach, which involves establishing priorities among the needs of all institutions within the system, not atypically resulted in white institutions' needs ranked higher than those of African-American institutions. Title VI enforcement in its most basic element involves recognizing such decision-making tendencies and remedying them. Federal civil rights lawmaking would seem to require a different approach that gives priority to TBIs' needs.

Noncompliant unplanned response elements also get displayed in the plan. Simply recommending funding gets presented in the 1978 plan and in compliance reports as actually obtaining funds. The governor first must agree to include funding for TBIs in the budget he submits to the state legislature; moreover, the legislature must approve such a request, authorizing the chancellor to make such expenditures. From the point of view of federal law, compliance does not consist of the regents requesting funds for TBI enhancement and the governor or legislature rejecting their request. Adequate effort is not reasonably defined along these lines. State government culpable for past race discrimination in public higher education includes the legislature, the regents, and the governor. Reporting with regret that the governor or legislature failed to approve a request indirectly expresses the view that the governor and legislature can righteously and legally avoid funding TBI enhancement and other civil rights compliance by asserting more important priorities for overall governance of the state system.

The plan also reifies enrollment projections. These are presented as an irreconcilable fact of life, justifying limited actions to increase African-American student enrollment. In this way, the plan incorporates the view that uncontrollable factors prevent accomplishment of desegregation goals. Enrollment projections for "minority," not African-American, students specifically suggest lack of clear understanding or disregard for the enforcement requirements. Systemwide Title VI enforcement in higher education concerns itself specifically with vestiges of prior discrimination against African-Americans and Latinos.

Summary of the 1983 Georgia Addendum

Deficient formal and informal responses of this kind may have led the court to declare the 1978–1979 plan inadequate. The 1983 plan, as described earlier, got developed when the federal district court judge in Washington ruled in favor of LDF's plaintiffs and ordered additional relief. The judge ruled that Georgia's plan was unsubstantial and partially implemented. State officials refer to the 1983 Georgia state Title VI plan for desegregation as an Addendum (Georgia State Board of Regents, 1983), presumably suggesting that actions it contains extend progress planned and achieved in the 1978–1979 plan. By some standards, this view holds substance. The Addendum shows limited improvement but contains many of the same flaws. Striving to establish an appropriate voice, it begins by specifying areas in which additional effort is required: racial parity of student enrollment; racial imbalance of students, faculty, and staff; and African-American college enhancement. Identifying problems in each area, the Addendum provides assurance that appropriate action will be taken. It then describes remedies in greater detail.

Student Enrollment Problems and Remedies

Reported student enrollment trends entail:

failure to meet systemwide and new African-American undergraduate student goals;

failure to meet systemwide African-American graduate student goals. The goal for 1981–1982 was 166 new students, but only 133 were enrolled. This shows improvement, though, because, in 1978, only 72 enrolled. With medical school enrollment goals noticeably deficient, total African-American graduate and professional enrollment declined from 2,156 in 1978 to 1,451 in 1982; and

increased enrollment of whites at two or three TBIs because of special academic programs being added — Albany State's white enrollment increased from 3.6 percent to 15.6 percent between 1978 and 1982 and from 10.4 percent in spring 1982 to 16.1 percent in spring 1983.

Factors accounting for these trends according to the plan include:

two state policy programs — the state's Equalization Grant Program for private institutions and community college expansion program — have syphoned off African-American students from four-year TWIs and TBIs;

the proportion of student aid awarded to blacks also declined, because the federal Middle Income Assistance Act disproportionately enabled middle-income white students to borrow money for college;

white systemwide graduate and professional enrollment declines also took place, suggesting race equity defined as mutual enrollment reduction; and

state scholarship support for graduate students declined from about $2.5 million to $2.2 million over the period 1978–1982.

In response to these problems, the Addendum reports having adopted or planned a variety of remedial measures. Concerning improving African-American student enrollment parity:

The regents and State Board of Education endorsed a college preparatory curriculum as a guide for students planning to enter college and for high-school counselors.

Student recruitment tasks inaugurated included preparation of a student brochure, hiring college recruitment officers, inaugurating a high-school visitation program (students visit college campuses), and advertising through black news media, churches, and civic organizations.

Special student financial aid incentive scholarships are established to encourage white students to transfer from Albany Junior College to Albany State, and Porter Merit Scholarships are established at TBIs.

Junior- and senior-college articulation is improved through formal arrangements that encourage students to transfer.

Summer enrichment programs at six institutions, beginning in summer 1984, and on-campus minority advisory programs during the academic year are established to increase unspecified retention rates.

Increased funding is provided for the Regents Opportunity Scholarship Program for blacks aspiring to attend graduate and professional school.

An unspecified program is established to identify and encourage black enrollment in graduate programs.

Developmental studies and state scholarship programs will be continued as a means of increasing retention and recruiting new black students.

In 1982–1983, each institution will report results of retention studies to the Georgia chancellor.

A systemwide conference will be conducted.

To remedy declines in graduate and professional enrollment, special recruitment and early identification programs will be inaugurated at the schools of medicine, law, and veterinary medicine.

The Addendum acknowledges only partial funding for the campus enhancement provisions promised over the past five years. It proclaims good faith effort, identifying the following actions taken:

In levels of appropriations, TBIs between 1979 and 1983 received a total of slightly more than $16 million, with a noncapital share of $7.6 million; about $5.1 million for new instructional programs at TBIs, and $3 million for campus enhancement.

A research building was constructed at Fort Valley.

A joint Armstrong-Savannah Continuing Education Building was constructed.

FTE allocations were made, averaging $3,500 for TWI senior colleges in comparison with $5,700 for TBIs.

Under design were a criminal justice building at Albany State, a farm and community life building at Fort Valley State (totaling $5.4 million), and a $9.7-million business administration building at Savannah State.

Special capital outlays were made for TBIs, totaling $1 million for 1980, $1 million for 1981, $500,000 for 1982, and $500,000 for 1984, occurring while capital funding systemwide decreased by $18 million in 1978, by $45.8 million in 1979, and by $40.7 million in 1984.

Joint degree programs were created involving Albany Junior College and Albany State.

A Student Incentive Program, providing scholarships for white students at Albany State and African-American students at Albany Junior College, was funded at $300,000 for each year 1980–1984.

Departments were transferred between Savannah State and Armstrong State, with growing enrollments in transferred degree programs.

A "productivity/ management review" was completed at Albany State, Albany Junior College, Armstrong State, Savannah State, and Fort Valley State, resulting in changes in campus management rules and processes, academic programming, and internal resource allocations.

Twenty-one new instructional programs were inaugurated at the three TBIs — 7 at Fort Valley State, 6 at Savannah State, and 8 at Albany State.

Improvements were made in teacher education.

New faculty evaluation systems were put to use for the first time at Armstrong State and Fort Valley State.

The Addendum also promises to request a special capital outlay of $1 million for each TBI in each of five consecutive years.

Employment Problems and Remedies

The Addendum asserts the regents' intention to achieve improved racial balance among employees of the higher education system. There were, at the time, 2 African-American regents out of total of 15, and the Addendum promises improvement in this area. Without suggesting progress or failure or specifying factors that account for either outcome, the Addendum promises the following (Georgia State Board of Regents, 1983):

The state chancellor will hold each college and university president responsible for affirmative action, requiring them to prepare detailed three-year plans for hiring African-Americans in administrative jobs.

The chancellor and presidents will establish "objectives," and the presidents will submit evaluations of progress to the chancellor.

The system will identify a maximum of ten black faculty for an Administrative Internship Program, which will provide administrative training and work experience under the supervision of college and university presidents.

The regents central staff will conduct a survey to locate African-American doctoral candidates, reorganize the job clearinghouse to ensure African-American awareness of opportunities within the system, establish an African-American vitae bank, and develop an affirmative action manual.

Revised black employment goals and timetables will be prepared by August 1983.

Campus affirmative action officers will maintain resume files.

Potential African-American applicants will be notified of position openings.

Institutions will be forwarded resumes at appropriate times.

State academic affairs officers will periodically notify institutions of the need to increase black employment.

Quarterly progress reports will be compiled.

The regents and chancellor will issue written notice to presidents to improve hiring records.

Discussion and Analysis

The 1983 Addendum shows improved clarity over the 1978–1979 plan; pressuring states to comply with the 1978 guidelines apparently produced such improvements. However, the second plan also contains flaws similar to those found in the earlier one: information required by the guidelines is missing, remedial programs and actions are insufficiently detailed, all elements taken together provide a limited scope of remedies, and obfuscation and false reification reoccur.

Concerning student enrollment, like the 1978–1979 plan, the Addendum fails to fulfill guideline requirements for setting various kinds

of enrollment goals. In this way, it poorly diagnoses continuing segregation problems within the state system. The four indices of enrollment
progress requested in the guidelines are not all applied. Analysis of retention barriers is not included. In an arrogant display, the Addendum associates two new state policy programs of financially assisting private and
two-year colleges with failure to achieve African-American student
enrollment goals. These apparently enabled private colleges to compete
for African-American high-school graduates and two-year institutions to
draw students away from four-year institutions. In the view of Georgia
officials, this explanation is acceptable, because, even though public
sector African-American enrollment declined, private sector and two-year
African-American enrollment may have increased. Their explanation
implies that providing aid to private institutions and expanding support for
two-year colleges is the best overall strategy for the state to follow, civil
rights enforcement constituting a comparatively minor element of the
regents' responsibility. Shifting African-American student enrollment
from public to private institutions and from public four-year to two-year
institutions, a state priority, took precedence over federal civil rights
requirements.

Like the earlier plan, remedies proposed and underway continue to lack
substance. Publishing guides for college preparation — an action that
coincided with change in systemwide admissions standards and may actually have little to do with civil rights enforcement, unspecified recruitment, summer enrichment, and on-campus "minority" advising programs
— does not, by modest standards, constitute a substantial remedy for
unanalyzed retention problems or even for poorly reported African-
American enrollment declines. Interestingly, the Addendum promises to
continue unchanged the state's developmental studies and state scholarship programs, even though they seem to have shown little positive
impact upon African-American student enrollment. While these programs
were in operation, African-American student enrollment declined. The
two programs apparently could not offset the strong effect of the new state
policy of aid to private institutions and community college expansion.
Perversely, it seems, the Addendum promises new academic programs
and additional student scholarships to attract whites to TBIs, even though
programs already underway have produced the only student enrollment
increase. It also promises, as a remedy for declining African-American
enrollment, to review transfer arrangements between junior and senior
colleges. Ironically, the 1978–1979 plan asserted absence of a problem
in this area, celebrating statewide rules facilitating transfers that already
had been put into place. State officials also promise to analyze retention

problems, apparently for the first time, by requiring colleges and universities in the system to conduct retention studies. Nevertheless, the summer enrichment and campus advising programs aim at improving African-American retention. Establishing a prevention program prior to understanding trends in retention may appear to some stakeholders as putting the cart before the horse. By specifying plans for campus "minority" advising programs, the Addendum, like the 1978–1979 plan, responds inattentively to federal policymaking.

Interestingly, concerning African-American college enhancement, the 1983 document proposes only one new enhancement strategy: a $3 million special capital outlay request for five years. Description of previous and ongoing enhancements camouflage this meager proposal. Although no standard gets used in the Addendum for measuring comparability between the state's TBIs and its white institutions, the amounts indicated, measured against imagined need from years of neglect and 1980 construction costs, are paltry.

Concerning increased African-American employment, the Addendum is equally unforthcoming. Its promises amount to detailing an administrative approach to affirmative action, which probably was already underway. If advertising jobs, establishing vitae banks, and producing affirmative actions plans were not underway in Georgia, in other states, they constitute widely recognized standard but minimal recruitment and hiring approaches. The Addendum's apparent focus upon inceasing African-American system and campus administrators probably reflects two facts: first, that Georgia actually reported progress in hiring African-American faculty and, second, that hiring high level administrators may have been advocated by OCR regulators, noting that absence of qualified applicants may not, at the time, constitute a reasonable barrier for the Georgia system. Focusing on this job category also makes sense because top-level administrators can play an active role in increasing employment in other job categories.

This analysis emphasizes flaws with the Addendum because, in this investigator's judgment, it contains no well-designed, adequately detailed information that might evoke an enthusiastic, positive response. Most of all, the scope of the 1983 plan — whether the comprehensiveness of proposed remedies matches the deep nature of the civil rights problem to be remedied — is diffuse and most limited. Judged by face validity standards, it simply promises modest actions to resolve complicated problems. Providing additional recruitment information, continuing existing aid programs that do not enable public institutions to compete with a handful of state-assisted private institutions, conducting retention studies, and holding a conference are strategies unlikely to remedy reported African-American student enrollment declines, regardless of what form they take. Its limited scope also is revealed by continuing the precedent established in the earlier plan of viewing the legislature and governor's office as independent agencies, apparently immune from federal Title VI enforcement. Adopting this view, it almost perversely evaluates the state's record of limited new funding for TBI enhancement by suggesting that some funds were awarded at a time when the governor and legislature were wildly involved in cutting the state's budget.

It can be argued that more detailed responses are described in documents that supplement the herein summarized 1978–1979 and 1983 plans. Indeed, Georgia officials eventually submitted additional information, including enrollment goals. Regardless, such information should have played a role in constructing a more detailed systemwide plan. It does little good to increase information about the benefits of college attendance if financial aid is unavailable. Student enrollment data from individual institutions could have been used to portray problems of racial concentration in certain institutions and, in this way, set the stage for more specific remedies tailored toward redistributing students, allowing some colleges to recruit African-Americans disproportionately enrolled at other institutions. Moreover, additional background information submitted along with the plans in many instances also emphasizes unacknowledged problems and inadequate remedies.

PROFILE OF THE UNIVERSITY OF GEORGIA

For all 19 Title VI states, information about campus interpretations of federal compliance requirements, filtered through the lens of state desegregation plans, is difficult to interpret. Enrollment and other quantitative data submitted to OCR during the 1980s illustrate trends taking place on a campus-by-campus basis in the 19 states, but connecting trend data to specific problems and programs underway at each local campus is perplexing. To learn more about TWI campus activities and their connection to reported outcome trends, this case study next looks at a single institution within the Georgia system. The following summary of Title VI enforcement at the University of Georgia, the state's flagship institution, provides additional insight into the design and character of responses to federal enforcement, providing a description of campus-level activities aimed at increasing and diversifying student enrollment and employment. The section relies upon a report prepared in July 1985 by the university for submission to OCR. The report provides illustrative evidence of local

campus responses to Title VI enforcement in the area of student enrollment, retention, and staff employment. It suggests one institution's reinterpretation of state officials' interpretation of federal Title VI
requirements. In the voice of official university spokespersons, it
describes campus policies and programs aimed at achieving compliance.

The study begins with an equal educational opportunity goal statement:

This statement is a reaffirmation of the commitment of the University of Georgia
to the principles of equal opportunity in employment and education, as embodied
in federal law, institutional policy and the University System of Georgia
Desegregation Plan. The full reward of employment or study are possible only
when each individual can work to the extent of his or her capability, unhindered
by artificial or preferential restrictions or requirements. ("Desegregation at the
University of Georgia, A Status Report," 1985, p. i)

In this introduction, the report notably makes no mention of the federal
guidelines that, arguably, are different from vague "equal opportunity in
employment and education, as embodied in federal law." It also make no
further mention of specific provisions of the "University System of
Georgia Desegregation Plan." Overlooked, therefore, is the joint
University of Georgia–Fort Valley State Family and Community Life
Center, an important element of the Georgia Plan, which, according to an
OCR 1988 letter of finding, was incompletely implemented. By ommis-
sion, the University of Georgia report, perhaps unknowingly, suggests
why the center went unimplemented. The University of Georgia report,
instead, begins by identifying eight areas of work and accomplishment on
which to report. Four involve undergraduate and graduate student access,
one deals with minority student retention, one deals with minority student
advisement, one deals with teacher education, and the final two deal with
employment. Each of the eight sections is discussed separately, and each
section adopts the approach of reporting actions or activities undertaken to
produce a result.

A variety of recruitment strategies are reported in the first section,
"Minority Student Recruitment Efforts": hiring a minority recruiter, using
PSAT-SAT information, high-school visitations by a University of
Georgia recruiter, participation in recruitment fairs, recruitment through
black churches, establishment of contacts with other-race leaders and
organizations, and publishing a minority brochure. The report explains
each activity, suggests why it is appropriate, indicates the extent of each
effort (that is, number of recruitment visits), and, in some instances,
comments upon relative success. The report suggests, for example, that

attending Probe Fairs is relatively more successful than other recruitment activities because many students can be contacted in a single place at one time. Similarly, the appointment of a black minister as a recruiter will facilitate future recruitment through black churches, sidestepping difficulties like the spread of the misunderstanding among potential recruits and their families that contact through the church guarantees admission to the university.

The section describing "Minority Graduate Student Recruitment Efforts" is interesting because, over the period of the final desegregation plan, University of Georgia graduate school enrollment notably increased (NAACP Legal Defense Fund, undated, p. 5). This section describes a "program designed to increase the enrollment of minority students in System schools" carried out in 1983–1984 under the direction of the Administrative Committee on Graduate Work of the University System Advisory Committee, chaired by University of Georgia Graduate School Dean John Dowling. The program entailed holding recruitment seminars at Georgia four-year colleges and other institutions in the Southeast; mailing information to 781 minority juniors and seniors with a 2.6 average or above; organizing a special competition for minority graduate assistantships, resulting in 23 awards for 1985–1986 totaling $140,000; and organizing a Southern Connection under the leadership of the assistant vice-president for academic affairs to recruit students from historically African-American institutions.

The section of the report labeled "Minority Student Retention Efforts" discusses in the genre of a university catalog the broad subject of retaining University of Georgia undergraduates. It quotes widely from a document titled "A Review of Student Persistence, Retention and Causes for Attrition, Fall 1982–Fall 1983, University of Georgia, 1984." It reports that the "number of black students in some of the retention student groups under study is too small for valid and/or reliable judgements about retention difference." Undiscouraged by this substantial caveat, it appears that black students compare quite favorably with their classmates in persistence. Retention of black full-time students in 1982–1983 was higher than that of other students in several categories: new Developmental Studies students, all Developmental Studies students, sophomores, and new graduate students; it was the same for whites in the "new freshmen" category and lower among juniors and "new professional students." Between 1973 and 1984, 54.6 percent of entering first-year students and 51.2 percent of entering first-year transfer students graduated within five years. Twenty-nine percent of students who entered the university in the Developmental Studies Program graduated within six years (pp. 18–20).

According to the 1984 retention report, there exist many ways to conceptualize the dropout phenomenon and several causes for dropping out, including, most notably, inadequate finances. It also reports that the reasons black students withdraw are virtually the same as those cited by white students. University faculty and staff working closely with the black students, on the other hand, "sense that the financial, family and personal factors affecting retention press more intently upon black students than upon whites" (p. 23).

The University of Georgia report notes that some offices and programs hold specific responsibilities for matters associated with student retention, beginning with the admissions office. The university also established a special Office of Advising and Retention Services in fall 1983 to coordinate related retention activities and start new ones, like a credit-bearing orientation course entitled "University 101." Other important offices include the Development Studies Program, Office of Student Affairs, and the Counseling and Testing Center. It ends by reporting that "Black student retention at the University of Georgia has focused not so much on the creation of new programs as on the promotion of services available to all students" (p. 26).

In recognition, though, of the special needs of minority students, the Office of Minority Affairs was created in the Office of the Vice President for Academic Affairs under the leadership of the assistant vice-president, who holds responsibility for coordinating the counseling and advising of minority students. This University Minority Affairs Program "directs black students to the 'right spot' for solutions or help with their problems" (p. 26). It also sponsors guest lectures and a faculty and staff mentoring program. It monitors student academic progress, identifying blacks who are in danger of failing courses, and offers tutorial and other assistance. Services of the Minority Advising Program are expanding: sophomores will be served during the 1985–1986 school year. Moreover, the Counseling and Testing Center will add a new position to coordinate minority student services, and the Committee on Minority Awareness, a biracial committee of student affairs staff, has been conducting sensitivity training within the Office of Student Affairs, soon to be offered to other offices within the university. The Admissions Office is creating a "buddy system," matching University of Georgia faculty and staff with entering freshmen in fall 1985; the Department of Housing will soon hire students as "minority assistants" to advise, consult, provide resources, and facilitate programs for the housing staff and will recruit black dormitory resident assistants. The Committee for Black Cultural Programs has been expanded to provide entertainment and cultural programming that reflects "the black experience." The Black Affairs Council will replace the Black Student Union, serving as the voice of black students. The report then identifies several campus speakers and programs initiated by individual departments dealing with racial issues.

The next section of the report, "Minority Advisement Efforts," follows the pattern set by earlier sections. Offices that hold reponsibility for various activities are identified. Most of the offices identified in this section were mentioned and described in the previous section on retention.

The section on "Teacher Education Efforts" describes special attention, during the time of the report, to the absence of minority teachers for the nation's K-12 school districts. It describes steps the university has taken to increase minority students undertaking careers as public school teachers. This effort comes about in response to closing several teacher education programs throughout the state, including TBIs, and the potential impact of these actions. It also reflects OCR monitoring of the systematic failure of African-American teacher trainees on state-administered academic achievement tests.

The final two sections describe the university strategy for increasing the number of African-American administrators and other staff employed at the university. Actions reported in this section involve recruiting, nominating, and placing Regents' Administrative Interns, a systemwide program that recruits black faculty and others, places them in year-long administrative internship assignments, and promotes their permanent employment; in a local version of the systemwide internship program, identifying minority faculty and administrators for "institutional" internships at the University of Georgia campus; and appointing more minority administrators in visible positions that "have both advancement potential and role-model exposure" (p. 41). The university, it is reported, also posts its vacant administrative positions and conducts searches for job candidates in keeping with state policy.

The final section of the report, "Minority Hiring Efforts", recites various rules and procedures the university follows for recruiting and hiring in various job categories ranging from faculty to support service workers. It then cites information from the American Council on Education's Office of Minority Concerns describing factors that explain the shortage of minority Ph.Ds. It next suggests a "long-term" "grow your own Ph.D" approach and an "intermediate-term" "Southern Connection"-styled approach. Responding to OCR criticism of the university's 1985 status report, the University of Georgia reports organizing a visiting faculty program. It next provides data describing black hires as a percentage of new hires by June 1985: six out of seven Equal Employment Opportunity (employment) categories show an increase of 1 to 12 blacks. The last section of the report emphasizes the importance of consulting, networking, and informing individuals, associations, and agencies that can assist in identifying black employees.

UNIVERSITY OF GEORGIA REPORT — SUMMARY AND ANALYSIS

The University of Georgia report illustrates responses at the local level that parallel or follow from system responses. University of Georgia got singled out by the chancellor as exemplary when OCR undertook its final compliance review in 1987. First, as noted earlier, at least one important aspect of the state's plan directly affecting University of Georgia — the joint center with Fort Valley State — goes unacknowledged. Indirectly, the report in other ways communicates poor attention to compliance problems. It demonstrates that, at University of Georgia, some responses were incomplete and others were slow materializing. Why did the university only get around to establishing new minority retention programs in 1982 or 1983? Whether or not guidelines were available, student retention constitutes an important, widely acknowledged aspect of increasing race minority inequity. The report gives the unfortunate impression that many reasonable campus recruitment and retention programs got underway at University of Georgia in the early 1980s. OCR notified Georgia of noncompliance with Title VI in 1969, and flagship institutions in many other states began retention programs prior to 1969. Perhaps inadvertently, the report in more than one instance emphasizes the importance of having the correct staff to undertake certain programs. However, it reports recently hiring or promoting specific personnel to undertake minority student and faculty recruitment for the first time or adopting certain approaches for the first time. Again, the question is, what took so long?

To an experienced college administrator concerned with increasing minority enrollment and hiring, none of the activities and strategies identified in the report is unique or untried. They also are reflective of what gets reported in higher education literature on special efforts at minority student retention and faculty hiring. This observation can be interpreted in at least two ways: that University of Georgia and other campus officials' responses to Title VI compliance are well-considered, informed, and reflective of well-documented experience of other officials at other campuses or that campus responses, like the ones at University of Georgia, typically are superficial, faddish, and unresponsive to adequately diagnosed needs. Without close inspection, it is difficult to determine what was taking place at University of Georgia.

Curiously, the view of local policy implementation most reasonably associated with complicated civil rights problems is communicated briefly in the University of Georgia report: "Success being achieved now should not be characterized as 'sudden' or 'overnight.' Rather this success is the product of an extended good faith effort as well as the product of willingness to examine apparent 'non-successes' with a given approach and seek a new level of entry or a new combination of personnel which might bring about the outcome sought" (University System of Georgia, 1985, p. 1). This statement moves in the direction of interpreting local program implementation as problem solving, rather than systematically pursuing clearly defined goals. Interestingly, the report also associates this point of view with the issue of accommodating conflicting University of Georgia's flagship research mission with its land-grant research and service mission. In a progressive sense, Title VI compliance is aimed similarly toward reconciling sometimes divergent missions of educating both white and African-American students. However, this insight is not reflected in the rest of the report. The strategies reported are equal educational opportunity strategies, limited in many ways and unreflective of specific problem diagnoses.

Absent from the report is a sense or described system of campus-level policymaking aimed at analyzing race inequity problems and, later, proposing, discussing, and implementing reasonable remedies. The implementation strategy referred to in the previous paragraph involves empowering officially sanctioned problem-solving forums. Worse, no continuity exists among the various activities and strategies mentioned. More likely, individual units and leaders within different units of the university at times engage the problem and consult with others who have previously done so, prior to independently taking action.

One of the biggest challenges facing the chief executive of major research universities like University of Georgia is deciding upon the time, scope, and means of addressing civil rights problems. Most university leaders never reach such decisions, instead adopting steps more narrowly to avoid controversy and to provide cover for short-term, transactional changes to emerge — hiring a new minority recruiter, establishing a mentorship program or an office for minority affairs. Aspects of this approach characterize the University of Georgia document.

The report also exemplifies the unfortunate tendency in system documents to manipulate details for purposes of receiving government approval. Such responses do not a priori suggest limited intent. Many hard-working and committed educators on occasion adopt the narrow view of "giving them what they want" in order to obtain necessary government approvals. However, when such standards widely characterize anonymous compliance reports, conclusions along this line are difficult to overlook. The clearest evidence of obfuscation in the University of Georgia report takes the form of referring back and forth to "minorities" and African-Americans. The distinction between the two must be certain within a civil rights enforcement context. Painting over the race ascriptive element of Title VI constitutes an important aspect of failure preventing necessary transformation in the organization and character of college campuses.

Adopting the approach announced by University of Georgia writers of providing equal student access to existing university offices comes close to the strategy of reporting figures for minority students as a group instead of those for African-Americans and other ethnic categories. The problem always has been that existing offices do not provide equal access as they are currently constructed. Making African-American, Latino, Asian, and Native American students aware that such offices exist and offering advice about where they can go to obtain what they need simply does not constitute a credible civil rights strategy.

Office for Civil Rights' Report on Compliance in the State of Georgia

Providing a broader look at a wider range of planning and compliance responses submitted by Georgia state officials, OCR's 1987 "Georgia Higher Education Desegregation Plan Factual Report" (GFR) adds insight into the state's overall civil rights program. The GFR summarizes federal enforcers' interpretations of and responses to state plans and compliance assessments over the period of this study. It takes into account measures specified in the 1977 Plan and the 1983 Addendum, in two compliance reports submitted to OCR in 1984 and 1985, in letters of finding issued by OCR based upon evaluation of the compliance reports, and in information gathered during 1986 site visits. The GFR document reflects the three major content areas of the 1978 OCR "Criteria": enhancement of TBIs, desegregation of enrollment, and increased African-American employment (academic and nonacademic) and representation on governing boards. OCR's purpose in issuing the GFR involved providing an overall progress report that would serve as a basis for deciding either to require additional planning or to rule compliance with Title VI.

Following federal requirements, the GFR, thus, identifies Georgia's goals and remedies, explores implementation, and suggests achieved results and failures. For present purposes, the following GFR summary, like the two plan summaries, further illustrates state officials' responses to federal enforcement based upon information collected and interpreted by federal regulators.

In this sense, it exemplifies important enforcement interaction between the two levels of government. It also provides further insight into the state-response aspect of interactive civil rights enforcement. Also, the GFR enlightens federal civil rights officials' observed rulings of compliance in Georgia.

Enhancing Traditionally Black Institutions

Following Reagan administration Title VI policy, the goal of TBI enhancement, according to the GFR, involves "strengthening (their) educational quality," adopting measures that fall into three areas: budgetary resources, physical facilities, and academic and staffing services. To aid in persuading federal auditors that comparability had been accomplished, state officials in 1985 compared three TBIs to two TWIs with comparable student bodies, finding that:

Differences in faculty salaries were small. . . . The average per student expenditure at TBIs was at least 30 percent higher than the average expenditure at TWIs. However, Armstrong State College, a TWI, initiated more new programs (23) than any of the other four institutions. Seventeen of these programs were in the health profession or teacher education areas, which were assigned to Armstrong State College as part of the Plan. Major construction, repair and rehabilitation has been much more extensive at the TBIs than at the TWIs. The student/faculty ratio was lower at the TBIs than at TWIs. The number of faculty by highest degree held varied, with FVSC (a TBI) having the highest proportion of nondoctoral faculty. (U.S. Department of Education, 1987, pp. 3–4)

Conducting comparisons between TWIs and TBIs constitutes a response to compliance employed by many states. Such studies, when well-designed and -conducted, provide a useful point of reference for establishing appropriate compliance strategies, as well as suggesting accomplishments. Absence of standards derived from such studies characterized the vague portrayal of remedies in the Addendum, and such comparisons, missing clear standards, also can be misleading. Georgia's report is not definitive. The points of comparison involve student-faculty ratios, FTE funding rates, new instructional programs inaugurated, faculty qualifications, faculty salaries, and construction and repair of physical facilities. The report's conclusion is uncertain: for some indices — FTE student expenditures, major repair and construction, and student-faculty ratios — TBIs are better off than comparable TWIs; by one index — faculty salaries — TBIs are slightly worse off; for another — new programs inaugurated — TBIs are worse off than TWIs, but this is because one TWI was assigned 17 new health profession and teacher education programs by the desegregation plan; by one other — faculty qualifications — TBIs may be worse off. The results suggest no clear course of action adopted by the Addendum. If faculty qualifications constitute a problem at Fort Valley more than other institutions, a finding of the 1985 study, why are faculty enhancement remedies not provided? If the intent of the study is to demonstrate equity, its indices are unconvincing and findings inconsistent and difficult to interpret. Does the study suggest, for example, that, even though TBIs received fewer new instructional programs than Armstrong State, a TWI, equity has been achieved because the desegregation plan called for many more new programs to be awarded to Armstrong State? Poorly constructed studies of this kind contribute little to policy planning.

GEORGIA HIGHER EDUCATION DESEGREGATION PLAN FACTUAL REPORT FINDINGS

Equalizing College Resources

> The GFR finds that over a period of years, the Georgia regents provided TBIs considerably greater E&G funding measured by full time equivalent students, but this was accomplished by maintaining rather than increasing funding under circumstances of declining TBI enrollment.

Table 2.1 illustrates this finding. It reports student expenditure data comparisons and calculations of the difference between TBIs and the average for senior colleges for the 18 years since OCR charged the state with maintaining a dual system.

The data in Table 2.1 affirm a compensatory FTE funding strategy not atypical of states engaged in federal civil rights enforcement. Though compensatory state funding is acknowledged as having started in 1955–1956, data more accurately suggest that the strategy actually began in 1972; moreover, according to the 1978–1979 state plans, for the years

TABLE 2.1
Comparison of State Appropriations per Student

Year	Senior Colleges (dollars)	TBIs (dollars)	Percent +/–
1954–55	431	405	–6.1
1955–56	409	455	11.2
1969–70	1,073	1,082	1.0
1970–71	1,093	1,140	4.0
1971–72	1,073	1,268	18.0
1972–73	1,176	1,517	28.0
1973–74	1,467	2,207	50.0
1974–75	1,680	2,317	38.0
1975–76	1,568	2,024	29.0
1976–77	1,798	2,212	23.0
1977–78	2,010	2,609	30.0
1978–79	2,401	3,359	40.0
1979–80	2,696	4,080	51.0
1980–81	3,016	4,584	52.0
1981–82	3,335	5,068	52.0
1982–83	3,333	5,314	59.0
1983–84	3,891	6,324	63.0
1984–85 (Budget)	4,279	7,184	68.0
1985–86 (Budget)	4,615	7,484	62.0

Source: U.S. Department of Education, "Georgia Higher Education Desegregation Plan Factual Report," Table 1, p. A-1.

1972–1977, differential average FTE funding actually reflects declining TBI enrollment (U.S. Department of Education, 1987, p. 34). Not to be overlooked is the fact that many college systems that previously operated dual systems began overfunding TBIs shortly after the supreme court's *Brown* (1954) decision as a means of avoiding further compliance with desegregation laws.

Enhancing Physical Facilities

Though Georgia planned taking a strategy of enhancing campus facilities as one aspect of its TBI enhancement strategy, implementation of this strategy in 1987 was incomplete:

As earlier indicated, the Addendum called for a Special Capital Outlay Cash Appropriation of $1 million for each of five consecutive years for each of the TBIs, a total of $15 million. It appears that, by 1985, "only half the promised funds had materialized." Of the 12 capital improvement projects specifically listed, two had been funded and were under construction; two had been funded but construction was delayed because of design changes; one's "current status . . . ha(d) not been reported to OCR"; one "apparently had not been funded as of December 1985"; "one ha(d) been determined not to be substandard; one had been partially renovated; one has become a storage facility; and three were not discussed at all" (NAACP Legal Defense Fund, undated, p. 5).

Requests for special funds for fiscal years 1985 and 1986 were not recommended by the governor, though he did stipulate that $850,000 of $7,897,000 appropriated for repair and rehabilitation be earmarked for projects at TBIs. This represents approximately 10 percent of these funds but less than one-third of the $3 million annual expenditures requested under the first five years of the plan.

The GFR provides additional insight into the capital funding promised in the Addendum:

The Board of Regents sought (as promised in the Addendum) a $1 million cash appropriation for each of five consecutive years for each of the three TBIs. These funds were to be expended for campus enhancement through construction of new capital projects, in addition to the renovation of existing structures. When adverse economic conditions in Georgia caused a severe curtailment of such funding from the states, the Regents supplemented the amount allocated for the State to the TBIs with funds from state allocations for general institutional rehabilitation. Between 1980 and 1985, more than $15 million was provided for physical enhancement of the three TBIs. (U.S. Department of Education, 1987, p. 2)

This information amplifies the regents' decision making described in the 1978–1979 plan as "providing capital funds on a systemwide priority basis." Georgia regents prioritize "special" capital improvement project funds submitted to the governor for inclusion in his or her total state budget request from the legislature. If, for example, the regents list a special "TBI enhancement" request for $3 million in fiscal year (FY) 1983 as funding priority three and also list $5 million for a new dormitory at Georgia State and $10 million for a new science building at Georgia Tech as funding priorities one and two, the governor and legislature must fund Georgia State's and Georgia Tech's $15 million projects prior to funding TBI enhancement. If the total special capital funding for the year amounts to $15 million, TBIs receive nothing. The same outcome occurs if the governor decides to submit only items one and two to the legislature.

Specifying that the regents "requested" an amount for TBI enhancement, a practice exhibited year by year in Georgia's Narrative (compliance) Reports, does not mean that funds were received. According to the GFR, the regents received $15 million in special capital outlay in FY 1979, but the amount budgeted by the governor and legislature for FYs 1980–1984 totaled only $5.34 million. A fraction of this total was to be spent for TBI enhancement. The regents also requested special capital funds for TBI enhancement in FYs 1984–1987, but the governor did not recommend the funds to the legislature for FYs 1985 and 1986. He instead requested an increase in "major repair/rehabilitation funds" stipulating that at least $850,000 of $7,897,000, or 10.8 percent of the new total in this budget category should be allocated for TBIs. However, this amount constitutes less than one-third of the $3 million annual expenditure promised under the first five years of the plan.

How, then, did OCR reach the conclusion provided in the GFR that the promised $15 million "was provided"? Further information appears in OCR's letter of finding evaluating Georgia's 1985 "narrative report of progress":

In 1984 the State agreed to continue to request $3 million per year for the enhancement of TBI campuses until the total $15 million had been appropriated. The State explained that, throughout the years of the implementation of its Plan, the Board of Regents has allocated funds to the TBIs in excess of the amount normally expected absent Plan commitments. It has assigned to TBIs a larger proportion of the funds appropriated to the System for rehabilitation purposes than would be dictated by an allotment of funds among System institutions in proportion to the square footage of the institutions' buildings. According to the State's calculations, TBIs have received funds equivalent to 36 percent of all funds appropriated for the System (apart from the special $3 million appropriation specifically for the TBIs), although TBIs comprise only 6.5 percent of the total square footage of all buildings in the System. From FY 1979–84, TBIs have received an excess of $4.77 million over what would have been appropriated based on square footage alone. *The Board has added that amount to the $3 million allocated in special funding, for a total of $7.7 million. This leaves an additional $7.23 million to be appropriated before reaching the $15 million funding plan commitment.* (Thomas to Crawford, 1984, p. 25 [italics added])

Academic Enhancement

Academic enhancements met with limited success — many new programs were not implemented, and most others did not increase white enrollment.

Expanding the number and range of instructional programs at the TBIs also constitutes a strategy described in the state plans. Adding new programs that whites are likely to demand — so-called high demand programs — and making them available only at TBIs is an element of academic enhancement employed in Georgia. The 1983 Addendum and supplemental amendments described 21 new programs for TBIs: seven at Fort Valley State, six at Savannah State, and eight at Albany State. Planned new programs at Albany State were diverse: baccalaureate programs in political science, criminal justice, computer science, and social work; master's programs in teacher education, business administration, criminal justice, and social work; and a two-year degree program in criminal justice. Baccalaureate programs at Fort Valley included ornamental horticulture, agricultural economics, computer science, agricultural engineering technology, commercial design, and mass communications; there also was a two-year program in agricultural engineering technology. New four-year programs for Savannah State included environmental studies, marine biology, process engineering technology, and computer science technology; two-year degree programs were added in computer technology and marine technology.

The addition of these programs was designed "to achieve between 50 and 75 percent white enrollment" at these schools according to the Addendum and supplemental planning documents. In addition, the Addendum called for productivity and management reviews "to target resources and to strengthen and develop programs" (U.S. Department of Education, 1987, p. 9). However, this strategy occurred with considerable problems. After two years, one program — Environmental Studies at Savannah State — in 1987 verged on discontinuing, and according to the GFR, "three other programs also show low enrollment figures" that seemingly threaten their continuation as well. Though "all programs have special recruitment activities to increase student enrollment," the problems encountered are "attributed partly to the lack of funds for recruitment and scholarships" (U.S. Department of Education, 1987, p. 8). Data provided in the factual report contain the following "highlights."

These programs were to attract at least 2,100 students, but by 1985 total enrollment of all races numbered less than 1,000.

Two programs at Savannah State attracted no students in 1983 and 1984 and only one African-American student in 1985 (marine technology and process engeering technology).

Of 18 programs still in existence in 1985, 13 had fewer than 10 white students enrolled.

Although overall and African-American enrollment in Albany State's computer science program increased from 1983 to 1985, white enrollment remained fairly constant; white enrollment actually declined at Fort Valley State and showed only modest growth at Savannah State.

Although white enrollment in the 21 programs increased from 148 in 1983 to 176 in 1985, this represents a decline from 21.8 percent to 19.4 percent of total enrollment in these programs.

According to "knowledgeable persons within the School of Science and Technology at SSC . . . the real measure of success of the programs should be the amount of research done and the number of graduate students produced" (U.S. Department of Education, 1987, p. 8). Although data are not included that allow for such specific measures, information supplementing the Addendum projected 13.9 percent systemwide minority enrollment in graduate programs, but data show 7.67 percent for 1983, 8.76 percent for 1984, and 8.42 percent for 1985. In the biological sciences, minority enrollment was projected at 13.46 percent, but actual enrollment for these three years was 2.63 percent, 4.06 percent, and 3.57 percent.

An additional academic enhancement strategy in Georgia involves eliminating unnecessary program duplication between TBIs and TWIs. Toward this end, "all business administration programs in the Savannah area were to be offered by Savannah State College (a TBI) and all teacher education programs by Armstrong State College" (U.S. Department of Education, 1987, p.10). Once this program consolidation occurred, white enrollment in business administration at Savannah State increased in absolute and relative terms — from 196 to 213, 21.54 percent to 28.5 percent — between 1981 and 1985. African-American enrollment in teacher education at Armstrong State, on the other hand, fell from 188 to 74, from 29.28 percent to 18.93 percent, over the same period. Total enrollment in both programs declined: business administration at Savannah State falling from 910 to 754 (a 17.1 percent drop) and teacher education at Armstrong State from 642 to 391 (a 39.1 percent drop). Furthermore, "the number of black faculty in the Teacher Education program dropped from 11 in 1979 to 7 in 1985" (U.S. Department of Education, 1987, p. 10).

Another strategy for the academic enhancement of TBIs involved creating "various cooperative programs between TBIs and TWIs" (U.S. Department of Education, 1987, p. 11). The most ambitious of these was planned between Fort Valley State and University of Georgia through the creation of a Farm and Community Life Center. This center was to "coordinate FVSC and UGA activities to provide a center of excellence in agricultural resident instruction, research, and extension at FVSC." Both Fort Valley State and University of Georgia are land-grant institutions. By 1987, $3,650,000 had been allocated for the construction of a building at Fort Valley State, where cooperative programs were to occur, but the planned new structure remained under construction. More important, perhaps, although a permanent director of the center had been appointed in 1985, "there are indications that the [Farm and Community Life Center] is not presently operating in the mode envisioned by the Plan" (U.S. Department of Education, 1987, p. 12). Programs at the two schools remained largely autonomous, with the Farm and Community Life Center director given "authority only for continuing education funds and a special legislative appropriation of $55,000, approved each year since FY 1981 for the administrative support of the Center, to pay the salaries of the Director and his secretary." Current efforts were guided by a Joint Agricultural Committee appointed in 1984. Failure to implement this strategy resulted in OCR's decision not to rule compliance in 1988 and, instead, to request further action.

During Title VI enforcement in Georgia, the regents inaugurated several testing programs aimed at improving teaching and learning within the state's higher education community. Inasmuch as African-Americans disproportionately failed such tests and inasmuch as the failure rates at African-American institutions were disproportionately higher, as explained earlier, OCR got involved in monitoring implementation of the state's new initiatives.

Thus, information supplementing the Addendum set specific goals for improvement of teacher education and nursing. According to the GFR, in 1984 and 1985, the state provided "technical assistance" to both Albany State and Fort Valley State and several "measures have been adopted to improve teacher certification rates." The report notes that, although "all of these measures have been conscientiously implemented by the institutions . . . they have not resulted in a significant number of students passing the TCT" (U.S. Department of Education, 1987, p. 15). In 1977, only 38 percent of Albany State's nursing majors taking the State Nursing Examination passed, falling far short of the required 75 percent pass rate for National League for Nursing accreditation. The school was accredited in 1983 but stood in danger of losing its accreditation by virtue of a 1985 pass rate of only 43 percent.

The state outlined several policies to eliminate "disparities in admission, progression and graduation standards" between TBIs and TWIs. By 1984, "OCR found that the system was not providing necessary remediation to ensure that students at TBIs had an equal opportunity to that of students at TWIs to pass the Regents Test" (U.S. Department of Education, 1987, p. 15). In 1984 and 1985, the state conducted analyses of its systemwide Developmental Studies program and its Basic Skills Examination and established "minimal guidelines" for the writing sample required in Developmental Studies English classes. These efforts were targeted to address the disparities in a systematic fashion and appear to have succeeded. Average scores at TBIs for 1985 exceeded established goals and were nearly comparable to those at TWIs (Table 2.2).

TABLE 2.2
Basic Skills Examination Exit Scores

	Reading	Math	English
Albany State	68	71	70
Fort Valley State	71	71	71
Savannah State	68	71	68
Four-year TWIs	68	72	70

Source: U.S. Department of Education, "Georgia Higher Education Desegregation Plan Factual Report," p. A-5.

Another TBI enhancement aimed at increasing white enrollment in Georgia involved linking Albany State College and Albany Junior College, a proximate TWI. The centerpiece was a "2 + 2" program that linked five academic areas offered at both campuses, allowing Albany Junior College students to transfer to Albany State "with full credit for work completed at AJC, thus increasing white enrollment at ASC" (U.S. Department of Education, 1987, p. 17). A sixth area was added in 1985. Scholarship programs were established at Albany State, one offering an incentive award of $1,000 per student for 2 + 2 transfers and a second open to transfers in criminal justice from any system junior college. Adopting these strategies, caused white enrollments in the 2 + 2 programs to increase from 22 in 1980–1981 to 111 in 1985–1986. Strangely, the president of Albany Junior College indicated that the school's criminal justice program will be phased out because of "decreasing enrollment," though the criminal justice program at Albany State held the third highest total overall and the highest white enrollment. Albany State in response used special 2 + 2 criminal justice funds previously targeted for Albany Junior College at other junior college campuses. As part of an expanded total and white recruitment strategy, Albany State sought to establish formal 2 + 2 links with other departments at Albany Junior College and other junior colleges.

An Inter-Campus Unit also was established "to coordinate activities between AJC and ASC" (U.S. Department of Education, 1987, p. 19). This program focused upon continuing education and public service programs with general exchanges of ideas, resources, and faculty. No faculty exchanges occurred in 1985, but faculty participation was voluntary, with compensation only for travel expenses. An expanded strategy involved assigning faculty to different campuses for full-time work, rather than have them commute from one campus to another, and providing "additional compensation."

Desegregation of Student Enrollment

> In most respects the state has failed utterly in meeting its enrollment goals — both of desegregating its black and white schools, and of equalizing black participation in higher education. Indeed, in many ways Georgia's black citizens are worse off at the plan's expiration than at its initiation.
>
> — NAACP Legal Defense Fund, undated, p. 7

The second major area of the Title VI guidelines involves increasing African-American student enrollment as a percentage of enrollment at TWIs and within the system as a whole and increasing white enrollment at TBIs. The GFR describes enrollment goals and trends but provides little information about actual campus-based and state responses aimed at affecting student enrollment distributions. Enrollment trends are, nevertheless, summarized in the section that follows as a reminder of the limited impact of policy responses described in the plans.

Equalizing systemwide enrollment first involves equalizing college-going rates of African-American and white high-school graduates. As the data in Table 2.3 show, the disparity between the two rates grew from 16.8 percent in 1978 to 27.1 percent in 1985.

African-American college-going rates had only twice, in 1978 and 1980, exceeded 50 percent of goals the state set in planning its desegregation effort, at a time when 31.9 percent of state high-school graduates were African-American. Although the college-going rate for whites showed a fairly steady increase (from 34.3 percent to 44.0 percent of high-school graduates), the 1985 rate of 16.9 percent for African-Americans is lower than during the first year of the plan. African-Americans became an

TABLE 2.3
College-Going Rates

Year	Black Rate	White Rate	Percentage Disparity	Index
1978	17.5	34.3	16.8	51.0
1979	17.2	35.3	18.1	48.7
1980	18.0	34.0	16.0	53.0
1981	18.8	37.6	18.8	50.0
1982	18.5	38.8	20.3	47.6
1983	17.4	37.9	20.5	46.0
1984	18.3	42.0	23.7	43.6
1985	16.9	44.0	27.1	38.4

Source: NAACP Legal Defense Fund, "Comments on OCR's Proposed 'Factual Report' on Implementation of the Desegregation Plan for Public Higher Education — Georgia," Table 2A.

increasing percentage of high-school graduates in Georgia but declined as a proportion of overall undergraduate college enrollment.

Increased overall college-going rates were linked to a goal of increasing the *number* of first-year African-American students in TWIs to 3,118 per year systemwide. Though the number of such students grew from 1,355 in 1978 to 1,650 in 1985, 1,650 represents only 52.9 percent of the targeted number. The state also set numerical and percentage goals for African-American enrollment at TWIs, described in Table 2.4.

Although the absolute number of African-American students increased from 9,907 in 1978 to 11,587 in 1985, clear from Table 2.4, this modest

TABLE 2.4
African-American Enrollment at Traditionally White Institutions

Year	Number Blacks	Number Goal	Percent Goal Reached	Percent Blacks	Percent Goal	Percent Goal Reached
1978	9,900	10,896	90.9	10.1	11.6	87.1
1979	9,338	12,154	77.1	9.6	12.6	79.2
1980	10,266	13,222	77.6	10.5	13.0	81.2
1981	10,549	14,465	72.9	10.8	13.9	77.9
1982	10,935	15,513	70.5	10.3	14.6	70.6
1983	11,152	15,513	71.9	10.4	14.6	71.1
1984	11,421	15,513	73.6	10.7	14.6	73.0
1985	11,587	15,513	74.7	10.6	14.6	72.7

Source: NAACP Legal Defense Fund, "Comments on OCR's Proposed 'Factual Report' on Implementation of the Desegregation Plan for Public Higher Education — Georgia," Table 3B.

growth still constituted a steady decline in terms of projected goals. The 1978 enrollment represented 90.9 percent of the numerical goal and 87.1 percent of the percentage goal. By 1985, African-American enrollment met 74.7 percent of the numerical and 72.7 percent of the percentage goals.

Retention and Graduation of African-American Students

On the other end of the spectrum from first-time enrollment is retention of African-American students once enrolled. Although the gap between the retention rate narrowed markedly from a 7.48 percent to 1.02 percent disparity in 1978–1979, it climbed to 11.03 percent the following year. As Table 2.5 shows, it was narrowed and appeared to level off between 1981 and 1983, when the disparity averaged 2.60 percent, but rose in the next two years, exceeding the initial rate (7.81 percent and 7.71 percent for 1984 and 1985, respectively). The retention rate for African-American students in 1985 stands at 89.7 percent of the goal of parity.

TABLE 2.5
Retention of Students

Year	Black Retention Rate	White Retention Rate	Disparity	Disparity Index
1978	69.40	6.88	7.48	90.3
1979	71.81	72.83	1.02	88.6
1980	62.87	73.90	11.03	85.1
1981	71.52	74.15	2.63	96.5
1982	72.83	75.51	2.68	96.5
1983	70.31	72.80	2.49	96.6
1984	64.75	72.56	7.81	89.2
1985	66.92	74.63	7.71	89.7

Source: NAACP Legal Defense Fund, "Comments on OCR's Proposed 'Factual Report' on Implementation of the Desegregation Plan for Public Higher Education — Georgia," Table 5A.

Despite increased African-American student enrollment over the course of the Georgia plan, African-American baccalaureate degree earners average around 10.5 percent for each year (10.19 percent in 1979, 10.51 percent in 1984, 10.94 percent in 1985; and 10.30 percent in 1986).

A pipeline effect clearly emerges from Georgia's enrollment statistics: African-Americans average 19 percent of first-year enrollment, 15 percent of total undergraduate enrollment, and only 10 percent of baccalaureate degrees earned.

African-American Graduate School Enrollment

Data in Table 2.6 suggest progress in enrolling African-Americans in professional programs in Georgia's system, but rates at which baccalaure-ate-degree earners went on to graduate study were discouraging. The data show a steady decline from 1978 to 1985 for all students.

TABLE 2.6
Enrollment in Graduate Schools

Year	White		Black	
	Number	Rate	Number	Rate
1978–1979	2,940	30.83	531	48.67
1983–1984	2,682	26.90	386	32.41
1984–1985	2,394	23.83	303	24.07
1985–1986	2,315	21.42	291	23.02

Source: U.S. Department of Education, "Georgia Higher Education Desegregation Plan Factual Report," Table 16, p. A-16.

The rate of African-American degree earners pursuing graduate studies fell from nearly half the system graduates at the initiation of the plan to less than a quarter for 1986. Ironically, it should be noted that, measured in terms of parity, the state met its goal, but the steady decline in the rate of African-American enrollment suggests that future success would be difficult. This is also the case because, although African-Americans constituted 10–12 percent of entrants, they made up only 8–9 percent of total enrollment, 7–8 percent of master's degrees and 3–5 percent of Ph.Ds. Retaining African-Americans in graduate school also constituted a problem that later would result in failure to meet parity.

Although there had been an increase in the percentage of African-American college graduates enrolling in graduate professional studies, such enrollment still lagged behind first-time enrollment of white gradu-ates. Table 2.7 shows that the gap narrowed from 4.5 percent of white students and 2.7 percent of African-Americans (59.1 percent of parity) to

TABLE 2.7
First-time Graduate-Professional School Enrollment

Year	White		Black	
	Number	**Rate**	**Number**	**Rate**
1978–1979	429	4.50	29	2.66
1983–1984	560	5.62	36	3.02
1984–1985	491	4.89	52	4.13
1985–1986	522	4.83	42	3.32

Source: U.S. Department of Education, "Georgia Higher Education Desegregation Plan Factual Report," Table 16, p. A-16.

4.8 percent and 3.3 percent for whites and African-Americans, respectively (68.8 percent of parity).

The rate of growth of African-American first-time enrollment was, however, impressive. Although overall enrollment grew by 24.5 percent (from 429 to 522), African-American enrollment grew by 44.8 percent (from 29 to 42), more than double the 21.6 percent growth in first-time white enrollment (from 429 to 522). However, several provisos are in order regarding this apparently positive movement. First, the number and rate *declined* between 1984 and 1985. Second, the number of African-Americans is relatively small. Nevertheless, total African-American enrollment in graduate school is 80 percent of the state's original goal, and in professional schools, African-American enrollment constitutes 95 percent of the state goal.

White Enrollment at TBIs

Increasing white enrollment at TBIs is vaguely postponed in the federal guidelines and has been interpreted in most states to involve enhancing TBIs, as already described. However, Georgia established a goal of 50–75 percent white enrollment at TBIs. According to GFR data, creation of new programs at TBIs and "2 + 2" programs only modestly increased white student enrollment at Georgia's TBIs. The state's goal involved achieving "between 50 and 75 percent white enrollment" at Fort Valley State and Savannah State (U.S. Department of Education, 1987, p. 7). White undergraduate and graduate enrollment at TBIs increased from 7.67 percent to 13.99 percent, with Albany State showing the most dramatic increase from a low of 3.60 percent in 1978 to a high of 18.11 percent in 1985 (Table 2.8).

TABLE 2.8
White Enrollment at Traditionally Black Institutions

School	1978	1982	1983	1984	1985
Albany State	3.60	15.51	15.11	16.27	18.11
Fort Valley State	7.48	9.42	6.90	6.91	6.98
Savannah State	11.04	27.09	14.25	14.12	16.56
Total TBIs	7.67	17.87	12.22	12.52	13.99
Total Students	449.00	1,027.00	730.00	719.00	789.00

Source: U.S. Department of Education, "Georgia Higher Education Desegregation Plan Factual Report," Table 12, p. A-12.

Although this growth falls short of projections and although at Fort Valley State percent white enrollment actually declined, the total growth for the TBIs as a group was 75 percent (from 449 in 1978 to 789 in 1985).

Both Albany State and Fort Valley State exhibited declining white attrition rates, Albany State falling slightly from 40.70 percent to 39.70 percent and Fort Valley State from 64.29 percent to 52.94 percent. Though the rate at Savannah State rose from 21.22 percent in 1982–1983 to 43 percent in 1983–1984, it fell to 35.59 percent for 1984–1985. As a point of comparison, Georgia Southern, a TWI, had a 1984–1985 attrition rate of 27.41 percent, six others fell between 30 percent and 40 percent, and four had rates between 40 percent and 50 percent. Another point of comparison is that the attrition rate for African-Americans at eight TWIs increased for these three years, with only three TWIs showing a declining rate of attrition (U.S. Department of Education, 1987, Table 10). Data also are provided on graduate enrollment at Albany State. They show that white graduate enrollment increased from 44.8 percent to 51.3 percent, but African-American graduate enrollment declined from 54.4 percent to 46.6 percent.

Employment

Employment goals were not met even though in some job categories increased levels and increased hiring occurred.

The GFR also does not describe actual programs aimed at increasing and redistributing employment, but the data reported again show the extent of the system's failure to comply with Title VI requirements.

Faculty Employment

Although steady growth occurred in both the number and percentage of African-American full-time doctoral faculty at Georgia TWIs, the state's modest goals were not met. As Table 2.9 shows, the 1985 rate of 2.45 percent failed even to meet the goal set for 1978 (3.57 percent) and constitutes only 58.3 percent of the 1985 goal.

TABLE 2.9
African-American Doctoral Faculty at
Georgia Traditionally White Institutions

Year	Number	Percent	Goal (%)	Percent of Goal
1978	35	.98	3.57	27.5
1979	51	1.41	3.55	39.7
1980	62	1.72	3.55	48.5
1981	57	1.58	3.55	44.5
1982	66	1.79	3.55	50.4
1983	97	2.56	3.55	72.1
1984	86	2.28	3.80	60.0
1985	95	2.45	4.20	58.3

Source: NAACP Legal Defense Fund, "Comments on OCR's Proposed 'Factual Report' on Implementation of the Desegregation Plan for Public Higher Education — Georgia," Table 7A.

The picture is no more encouraging in terms of African-American full-time master's level faculty, a category that declined over the life of the plan. From Table 2.10 it is apparent that full-time employed faculty in this category in 1985 met only 63.2 percent of the state's revised and decreased goal.

Data in Table 2.11 also show a considerable increase in the number of full-time African-American faculty *hired* between 1984 and 1985. For the last three years reported, 1983–1985, hiring achieved at least 95 percent of the system's goals.

Staff Employment

One of the most discouraging and disturbing trends is the system's overall employment pattern. The following passage from a March 8, 1978, letter that stands as part of the plan states: "The proportion of Black non-academic personnel (by job category) at each institution and on the staff of the governing board or any other state higher education entity, shall at least equal the proportion of Black persons with the

TABLE 2.10
African-American Full-Time Master's Level Faculty

Year	Number	Percent	Goal (%)	Percent of Goal
1978	69	4.14	10.82	38.3
1979	67	4.20	—	—
1980	73	4.72	—	—
1981	68	4.49	7.63	58.8
1982	53	3.72	7.55	49.3
1983	65	3.92	7.67	88.5
1984	74	4.61	8.43	54.7
1985	82	5.25	7.29	63.2

Source: NAACP Legal Defense Fund, "Comments on OCR's Proposed 'Factual Report' on Implementation of the Desegregation Plan for Public Higher Education — Georgia," Table 7B.

TABLE 2.11
Full-Time African-American Faculty Hired

Year	Number	Percent	Goal *(%)	Percent of Goal
1978	25	3.97	6.2	64.0
1979	33	5.01	—	—
1980	32	5.68	—	—
1981	18	3.40	4.9	69.4
1982	9	1.89	4.8	39.4
1983	20	4.58	4.8	95.5
1984	41	7.65	5.2	147.2
1985	39	5.65	5.1	110.7

*Goal constructed on basis of ratio of doctor vs. master's faculty applied to their respective percentage goals.

Source: NAACP Legal Defense Fund, "Comments on OCR's Proposed 'Factual Report' on Implementation of the Desegregation Plan for Public Higher Education — Georgia," Table 7C.

credentials required in the relevant labor market area." Table 2.12 indicates specific goals for two important job categories — faculty and top level administrators.

Table 2.13 displays failure to accomplish these goals.

According to Table 2.13, an 11.8 percent growth rate occurred in employment of African-Americans at TWIs; regardless, African-American employees remained concentrated in nonprofessional categories, with the overwhelming majority being in the secretarial-clerical and service-maintenance occupations (67 percent of African-American employment in 1985). In fact, the only area in which African-American

TABLE 2.12
African-American Employment Goals — Faculty and
Executive-Administrative-Managerial
          (Same Goals for Both Job Categories, in Percent)

Year	Doctoral Degree Required	No Doctoral Degree Required
1978–1979	3.57	10.82
1982–1983	3.55	7.55
1983–1984	3.55	7.67
1984–1985	3.80	8.43
1985–1986	4.20	7.29

Source: U.S. Department of Education, "Georgia Higher Education Desegregation Plan Factual Report," Tables 18–21, pp. A18–A21.

employment *declined* is the borderline occupational category of technician-paraprofessional. As Table 2.13 also shows, the situation was almost reversed in terms of white employment at TBIs. Overall employment of whites rose by 62 percent, and the rate of white employment grew in professional job categories but remained low or shrunk in other categories.

Summary and Discussion

To reiterate the GFR findings:

Over a period of years, the regents provided TBIs considerably greater E&G funding measured by FTE student enrollment, but this mostly involved level, not expanded, funding, because TBI student enrollment declined.

Funding and actual improvements in physical facilities were incomplete.

Academic enhancement met with limited success — many new programs were not implemented, and most did not increase white enrollment.

In most respects, the state failed to meet its enrollment goals, both of desegregating its African-American and white institutions and of equalizing African-American participation in higher education.

Employment goals were not met even though, in some job categories, hiring and employment rates increased.

TABLE 2.13
Employment

Position	1978–1979		1983–1984		1984–1985		1985–1986	
	Number	Percent	Number	Percent	Number	Percent	Number	Percent
African-American Employment at Traditionally White Institutions								
Executive-Administrative-Managerial	42	2.8	67	3.8	79	4.5	88	4.9
Faculty	115	2.1	136	2.6	160	3.0	177	3.3
Professional-Nonfaculty	143	6.4	275	7.8	313	8.0	351	9.3
Secretary-Clerical	770	15.1	763	17.4	822	18.9	867	19.7
Technician-Paraprofessional	655	28.7	678	24.0	588	23.4	638	23.8
Skilled Crafts	118	15.5	149	17.1	161	17.1	229	23.4
Service-Maintenance	2,137	70.6	2,061	67.2	2,063	67.3	2,102	68.7
TOTAL	3,980		4,129		4,186		4,452	
White Employment at Traditionally Black Institutions								
Executive-Administrative-Managerial	4	4.3	15	9.8	15	9.3	13	8.4
Faculty	73	18.15	100	27.3	104	28.3	108	29.8
Professional-Nonfaculty	5	4.0	8	7.5	15	11.0	15	10.3
Secretary-Clerical	6	3.1	4	1.8	7	3.1	6	2.7
Skilled Crafts	6	10.2	7	11.7	5	9.1	5	8.6
Service-Maintenance	1	0.4	4	1.6	9	3.5	7	2.9
TOTALS	95		138		155		154	

Source: U.S. Department of Education, "Georgia Higher Education Desegregation Plan Factual Report," Table 24, p. A24.

The Georgia Chancellor's Response to OCR's GFR

The Georgia chancellor, H. Dean Propst, submitted a response to OCR's GFR in a June 4, 1987, letter to Alicia Coro, acting assistant secretary for civil rights at ED in Washington. Propst's response is summarized to illustrate further the depth and character of Georgia officials' responses to Title VI requirements. The first section corrects six factual details:

1. Minimum exit scores on the regents' test of students' basic skills required for graduation will not be adjusted each time the TWI average changes, adversely affecting TBIs.

2. "All senior and university level institutions participate in the Junior College Tour," apparently contradicting a GFR assertion of fact.

3. There was failure "to mention the OCR report on Student Financial Aid. The OCR B-3 surveys reflect a key factor in efforts to recruit and retain minority students."

4. "In Table 8 the 1982–83 white graduate student enrollment at Albany State College should be 53 (not 535) representing 51.4 percent of total graduate enrollment."

5. "In Table 10, the difference between the 1984–85 attrition rates of black student and white student at Fort Valley State College should be –22.75 rather than 22.75."

6. "Table 12, the fall 1982 white enrollment at Savannah State College (of) 573 students . . . was reported to OCR . . . by error," the correct number being 374.

The response letter next refers to three tables of financial data that FY 1987 budget figures as proof of the system's commitment to "funding desegregation." The first table indicates increased FY 1987 appropriation for the Farm and Community Life Center at Fort Valley State from $3.7 million to $5.1 million; a decreased sum for the Savannah State–Armstrong State Joint Continuing Education Center from approximately $528,000 to $543,000; and a decreased amount for Albany State–Albany Junior College from $264,000 to $226,000. The second table reports "Developmental Studies and Regents' Test Remediation Cost Per Equivalent Full Time [EFT] Student for Fiscal Years 1986 and 1987" at each of the state's senior colleges, showing a total budget in 1986 of $5 million, with an average FTE student cost of $186, and in 1987, a total of about $7.1 million, with an average FTE cost of $193. The third table displays "Total Budget and Projected Expenditures Per EFT Student for Fiscal Year 1987 (Amended)." Average "Amended Fiscal Year 1987

Budgets" for the three TBIs amount to roughly $36.7 million ($12.2 average per institution) with "projected FY 1987 expenditures per EFT student" averaging roughly $9,100. The 1987 total amdended budget for TWIs is roughly $183.5 million, with an average per institution of $16.7 million and an average EFT projected expenditure of roughly $5,700.

The letter then lists several physical facility renovation projects planned, underway, or recently completed at the system's three TBIs: seven at Albany State, nine at Fort Valley State, and ten at Savannah State. It then describes projects funded by the FY 1986 State Appropriations Act, which set aside $850,000 of $8.3 million total system funding for TBIs; by a $1.9 million TBI share of $19.6 million that "was designated to be spent"; and by a $2 million TBI share of roughly $20 million to be budgeted for FY 88. Recall that the governor turned down the regents' FY 1986 request for substantially more special capital outlay funds for the TBI, instead budgeting the stated $850,000. In previous years, the regents' requests also were turned down or substantially reduced.

The promised funds will be used for "campus enhancement" projects listed in the June 4, 1987, letter: three at Albany State, and six at Savannah State. They also will be used for facility construction: four projects at Albany State, three at Fort Valley State, and four at Savannah State. Although the letter suggests that the new funding mentioned will be used for future projects, some of the projects listed in the subsequent unintroduced section of the letter are reported completed. Notably as well, some of the same projects are repeated, like the Albany State criminal justice building, the Fort Valley State administration building, and the Savannah State business administration building from earlier reports and plans.

In the next section, the chancellor reports that five TBI teacher education programs had been removed from probation and that five others will be reviewed in summer 1987. The nursing program at Albany State was removed from conditional accreditation status and has obtained full approval. The number of white students increased from 19 percent in 1985 to 33 percent in 1986, from 18 percent of graduates in 1985 to 61 percent in 1986.

The subsequent section describes meetings, conferences, and information dissemination projects aimed at preparing all Georgia high-school students for college. Though including them in the letter suggests that they were undertaken as a compliance measure, they actually were designed to prepare Georgia high-school students, their parents, and public school officials for changes in admissions earlier undertaken by the regents. The letter goes on to describe new requirements proposed in June 1987, which, according to the letter, "should increase access to System institutions and should enable the System to serve populations of students that may not have been accommodated under the current policy." These include "students entering certificate or career associate degree programs would be exempted from taking the SAT or ACT for admission" and similar changes actually aimed at channeling low-scoring students, who cannot meet the recently increased high-school course completion and SAT entrance requirements, into community colleges, in this way raising the academic profile of students enrolled in senior colleges. In the next paragraph, the letter reports that TBI students' performance on the Regents' Test had increased during 1985–1986, a fact already confirmed in the GFR.

Boastfully, participation in the distinguished scholars program at Albany State increased from five to seven between 1985 and 1986, with a total of six in 1987 and plans for a grand total of seven in 1988. According to the chancellor's letter (Propst, 1987), "The program has been successful in establishing an improved relationship with the community. . . . This initiative has resulted in certain sectors of the community becoming acquainted with the college and others being reintroduced to the college." Translated, white faculty visiting Albany State gave public lectures and sponsored other events that whites in the Albany area were interested in attending, probably because the lecturers and sponsors were white.

Concerning student enrollment, the chancellor describes "statewide comprehensive workshops on the college planning and selection process," as it turns out, coincidentally aimed at recruiting African-American students. He also reports that individual institutions will continue to submit reports on "causes of attrition, retention rates, and special programs for retaining minority students." These include a statewide summer enrichment program; instructions from the chancellor for junior colleges to forward names and addresses of all graduates, identified by race, to senior colleges; recommendations for improving graduate recruitment seminars; and a statewide minority advising program of conferences and campus advisement, revamped at several campuses where reviews showed poor results were being obtained.

Over a three-year period, 26 minority faculty enrolled in the Regents Administrative Development Program (formerly the Administrative Internship Program), with 16 completions and 5 placed in permanent university system administrative positions. Faculty recruitment consisted of recruitment visits to several appropriate universities between November 1986 and January 1987; an inventory of available positions within the system; meetings between recruiters and chief academic offices to discuss available candidates and their interests: "Along with the resumes several letters were sent encouraging each institution to take a strong look at the minority students who had an interest in . . . the University System of Georgia."

The chancellor's response letter (Propst, 1987) attempts to convey a sense of the low expectations underlying enforcement by the end of the decade of the 1980s. His letter provides additional evidence of non- or unsatisfactorily limited compliance. It reports uncompleted remedies, it repeats unreasonable excuses for failure, and it provides additional evidence of incomplete implementation. The letter obviously is intended to undermine the findings of the GFR and to persuade federal officials to rule compliance. Doing so, the letter implies, requires little evidence of results, more of effort. The problems with enforcement intentionally and subtly repeated in the letter are, therefore, inconsequential.

It is worth repeating that OCR officials responded to their own above-summarized findings and the chancellor's responses by ruling substantial compliance. The 1988 Georgia letter asked for more complete implementation of TBI enhancements, and once the state provided evidence of effort as requested, OCR ruled compliance. In fact, the state's remedies contain poor program theories and are poorly designed, planned responses are incompletely undertaken, and many obfuscate limited action.

GEORGIA ENFORCEMENT, 1978–1989: SUMMARY AND ANALYSIS

This case study began with questions about the nature of state civil rights policy responses that the federal courts viewed as inadequate but that OCR, representing the nation's new conservative leadership, viewed as achieving compliance. Illustrated by the two state plans, state responses repeatedly reified barriers to compliance, limited the scope of planned remedies, provided only a portion of information required by the guidelines, and engaged in obfuscating actual actions taken. The fact that responses along these lines get repeated throughout the documents establishes a pattern of noncompliance. Though demonstrating the impact of a response pattern characterized in this way does not constitute a primary goal of this study, the GFR clearly provides evidence of their negative impact. According to the GFR, many TBI physical facility enhancements went unimplemented, student enrollment goals were unmet, TBI academic enhancements met with limited success, and employment goals were not accomplished. Ironically, the chancellor's response (Propst, 1987) confirms and amplifies the GFR findings.

Reinterpreted, the identified response pattern infers an overall strategy of refusing to acknowledge noncompliance, failure to diagnose civil rights problems, taking limited action, explaining limited action and poor results by falsely reifying outside forces, and relying upon broadly interpreted adequate effort as an ultimate standard for compliance.

Refusing to clearly acknowledge noncompliance with Title VI, the Georgia state desegregation plans do not establish a constructive tone for undertaking compliance. The 1978–1979 plan begins by simply denying the existence of current policies and practices that promote segregation. Asserting that no current policies deliberately segregate students suggests an interpretation of federal law similar to Mississippi's claim in the *United States v. Fordice* (1992) case — that removal of purposeful segregation laws alone constitutes compliance. Adopting such a strategy instead conveys the sense that federal laws are uninformed and intrusive, even though they must be complied with. No public leaders in the south could today wildly endorse civil rights problems because federal officials bring them to his or her attention. However, strong leaders can reasonably be expected to find ways of acknowledging race inequity problems constructively and set the tone for policy implementation aimed at improving critical situations in higher education. Such is the responsibility of leadership — to lead others toward compliance with public laws.

In fact, Georgia officials seemed to have made little effort to connect any system or institutional policy with past or present segregation. Knowing what institutional and system policies promote race inequity would seem to be necessary for planning remedies. Systematically and operationally describing campus and state race minority underenrollment and underemployment may contribute toward public acceptance of a problem, but certainly, such diagnoses lead toward proper design of remedies. The Georgia documents reviewed never fully describe race enrollment and employment problems and exhibit little enthusiasm for doing so. They repeatedly fail to provide data, required by the guidelines, that are intended to diagnose civil rights problems.

The materials, instead, partially describe solutions already underway to problems that were identified in unknown ways in the past. Though remedial actions are unclear and incompletely presented, it is certain that their scope is very narrow. Georgia officials simply designed programs that seemed to suit vaguely defined problems marginally disruptive of the current system. The Addendum, for example, promises to repeat old programs that accompanied declining African-American enrollment and, at the same time, to increase programs aimed at increasing white enrollment, when white increases already were firmly established through existing policymaking. Similarly, the University of Georgia report clearly states an institutional policy of improving African-American student access by expanding existing services and making African-Americans more aware of them. The undiagnosed civil rights problem at University of Georgia may be that existing services do not work well for African-Americans because, for years, the institution engaged in both formal and informal segregation practices. Expanding them and disseminating information is unlikely to address this more fundamental problem. Similarly, the legislature and governor refused funding for TBI enhancement, choosing instead to promote the current system social structure by giving priority to the needs of other campuses.

By no stretch of the imagination are the remedies proposed likely to produce substantial changes in civil rights with Georgia's college and university system. Activities planned simply do not involve sufficient financial and other resources to recruit other-race students, to establish new instructional programs and new facilities, and to develop new campus structures and programs that facilitate race minority participation.

The scope and pace of compliance policymaking depicted in the documents summarized also are incomplete and slow. Some remedies eventually got funded and implemented, perhaps even producing results like increased African-American graduate school enrollment, though such conclusions are extremely difficult from the compliance materials presented. However, clearly, many of the planned actions, like constructing new facilities at TBIs, were undertaken at a very slow pace only when federal regulators compromisingly but persistently insisted upon their completion. Similarly, new programs at University of Georgia were planned almost 15 years after Title VI enforcement began.

Quantifiable measures of the scope and pace of Georgia's responses are difficult to identify because of the inconclusive details provided. Whether the state spent sufficient funds to enhance TBIs depends upon needs that never were clearly established in the compliance documents. The 1983 study comparing TBIs and TWIs (U.S. Department of Education, 1987, p. 3) lacked sufficient substance to reach such conclusions. It appears aimed at providing limited but publicly persuasive evidence of active compliance. Similarly, state responses do not contain sufficient standards for judging adequacy of new instructional programs at TBIs. Does the "program theory" underlying a strategy of adding new programs involve establishing robust TBIs in which whites will choose to enroll because they are demonstrably high quality? Or does the state's underlying program theory involve, regardless of overall robustness, establishing a physically neat and safe campus that offers a handful of instructional programs in which whites choose to enroll because they are not offered at other colleges? Measures of adequate scope of remedies, derived from clear understanding of problems and clear goals, are not possible in the case of Georgia. Adopting less precise and more informal measures, by no stretch of the imagination, will the ten actions specified in the 1978–1979 plan improve African-American participation within Georgia's system. The actions outlined in the Addendum are clearer but equally limited.

Exhibited by plans and compliance documents, it is also the habit of Georgia state officials to rationalize limited action by drawing attention to perceivably uncontrollable factors that constitute a barrier to enforcement. Near the end of the 1983 plan's effective time period, Georgia officials submitted a paper describing barriers to minority student retention that mentions only those that are student centered and does so in a manner suggesting that the student-centered barriers provide an unassailable explanation for state failure to accomplish desegregation goals ("External Factors Which Constrain Achievement of Desegregation Goals in the University System of Georgia," undated).

Georgia officials also justify weak remedies by asserting or assuming unremediably limited capacity and responsibility. In the Addendum, enrollment declines are uncontrollable, the unevidenced result of student factors portrayed in the literature review, of changes in federal student aid policy, and of race-neutral state policymaking. These are all factors under the control of others. Moreover, the legislature and governor play no compulsory role in federal civil rights compliance, preserving the right not, or only partially, to fund remedies that state higher education officials promised to undertake. Such assumptions strongly suggest evidence of a much broader negative response.

Another apparent aspect of the Georgia compliance strategy involves attempting to show that policies aimed at other goals in fact are intended to accomplish civil rights outcomes. The counseling sessions held throughout the state actually supported the regents' new admission criteria. Although African-American student needed to know about them, the sessions did not exemplify a special effort or remedy for past race discrimination. Other examples of this kind emerge from Georgia plans and compliance reports, enough to characterize the state's responses as misleading and misguided.

Viewed negatively, Georgia state responses become a strategy of purposeful guile and obfuscation, presumably aimed at minimal or continued noncompliance. Misguided assumptions of limited authority, sole reliance upon uncontrollable external factors as an excuse for taking limited action, adopting policies of expanding (but not changing) existing campus services, and suggesting that state policies unrelated to desegregation constitute civil rights responses characterize the state strategy. Targeting "minority" students, vaguely reporting with triumph that proposals got made, and submitting poorly designed studies and policy analyses that, by weak academic standards, are unacceptable within any college and university community also display its true character. Unarguably, some officials of goodwill involved in undertaking the Georgia strategy simply do not recognize its true characteristics, believing that proposed responses will advance civil rights outcomes; others may cynically have endorsed its characteristics in pursuit of goals of their own; and still others failed to reconcile fear of disrupting the system with the perceived unimportant challenge of civil rights compliance. These three state interpretations and responses to federal civil rights regulations, each amounting to resistance, to some extent explain enforcement in Georgia, and probably other states as well.

What took place in Georgia may not duplicate other states' responses. However, careful (though unreported) reading of other state plans and reports suggest to this author the opposite conclusion — that Georgia's are not atypical. Certainly, Georgia's results duplicate those of other states. The next two chapters take a look at more recent state responses in Mississippi, Alabama, and Louisiana after OCR ruled compliance in Georgia. Information about these three other states will suggest the extent to which Georgia's enforcement episode is being replicated. The next chapter , like this one, also provides an opportunity to place into perspective the two competing interpretations of enforcement.

NOTE

I gratefully acknowledge the assistance of David Harris, at the time a Ph.D. student at the Harvard Graduate School of Arts and Sciences, in preparing the summary of the Georgia Factual Report.

REFERENCES

Adams v. Bell, D.C. Civil Action No. 70-3095 (March 24, 1982).
Brown v. Board of Education, 347 U.S. 483 (1954).
Daniels, Legree S., Assistant Secretary for Civil Rights USED to Honorable Joe Frank Harris, Atlanta, Georgia, February 9, 1988.
"Desegregation at the University of Georgia: A Status Report." July 18, 1985. Attachment to H. Dean Propst to Lamar Clements, December 31, 1987.

Mimeographed.

"External Factors Which Constrain Achievement of Desegregation Goals in the University System of Georgia." Undated. Attachment to Propst to Clements, December 31, 1985. Mimeographed.

Georgia State Board of Regents. 1983. "Addendum." Mimeographed.

Georgia State Board of Regents. 1977. "A Plan for the Further Desegregation of the University System of Georgia." Atlanta, Georgia. September 1977. Mimeographed.

Hunnicutt v. Burge, 356 F. Supp. 1217, 1238 (M.D. Ga 1973).

NAACP Legal Defense Fund. undated. "Comments on OCR's Proposed 'Factual Report' on Implementation of the Desegregation Plan for Public Higher Education — Georgia." Mimeographed.

Propst, H. Dean, Chancellor, University of Georgia System, to Alicia Coro, Acting Assistant Secretary for Civil Rights, ED, June 4, 1987.

Propst, H. Dean, Chancellor, University of Georgia System, to Lamar Clements, Acting Director, OCR Region IV, December 31, 1985.

Rilling, Paul, OCR Region IV Director, to Charles Simpson, Georgia Chancellor of Higher Education, February 26, 1970.

Thomas, William H., Regional Civil Rights Director, to Honorable Joe Frank Harris, Governor of Georgia, May 15, 1985.

Thomas, William H., Director, OCR Region IV, to Vernon Crawford, Chancellor, University System of Georgia, March 7, 1984, with "Statement of Findings: The University System Operates A System of Higher Education in Which the Effects of Past Discrimination Against Students at TBIs Have Not Been Eliminated." Undated. Mimeographed.

United States v. Fordice, 112 S. Ct. (1992).

University System of Georgia. 1985. *Annual Progress Report: Implementation of a Plan for the Further Desegregation of Georgia.* May 15, 1985. Mimeographed.

U.S. Department of Education. 1987. "Georgia Higher Education Desegregation Plan Factual Report." March 27, 1987. Mimeographed.

3

Mobilizing Civil Rights Enforcement in Mississippi, 1992–1996

In 1992, the U.S. Supreme Court ruled that Mississippi's state system remained noncompliant with Title VI and the Fourteenth Amendment to the Constitution. The Fifth Circuit Court previously determined that removing segregation laws alone constituted compliance with federal civil rights requirements. *United States v. Fordice* (1992) opened a new chapter in Title VI enforcement. By the end of the 1980s, the Office for Civil Rights' (OCR's) systemwide monitoring and compliance policy-making essentially had ended, as described in the previous chapters. The Supreme Court had not issued a major civil rights ruling in higher education for 20 years. Leaders of the nation's civil rights community hailed the *Fordice* decision, the Legal Defense Fund's former director, Julius Chambers, referring to it as a modern version of the 1954 *Brown v. Board of Education* decision. The following chapter describes the unfolding episode of civil rights enforcement in Mississippi brought about by *Fordice*.

BACKGROUND

During the 1960s, the state of Mississippi became a well-known symbol of southern resistance to racial justice and equality. Many dramatic events of the civil rights movement occurred there. News media reports and policy studies illustrated in Mississippi the greatest physical violence against African-Americans and most thorough denial of basic human and political rights. White leaders like Governor Ross Barnett gained national notoriety from personal appearances on television news programs and other public policy forums in the north, personifying dogged determination to maintain the "closed society" of his home state. Life in Mississippi was characterized by repeated acts of heroism by African-American social activists like Medgar Evers, Winnie and Dovie Houston, and Fannie Lou Hamer, to name a few. Battle-scarred SNCC veterans were the only civil rights workers brave enough to set foot, let alone register voters and organize demonstrations, in isolated rural areas of the celebrated state. The Whig-Cliosophic Society invited Barnett to speak at Princeton University, where the author of this study, a freshman at the time, staged his own personal protest, walking out of the lecture hall shortly after the governor began to speak. Perhaps more significantly and insightfully, Nina Simone, an African-American jazz singer well-known during the 1960s, recorded a song entitled "Mississippi Goddamn (And I Mean Every Word Of It)."

Mississippi's socioeconomic status to a certain degree explains its civil rights history. It is a poor state with problems not atypically associated with poverty. The following recent demographic trends illustrate Mississippi's continuing socioeconomic problems (Mississippi Board of Trustees of State Institutions of Higher Learning, *Ayers Decision*, Vol. 1, mimeo undated and unpaginated, in Appendix):

According to the 1990 census, the population of Mississippi is 2,573,216, reflecting an out-migration of 144,000 people between 1980–1990, atypical for the South.

The state median household income is $20,136, compared with the national average of $35,225, with 25.2 percent of the state population living in poverty.

During the 1980s, the number of families living in Mississippi in poverty grew at the rate of 13.6 percent. The poverty rate for 18–24 year olds was 29.6 percent in 1990.

About 11 percent of the state's 16–64-year-old population suffers from a health problem that affects their ability to work.

Roughly 15.6 percent of Mississippi's adult population (compared with 10.4 percent nationally) achieved less than a ninth-grade education.

Notably, 12 percent of the state's 16–19 year olds in 1990 were high-school dropouts, and two out of three teenaged dropouts were unemployed.

African-Americans long have constituted a substantial proportion of Mississippi's population and are disproportionately affected by its socioeconomic problems. Today, about 35.6 percent of the total state population is African-American, compared with an average among the states of roughly 12 percent. The combination of a high population of African-Americans, the negative history of race relations, and continuing poor socioeconomic conditions nourish continuing race conflict. No set of Mississippi institutions has been immune, including higher education.

In fact, higher education was among the first set of Mississippi institutions affected by the stresses and strains of race conflict of the 1960s variety. Civil rights conflict for which Mississippi became famous emerged in 1962, when the Fifth Circuit Court ordered state leaders to admit African-American Mississippian James Meredith to the state's flagship university, the University of Mississippi at Oxford. Accompanied by federal marshals and the national guard troops, Meredith arrived at the University of Mississippi campus on September 30, 1962, and several violent days of white protest ensued. Conflict between federal marshals and local citizens and students resulted in physical injury and death. Events and conditions surrounding this widely known episode in the history of the civil rights movement have been well-chronicled (Silverman, 1964). Legal assaults upon southern states' policies of segregating colleges and universities, like the law cases leading to Meredith's admission to Ole Miss, constituted a prominent element of an overall strategy for opening the closed system of the south. Although heightened awareness of racial segregation reflecting the strong violence that accompanied Meredith's arrival could not have been arranged by civil rights leaders, certainly it could have been anticipated.

The dramatic and uncomplimentary Meredith episode shortly preceeded expanding OCR enforcement of Title VI of the 1964 Civil Rights Law. Based upon compliance reviews, OCR in 1969 notified Mississippi and nine other states — Virginia, North Carolina, Maryland, Pennsylvania, Louisiana, Georgia, Florida, Oklahoma, and Arkansas — that civil rights violations had been uncovered. In response, Mississippi's Board of Trustees of State Institutions of Higher Learning (popularly referred to as "the College Board") submitted a plan for eliminating vestiges of prior de jure segregation in public higher education in 1973, but OCR never approved it.

Dispute between Mississippi and OCR centered upon at least two problems with the state's desegregation plan: Mississippi's refusal to include two-year colleges, claiming that they all were founded after 1954, when de jure segregation laws already had been repealed, and OCR's judgment that its contents simply did not go far enough in such areas as student enrollment, faculty hiring, and eliminating duplicative instructional programs. Substantial tension accompanied expanded federal civil rights enforcement, and after negotiations broke down, Mississippi's central governance body, the Board of Trustees of State Institutions of Higher Education, approved the state's desegregation plan anyway. The Mississippi legislature slowly got around to funding it in 1978, awarding one-half the funds the College Board requested five years earlier. As required by law, OCR asked the Justice Department to instigate judicial proceedings against Mississippi, but the leaders of the Justice Department moved neither quickly nor deliberately. After federal enforcement diminished following Richard Nixon's election in the mid-1970s, a group of private African-American citizens of Mississippi initiated federal court action.

EARLY LITIGATION IN MISSISSIPPI

On January 28, 1975, a group of private petitioners filed a class action suit against the state of Mississippi's governor, College Board, Commissioner of Higher Education, other public officials, and the five historically white universities. Accompanied by the U.S. Justice Department as intervenor, the petitioners claimed that the state of Mississippi continued its policy of de jure segregation in its public university system by maintaining five predominantly white universities and three almost completely black universities. By doing so, the state failed to meet the obligation set forth by the Fourteenth Amendment and Title VI of the Civil Rights act of 1964. After several years of trying to reach a settlement, a six-week trial took place between April 17 and June 1, 1987. The outcome favored the defendants. On December 10, 1987, the district court found that the state of Mississippi had fulfilled its obligation by having earlier established race-neutral policies not animated by a discriminatory purpose. In other words, all that the law required of the state was repeal of statutes and policies that barred black students from attending white institutions, requiring separation of students by race.

Dissatisfied with this outcome, petitioners appealed, and in 1990, the Fifth Circuit Court of Appeals affirmed the district court decision, ruling that the adoption and implementation of race-neutral policies alone satisfied the state's obligation to abandon its prior dual system: "The record makes clear that Mississippi has adopted and implemented race-neutral policies for operating its colleges and universities and that all students have real freedom of choice to attend the college or university they wish" (*Ayers v. Allain*, 1987).

The circuit court ruled that college and university systems are different from public school districts in that college attendance is voluntary: qualified students normally enjoy free choice among unfungible institutions within the system. Because this is true, race-neutral policies constitute sufficient remedies for past de jure segregation. This is the case even though the Supreme Court ruled in 1968 that free choice and race-neutral policies were, alone, insufficient where public elementary and secondary education is concerned (*Green v. New Kent County*, 1968). Discounting the school desegregation cases, the circuit court relied upon the Supreme Court's 1986 ruling that single-race identity of a subset of 4-H and Homemaker clubs, holding voluntary membership like college and universities, does not a priori constitute evidence of violation of Title VI or the Equal Protection Clause.

The Court of Appeals concluded that the state had fulfilled its affirmative obligation to disestablish its prior *de jure* segregated system by adopting and implementing race-neutral policies governing its college and university system. Because students seeking higher education had "real freedom" to choose the institution of their choice, the state need do no more. Even though neutral policies were not enough to dismantle a dual system of primary and secondary schools, *Green v. New Kent County School Board, supra*, the Court of Appeals thought that universities "differ fundamentally" from lower levels of schools, 914 F. 2d, at 686, sufficiently so that our decision in *Bazemore v. Friday* justified the conclusion that the state had dismantled its former dual system. (*United States v. Fordice*, 1992, p. 9)

Bazemore (1986) "raised the issue whether the financing and operational assistance provided by a state university's extension service to voluntary 4-H and Homemaker Clubs was inconsistent with the Equal Protection Clause because of the existence of numerous all-white and all-black clubs." A previous district court found that the clubs' race discrimination policies ended in 1965 and no evidence existed of lingering effects of such policies; current racial imbalance resulted from free choice of private individuals. The Supreme Court justices approved this finding after "satisfying ourselves that the state had not fostered segregation by playing a part in the decision of which club an individual chose to join" (*United States v. Fordice*, 1992, p. 11).

At the time of the circuit court ruling, the Mississippi state university system consisted, as it currently does, of eight institutions. (The state's 15 community colleges are not directly affected by *Fordice*.) In accordance with the state's 1981 long-range plan, the University of Mississipi, Mississippi State University (MSU), and the University of Southern Mississippi are "comprehensive" universities, offering a wide range of undergraduate and graduate degree programs; two of the state's three traditionally black institutions (TBIs) — Mississippi Valley State and Alcorn State — traditionally white Delta State and Mississippi University for Women are "regional," offering fewer degree programs concentrated at the undergraduate level; and Jackson State, the third TBI, holds an "urban" university mission.

The total operating budget for the state system in fiscal year 1993 was roughly $980,000,000, with a state appropriation totaling roughly $308,000,000, or approximately 31 percent. Table 3.1 displays total fiscal year 1993 operating budgets and state appropriations for each of the eight universities:

TABLE 3.1
Fiscal Year 1993 State Appropriations and Operating Budgets
(in Dollars)

University	State Appropriation	Total Operating Budget
Traditionally Black Institutions		
Alcorn State	8,681,397	23,120,788
Jackson State	19,121,928	46,425,053
Mississippi Valley	6,861,538	15,897,113
Traditionally White Institutions		
Delta State	11,611,252	25,819,662
Mississippi State	47,807,919	127,115,882
Mississippi University for Women	7,125,299	16,897,000
University of Mississippi	38,437,194	111,571,286
University of Southern Mississippi	41,356,955	106,746,519

Source: Mississippi Board of Trustees of State Institutions of Higher Learning, *Ayers Decision*, Vol. 1, 1992, Appendix.

Other important demographic facts about the Mississippi system are adapted from the Southern Education Foundation's recent report "Redeeming the American Promise" (1995) and are included in the Appendix.

In *Ayers v. Allain* (1987), Mississippi defendants made no claim that problems of race inequity, perhaps reflected in the differences in funding depicted in the above information, do not today exist in Mississippi. The following more recent data illustrate other kinds of race inequity problems that the Missisippi government officials, the district court, and the circuit court dismissed:

Fewer African-Americans earned bachelor's degrees in Mississippi in 1991 than in 1979. White students' degrees increased by 11 percent, but African-Americans' degree earning decreased by 16 percent.

Although the number of doctoral degrees earned by African-Americans increased from 16 in 1979 to 22 in 1991, black representation remained substantially below the state's population norm — 6 percent versus 36 percent — in 1991.

Although undergraduate African-American enrollment at traditionally white institutions (TWIs) increased substantially over the decade of the 1980s, from 4 percent to 21 percent, it never reached population parity and did not match a corresponding increase in the rate of high-school graduation attained by African-Americans.

African-American graduate school enrollment declined by 6 percent during the 1980s (from very low beginning levels).

At the first professional school level, African-American enrollment increased, but only to 6 percent between 1980 and 1992.

THE SUPREME COURT'S *FORDICE* DECISION

On appeal, the U.S. Supreme Court on June 26, 1992, ruled that the circuit court erred by overlooking the district court's failure to conduct an inquiry about factors traceable to past policies that continue to operate and result in racial segregation even though an overall nondiscrimination policy has been adopted. The court observed that race-neutral admission policies are not the sole factor determining admission to college. Some, traceable to past discrimination policies, may continue to operate: "If the state perpetuates policies and practices traceable to its prior system that continue to have segregative effects — whether by influencing student enrollment decisions or by fostering segregation in other facets of the university system — and such policies are without sound educational justification and can be practicably eliminated, the state has satisfied its burden of proving that it has dismantled its prior system" (*United States v. Fordice*, 1992, p. 12).

The Supreme Court's ruling vacated the previous decisions, because the district and circuit courts failed to consider whether the significant lack of racial integration still existing at that time had anything to do with policies and practices stemming from the prior de jure system. The court ordered that the district court reexamine "in light of the proper standard, each of the other policies now governing the State's university system that have been challenged or that are challenged" (*United States v. Fordice*, 1992, p. 14).

The court identifies, as examples, "four policies of the present system: admission standards, program duplication, institutional mission assignments, and continued operation of all eight public universities" that appear to restrict student enrollment choices, foster segregation, hold weak educational justification, and can be easily remedied (*United States v. Fordice*, 1992, p. 13). Admissions standards, the court points out, can be race neutral on the surface but still reflect past restrictive purposes, and in the way they are formulated and implemented, this seems to be the case in Mississippi. The problem is that current policies channel African-American students' choices in the direction of enrolling at TBIs and whites' in the direction of enrolling at TWIs: "The present admission standards are not only traceable to the *de jure* system and were originally adopted for a discriminatory purpose, but they also have present discriminatory effects. . . . Without doubt, these requirements restrict the range of choices of entering students as to which institutions they may attend in a way that perpetuates segregation" (*United States v. Fordice*, 1992, p. 14).

For example, in 1963, the system admitted to all but one of its TWIs any student who scored at least 15 on the ACT admissions test. Students scoring 13 or 14 who applied to the state's two TBIs were admitted automatically. According to the court, in 1985, 72 percent of white high-school seniors in Mississippi scored 15 or above; less than 30 percent of black high-school seniors did as well. Interestingly, Mississippi University for Women requires an ACT composite score of 18 for automatic admission, even though it is one of three universities designated as having a "regional," as opposed to "flagship," mission. The other two regional universities — Alcorn State and Mississippi Valley State — are predominantly black.

The court argues that lower-scoring black students are barred from attending predominantly white institutions by test score policy of this kind. Furthermore, the case reports, the American College Testing Program and the Educational Testing Service, which construct standardized college admissions tests, strongly recommend against using test scores as the sole determinant of college admissions. By citing such

evidence, the court provided examples of unjustifiable and easily remedied factors traceable to prior practice that continue to foster segregation.

In the court's view, decisions about where to locate institutional
programs clearly were reached with the goal in mind of segregating
students: "It can hardly be denied that such duplication was part and
parcel of the prior dual system of higher education — the whole notion of
'separate but equal' required duplicative programs in two sets of schools
— and that the present unnecessary duplication is a continuation of that
practice" (*United States v. Fordice*, 1992, p. 19).

The court's reasonable expectation is that "elimination of unnecessary duplication would decrease institutional racial identifiability,
affect student choice, and promote sound educational policies": it admon-
ishes the district court for, on the one hand, failing to request proof in
support of this concept and, on the other hand, noting absence of proof of
this assertion.

The court centers upon the system's mission designation because: "The
institutional mission designations adopted in 1981 have as their
antecedents the policies enacted to pepetuate racial segregation during the
de jure segregated regime. The Court of Appeals expressly disagreed with
the District Court by recognizing that the 'inequalities among the institutions largely follow the mission designations, and the mission designations to some degree follow the historical racial assignments'" (*United
States v. Fordice*, 1992, p. 21). The problem is that "different missions . . .
assigned to the universities surely limits to some extent an entering
student's choice as to which university to seek admittance" (*United States
v. Fordice*, 1992, p. 21).

Similarly, in the court's view, "The existence of eight instead of some
lesser number (of universities) was undoubtedly occasioned by state laws
forbidding the mingling of the races." It then directs the district court to
determine "whether retention of all eight institutions itself affects student
choice and perpetuates the segregated higher education system, whether
maintenance of each of the universities is educationally justifiable, and
whether one or more of them can be practically closed or merged with
other existing instututitions" (*United States v. Fordice*, 1992, p. 23).

The recent Supreme Court judgment about Mississippi's efforts to
desegregate sets a long-needed standard for judging states' dismantling
of prior de jure segregated systems, and it provides a new policy resource
for continued Title VI regulatory intervention. *Fordice* presents the new
standard for judging compliance in the following terms: "If the state
perpetuates policies and practices traceable to its prior system that
continue to have segregative effects . . . and such policies are without

sound educational justification and can be practicably eliminated, the state has not satisfied its burden of proving that it has dismantled its prior system" (*United States v. Fordice*, 1992, p. 12).

It suggests a course of action that involves identifying factors preventing access and "free choice" that meet the court's three criteria — traceability to the prior system, educationally unjustifiable, and practically remedied. To achieve compliance, Mississippi must identify factors that not only limit African-American initial enrollment in college, but also foster "segregation in other facets of the university system." The case leaves unclear standards for judging evidence of traceability and reasonableness, although clear examples are provided.

The state cannot comply until it eliminates all policies and practices traceable to prior segregation that continue to foster the same result. Clearly, TBIs can be traced to prior de jure segregation and today segregate the African-American students who attend them. Absent any sound educational justification or substantial incapacity to resolve this problem, operating traditionally black colleges as such clearly is unlawful. Following this reasoning, the court identifies the mix of eight similar institutions — three African-American and five white — with clearly duplicate instructional programs as evidence of unlawful governance.

By this logic, any policy at previously segregated systems of operating institutions with predominantly African-American enrollments is suspect. There must exist a sound educational justification for doing so or a substantial difficulty for remedy. Traditionally black colleges and universities, in the court's current view, are not "exclusively black enclaves by private choice" in which students freely choose to enroll for private reasons of their own. They are, instead, "facilities for all . . . citizens" within a system that cannot perpetuate separate but more equal institutions (*United States v. Fordice*, 1992, p. 23). Acceptable educational justifications for the existence of such institutions must stand on their own, independent of providing private choice for African-Americans.

RESPONSES TO *FORDICE*

Responses to *Fordice* within the state of Mississippi were high-spirited. Anticipating the court's judgment, the governor, Kirk Fordice, who vowed three years earlier to call out the national guard if the federal courts forced increased state spending on higher education, appointed three advisory groups in January 1992. Similarly, the College Board, soon after the decision was announced, organized a strategy for developing a remedy that involved convening three "advisory panels" (*Clarion-Ledger*, July 27,

1992, p. 27) and publishing a statewide desegregation plan in October 1992. According to Ray Cleer, the former Mississippi commissioner of higher education, the board considered several alternatives and then adopted a system restructuring strategy toward planning a remedy (Cleer, 1994). The board's plan, along with a claim to save the university system $12 million annually, contained several controversial provisions (*Ayers v. Fordice*, Civil Action No. GC75-9-B-O, 1992):

Mississippi Valley State, a TBI, and Delta State would merge to form a new unit of the University of Mississippi, one of the state's flagship instititutions.

Mississippi University for Women would become a unit of the University of Southern Mississippi.

Alcorn State, the second TBI, would become a unit of Mississippi State University, with some of Mississippi State University's undergraduate programs being shifted to Alcorn.

Jackson State, a third TBI, would be expanded, receiving new programs — some from other institutions — and new facilities.

The school of veterinary medicine at Mississippi State and the dental school at the University of Mississippi, the only ones of the kind in the state, would be closed, and students in these program would be funded at out-of-state universities.

The U.S. Justice Department presented recommendations to the court, including a very controversial suggestion for merging Jackson State and the University of Mississippi's medical school, which are both located in the city of Jackson. The Justice Department recommendations also suggested reassigning Ole Miss' and Mississippi State's undergraduate architectural programs to Jackson State (U.S. Department of Justice, 1993). The plaintiffs did not submit a plan.

Once the College Board and Department of Justice plans were made public, widespread and vigorous disagreement emerged. Those protesting the plan included all parties to the case, including virtually all the universities in the system. Among the most vocal opponents were officials of the Mississippi University for Women (MUW), which, according to the board, should be merged with Mississippi State. The often-outspoken enrollment director at the Mississippi University for Women claimed that "They're picking on blacks and women. It's always the same damn thing — we're dispensable" (*St. Petersburg Times*, 1994, p. 1A). Leaders of the Mississippi University for Women claimed that the plan disturbed its mission to educate women, but then-Commissioner Cleer disagreed: "It (MUW) is making no more of a unique contribution to women than any other institution" (*St. Petersburg Times*, 1994, p. 4). "One need look only a few miles away from MUW to find an institution (Mississippi State) that has a broad interest in women in its curriculum" (*Commercial Appeal*, 1994, p. 17). According to the Mississippi University for Women President Clyda Rent, "We're all dedicated to keeping higher education in Mississippi intact, and to not doing anything that would be devisive" (Mercer, 1992). Ricki Garrett, the only graduate of the Mississippi University for Women on the College Board, voted against the plan and later voiced opposition to it, expressing hope that "We can go back to the drawing board and begin again to devise a plan that will address the issues of the Ayers case (*Northeast Mississippi Daily Journal*, 1992, p. 5A).

Two of the three historically African-American institutions — Alcorn State and Mississippi State — also stood to lose in the board's plan. William Sutton, president of Mississippi Valley State, suggested that, "In the foreseeable future, we believe Mississippi will not implement a plan that will tear the higher education system apart, as this (plan) would" (Mercer, 1992). Other TWIs also stood to lose. Mississippi State University's dean of the school of agriculture responded that "the question is not how can we divide the sack of marbles and distribute them, but how can we bring the resources we have to bear to educate our citizenry?" (Mercer, 1992).

One of the universities' major complaints was lack of involvement in planning. This point of view was expressed publicly by Dean Dwight Mercer of Mississippi State University's College of Veterinary Medicine, which was scheduled for closure: "We've been lumped into the board recommendation, without any input from us or the groups we serve. . . . All of the students are concerned, but our posture has been we are not in the business of demonstrating or raising a ruckus. . . . But we're taking a quiet, person-to-person approach and we're saying 'Here's what the school does'" (Mercer, 1992). The local press' approach was less "person-to-person." Reporters were annoyed by the board decision to hold closed meetings to prepare the plan. State law allows for public officials to conduct closed sessions when matters of litigation are under discussion. A newpaper campaign decrying the board's decision accompanied the closed deliberations. It continued once the plan became public. When the plan got introduced at an October 22, 1992, court session, hundreds of protestors, led by Joseph Lowery, president of the Southern Christian Leadership Conference, which Martin Luther King founded, gathered in protest outside the courtroom. The leadership of the state National Association for the Advancement of Colored People (NAACP) called for the resignation of the eight College Board members who voted for the plan (*Sun Herald*, 1992).

Mirroring Mississippi's earlier civil rights history, reactions to some elements of the proposed merger — for example, assigning Ole Miss' medical school to historically African-American Jackson State — were less tactful. The student quarterly at the medical center printed a notice: "Reserve your copy of an official University of Mississippi Medical Center diploma today. Supplies are limited so you must act now if you want to beat the rush. Once Jackson State takes over, you'll be SOL, so get a move on. Get yours now." The *Murmur* also offered bumper stickers for sale that read "Non-JSU M.D. I GOT MINE BEFORE RENO GAVE IT AWAY" (*Jackson Advocate*, 1994). Along the same line, 17 Jackson State students were arrested at the College Board headquarters. They arrived demanding a meeting with the commissioner and the board but were jailed after they refused to leave the building when it closed (Mercer, 1994).

After submission of the board's plan, three studies were undertaken, two by higher education lobbyists and representatives and one by a subcommittee of the state legislature; all three recommended no closures. A local legal advocacy organization organized a summit meeting of numerous groups opposing closure of institutions in Jackson, Mississippi, on January 9–10, 1993. The purpose of the meeting was to agree upon alternatives to the board's proposals and to establish a strategy for being heard by the court, including further litigation.

Thirty-eight members of the Mississippi Legislature responded by introducing legislation asserting the legislature's exclusive right to close down state colleges and universities. African-American legislators' analysis of the board's proposals included the following observations:

Merger of Delta State, the TWI with the highest black enrollment in the state, with Mississippi Valley actually increases racial isolation and identifiability.

The proposed mergers are pro forma, because enrollments would not be displaced from one campus to the other and institutions, thus, would remain racially identified.

Except for shifting some programs to Jackson State, very little program duplication measures are included.

Closure of the state's veterinary and dental schools would not affect desegregation.

The same proposals for merger and closure were presented by the board chairperson in 1986, long before the *Fordice* ruling.

In this view, the board proposals demonstrate continuing bad faith and deception (*Sun Herald*, 1992). At least one College Board member displayed second thoughts. James Luvene, who voted for the plan, later indicated that he was "open to listen. . . . I don''t want to close any school" (*Northeast Mississippi Daily Journal*, 1992, p. 4B). Disagreement also reached the legislature. Although some state leaders characterized the plan as fair and referred to its provisions in Ross Perot language as sharing the pain, others disagreed. State senator Robert Crook, for example, once the decision was announced, appointed a state senate committee to develop a desegregation plan, action separate from the governor's three advisory panels. Crook later requested a special session of the state legislature to address the College Board remedy, but the governor denied his request (*Northeast Mississippi Daily Journal*, 1992, p. 11; Barton, 1992, p. B1).

Attempts to negotiate a settlement between 1975 and 1993 met with little success, because substantial mistrust seemed to expand over the years, at a personal level among negotiators and more broadly among the groups they represented. This problem was apparent to a variety of parties to the case, including Jackie Robinson, president of the Jackson City Council and one of the plaintiffs in the original *Ayers* case (Robinson, 1994); William Winter, former governor of the state (Winter, 1994); and former Commissioner Ray Cleere (1994). Illustrating this problem, a local newpaper reported a February 16, 1993, meeting to discuss the plan between the College Board and the presidents of the TWIs. African-American university presidents were not invited. (Editorial, *Clarion-Ledger*, 1994). Similarly, Sutton, president of Mississippi Valley State, recalls a private meeting among all the college presidents in which difficult changes were discussed and tentatively agreed upon, including potentially disagreeable reallocations of programs and funding to traditionally African-American universities. College Board representatives, the president pointed out, did not attend this meeting, and their absence may have contributed to its success, even though recommendations from the meeting were never officially concluded, presented, or seriously considered by the board (Sutton, 1994).

An editorial in a local newspaper, the *Clarion-Ledger*, observes that "With some tinkering, the state College Board basically dusted off an old proposal from the 1980s. It was a plan to close some schools and merge others that was entertained during the administration of former Gov. Bill Allain. This plan originally was a cost-saving move, not one to desegregate schools. The board did this in secret and laid it upon a stunned public like a bombshell" (Editorial, *Clarion-Ledger*, 1994). This editorial refers to apparent attempts by the board in 1986 and 1991 to downsize and to close some universities. On Neal Biggers' behalf, U.S. Magistrate Jeremy Davis made a final attempt at a negotiated settlement among higher education officials in Oxford on March 23, 1993, at an unannounced meeting of all college presidents and board members, but this effort also led nowhere.

THE DISTRICT COURT TRIAL AND REMEDY

Viewing opposition from the many groups involved, the district court judge entered a scheduling order requiring parties involved to submit by October 15, 1993, descriptions of factors that meet the Supreme Court's criteria — factors that restrict African-American participation — are traceable to prior legal segregation, are amenable to reasonable remedy, and are educationally unjustifiable. Defendants needed to respond by November 1, 1993, and plaintiffs were asked for a response by December 10, "identifying the practicable alternatives they contend are available to policies and practices the state contends are supported by sound educational justification" (U.S. Justice Department, 1993).

District Court Judge Biggers then ordered a trial beginning May 9, 1994. Alvin Chambliss, lead lawyer for the plaintiffs, Mississippi State Representative Bennie Thompson, City Councilman Louis Armstrong, and leaders of the national and state NAACP, the Historically Black College and University Watch, the A. Phillip Randolph Institute, and the state American Federation of Labor and Congress of Industrial Organizations immediately affirmed the importance of the trial by organizing a student demonstration in Oxford at the University of Mississippi (*Jackson Advocate*, 1994). National attention through the news and professional media, though limited, bolstered local strategies aimed at drawing attention to the case. For example, the American Association of University Professors released a study in January 1995 that reaffirmed the "essential" contribution of historically black institutions and condemned attempts, like the one in Mississippi, to merge them with white colleges and universities (American Association of University Professors, 1995). Similarly, an editorial appeared in *The Wall Street Journal*, headlined, "Save the W." The writer observes that "How closing the W (MUW) would advance the goal of desegregation is a mystery. The W has an exceptionally strong record attracting minorities. . . . Nor would merging the W into Mississippi State save money: Mississippi State costs the state $500 more per student than the W does" (*The Wall Street Journal*, 1994).

While waiting for the judge's decision, the plaintiffs requested an injunction to prevent the College Board from implementing parts of its desegregation plan. In particular, the plaintiffs sought to postpone, until after the judge's ruling, several actions scheduled to take place prior to or during the 1995–1996 academic year — elimination of the Mississippi Guaranteed Student Loan Agency; transfer of remedial programs and departments at the historically African-American universities to the new supervisor of the College Board Summer Remediation Program; implementation of the new admissions standards, referred to as "Project 95"; and increases in out-of-state tuition (*Ayers v. Fordice*, 1994). Biggers and the Fifth Circuit Court denied the request. The U.S. Supreme Court followed suit on April 22, 1996.

At the beginning of the trial, plaintiffs alledged 14 vestiges of prior segregation. In his ruling of March 1995, the judge dismissed seven of them (for varying reasons, described in greater detail in Chapter 4). He recognized the remaining seven areas of undergraduate admissions, institutional missions, duplicative offerings, land-grant programs, funding, equipment availability, and library allocations, and the operation of eight universities. He ruled that these remnants were traceable to de jure segregation and, at that time, continued to have segregative effects.

Regarding undergraduate admissions, standards in place at the time of the trial in 1987, although racially neutral on their face, were discriminatory when viewed under the legal standard established in *Fordice* and should be altered. The court endorsed the 1995 admissions standards proposed by the College Board for incoming freshman, effective for the 1995–1996 academic year. The new standards eliminate the prior segregative effects of the previous ones. They include the use of ACT scores in combination with a prescribed high-school grade point average (GPA) and provide for a systemwide intensive summer program for students in need of remediation.

Regarding mission designation, the judge ruled that the limited missions of the TBIs, in relationship to the TWIs, were, indeed, vestiges of the past supported in a variety of ways by the state's past educational policies and practices. He ruled that the 1981 mission statement had the effect of maintaining the status quo with respect to programmatic offerings and was consistent with the development of institutions during the de jure period. However, the judge accepted the board's proposal not to revise the mission designations of the various institutions; instead, he agreed with board proposals to enhance the programmatic offerings at Jackson State and Alcorn State. These involve adding engineering, law, and pharmacy schools at Jackson State and a master of business administration program at Alcorn State. The judge also adopted the board's proposal for a $5 million endowment for Jackson State and Alcorn State for educational enhancement and race diversity, $15 million over five years to enhance physical facilities at Jackson State, and up to $4 million annually over a five-year period to be matched by Alcorn State for the Small Farm Development Center.

In regard to program duplication, the court acknowledged that the duplication existing at that time was a remnant of the old dual system of higher education that developed out of the separate but equal era. The duplication issue did not stand alone: when combined with different admissions standards, it was quite possible that it could promote segregation. Specific remedial steps described above also were intended to address this problem.

Concerning the number of universities, there was agreement by all parties that the policy to maintain eight universities was a vestige from the past that still had segregative effects, without sound educational justification, and needed reforming. The judge ordered a study of the possibility of merging Mississippi Valley State and Delta State.

The court acknowledged that the funding formula and other funding inequities were traceable to prior de jure, but only to the extent that they followed the mission designations. In 1987, the state changed its funding formula so that each institution was treated the same. Consequently, current funding policies and practices were not unlawful and, therefore, did not need to be altered. The state could not address the funding inequity found between the TBIs and the TWIs in a practical and educationally sound manner. Policies and practices related to library allocations and equipment availability followed the state's mission designations and, like the funding formula, were traceable to de jure segregation. However, the court saw no need to mandate additional remedies when adequate expansion already was underway.

With regard to the land-grant programs, the court confirmed that differences found in the size and breadth of Mississippi State and Alcorn State's land-grant institutions are traceable to the de jure past and to the state's assigned mission designations for these two institutions. However, it could not find at that time any policy or practices that prevented or discouraged black students and white students from enrolling in either institution. Consequently, the court could not alter the current allocation that was already educationally sound.

Finally, the court ordered the establishment of a committee to monitor implementation of its instructions. This body was to be composed of three disinterested individuals with experience in the field of higher education.

The court set the expectation that the board would provide several reports to this committee relating to the following: the nature and extent of program duplication involving Jackson State and other institutions in the system, a resolution on the decision to consolidate Delta State and Mississippi Valley State in light of no other educationally sound alternative, a review of all the graduate school catalogs that outline admissions requirements, a feasibility study of developing statewide coordination of the community colleges in Mississippi, and articulation between Jackson State and surrounding community colleges to promote racial diversity at Jackson State.

RESPONSES TO THE REMEDY

The College Board quickly reacted by calling a press conference where Diane Miller, the chairperson, announced the board members' decision not to appeal the judge's ruling and the board's intent to request $35.8 million from the legislature to fund the court's remedies. She was quoted as saying, "This is a historic day. We are very hopeful we can finally put all of this behind us. We look at this as a cloud that has been lifted over Mississippi" (Jaschik, 1995). Governor Kirk Fordice, who vowed in 1992 to call out the national guard if the federal court ordered increased state funding, also agreed not to appeal the decision (*New York Times*, 1995).

Agreeing with the College Board, many white college officials backed the new standards. A University of Mississippi history professor's remarks exemplify the views of many in this group: "This is sending the exact right message to black students: 'College is there for you, but you are going to have to study more and work harder.' . . . This is the message we should be sending to all high school students. . . . This could be the beginning of a great period in that (Jackson State's) history" (Jaschik, 1995).

However, the plaintiffs disagreed. They especially objected to the new admissions standards, fearing that African-American enrollment would decline. Applied for the first time in September 1995, the new standards require a 16 ACT score and a 2.5 GPA for admission to all universities in the system. Apparently, they have negatively affected African-American 1995–1996 application rates, as suggested by the plaintiffs. As of March 1996, total applications to Jackson State, a TBI, declined 25 percent from the previous year; applicants admitted declined 60 percent; and applicants eligible for remedial summer courses rose 61 percent. These numbers suggest a final enrollment decline of 60 percent for the coming year once all applications are submitted and reviewed. (Applebome, 1996).

The plaintiffs and the Justice Department appealed the district court remedy, including the admissions standards, to the circuit court in late June 1995. Strangely, one week before the filing deadline, North Mississippi Rural Legal Services, the agency that has led the lawsuit in which Alvin Chambliss, the lead attorney for the private plaintiffs, is employed, told the plaintiffs that it would not support an appeal. The agency's trustees voted 8 to 7 not to support the appeal, with ten board members absent. Robert Black, the board chairperson, explained that funds are limited; moreover, the agency's mission involves helping poor people, not middle-income African-Americans who benefit from the court case. According to Black, the board also favored sticking with the provision of the current court decision — particularly, enhancing the historically African-American universities — rather than risking reversals by higher courts. At least one board member suggested political intrigue as a possible explanation for what took place. She claimed she left the board meeting after reassurance that the matter of supporting the appeal would not be voted upon (Healy, 1993).

Undeterred by outside reactions, the board fired Chambliss in August, after the appeal was filed, saying that they could no longer afford his salary and the costs associated with the appeal, previously amounting to more that $3 million. Subsequently, a county judge ruled that Chambliss was fired unfairly. The board then asked the U.S. District Court to overturn this decision. Ironically, the case was assigned to Judge Biggers, who presided over the *Ayers* case, a move that Robert Buck, chairman of the legal services board, protested. Biggers advised Chambliss to seek redress through his union, the National Organization of Legal Services Workers, refusing to enforce the county court decision until Chambliss did so. Other members of the legal services board, after failing to get Chambliss reinstated, are suing the organization's executive director in another attempt to get him his old job back (Healy, 1995a).

The Fifth Circuit Court was scheduled to hear the appeal during the week of November 15, 1996. Preparations were slowed by state officials' failure to reconcile enrollment data collected and reported by the College Board, the court, and the individual African-American institutions. For example, according to the College Board, the number of African-American first-year students declined by 9.1 percent statewide, compared with the previous year, but numbers submitted to Biggers by his advisory group show a 6.6 percent decline. Adding to the confusion, Mississippi Valley State, an African-American institution, reported a 20 percent decline rate from 512 new students in fall 1995 to 409 in fall 1996, with court data showing an 80 percent increase to 328 from 183 (Healy, 1995b).

Not relying upon the courts' favorable judgments, African-American legislators for a time blocked funding of the board's $5.4 million request for remedial summer programs. Representative Charles Capps, chairman of the House Appropriations Committee, reported that "The blacks in the House are just so vigorously opposed to the new standards that they were able to influence legislators to ignore them" (Healy, 1995). College Board staff requested $35.8 million in 1995 to fund the judge's remedy, but the legislature acted slowly. House Speaker Tim Ford reportedly announced that "$7 million is all the state can afford right now. . . . [L]awmakers have to wrap up action on the $2.7 billion state budget by Wednesday (March 15th), and that is too little time to find $36 million" (*Atlanta Journal-Constitution*, 1995).

A portion of the $7 million approved by the Mississippi legislature apparently got used to conduct the studies mandated by the court. In accordance with the court's decision, the College Board appointed a three-person panel, including Robert Kronley, senior consultant at the Southern Education Foundation; William Butts, special assistant to the Mississippi Commissioner of Higher Education and former president of Kentucky State University (an historically African-American institution); and Walter Washington, president emeritus of Alcorn State, to consider merging Mississippi Valley State and Delta State. The panel found that a merger would cost about $30 million and argued instead for several alternative recommendations in its report entitled "Transformation Through Collaboration" (Kronley, Butts, & Washington, 1996).

$10 million over ten years for new academic programs at Mississippi Valley State in areas like recording-industry management, history, therapeutic recreation, and public policy;

$5 million over ten years for scholarships to attract white students and faculty to Mississippi Valley State, and $2 million for black students and faculty at Delta State;

$10 million over five years for campus construction at Mississippi Valley State;

Student cross-registration and a transportation system between the two institutions.

The College Board approved the panel report by a vote of 9 to 1 on March 27, 1996, in this way agreeing to keep Mississippi Valley State open. It reserved, however, opinion about the other specific elements of the report (Guernsey & Healy, 1996).

The Legislative Black Caucus also blocked recently reelected Governor Fordice's four nominations for the College Board. Membership on the board is staggered, allowing each newly elected governor to appoint four new members. Fordice nominated four white men, and the caucus responded by demanding minority and female nominees. At the time, membership of the caucus totaled 45 individuals. This dispute continued into October 1996, when Fordice resubmitted a new slate of appointees including a white woman, an African-American man, and two white men. The legislature rejected his appointments on two occasions prior to this date. Determined to have his way, Fordice, in June 1996, invoked emergency powers while the legislature was in recess and appointed his nominees without confirmation. However, several senators sued, and after a favorable court ruling, the senate rejected the governor's candidates a second time (Healy, 1996).

SUMMARY AND ANALYSIS

More than in other states, Mississippi political leaders and higher education officials for many years successfully avoided making any substantial response to changing federal interpretations of civil rights requirements. Litigation postponed having to take difficult steps for many years. Other states, like Georgia, got involved in a ritual of masking actual effort and receiving federal approval; Mississippi leaders slogged their way through the courts. As Chapter 1 indicated, Louisiana and Mississippi, among that group of several states OCR early identified as noncompliant, chose not to engage in the enforcement ritual that emerged in other places.

Although federal interpretation of Title VI requirements did not compel compliance in Mississippi in the early years, interpretations during the Reagan administration and the overall tone of enforcement adopted by the late 1980s may have facilitated Mississippi's briefly successful legal strategy of claiming complete compliance by simply eliminating segregation laws. Such a claim was not incompatible with recent conservative concern for overstepping the bounds of federal policymaking and ignoring local prerogatives, nor is such a view incompatible with emerging consensus that federal enforcement of civil rights law and other factors by the 1980s sufficiently reduced race discrimination to the point of no longer requiring extreme forms of enforcement from the past.

Extreme negative responses of refusing to comply or to negotiate also may illustrate the strength of opposition within the state of Mississippi, not inconsistent with its broader civil rights history. Strong local opposition to civil rights enforcement certainly illustrates the contin-ued existence of race discrimination. Strong, persisting resistance coupled with many aspects of early enforcement, once it got underway in the early 1990s, calls into question any negative interpretation of the need for enforcement. Among the states, it took a Supreme Court decision to get Mississippi to desegregate its public higher education system.

Having successfully prevailed in lower federal courts, Mississippi defendents may have been surprised by the 1992 Supreme Court ruling. However, among most legal experts, *Fordice* demonstrates clear continu-ity with prior Supreme Court civil rights cases. The justices simply reaf-firmed two important rulings upon which the court has relied for 30 years: that states and local school districts must not only repeal race segregation laws but also eliminate or replace traceable policies and practices that reflect such laws with new ones that accomplish a race-neutral purpose; and that students' right to choose where they attend college (or elementary and high school) must not be constrained or restricted by policies that reflect past segregated system making.

In the court's view, concerning higher education in 1992, "In a system based on choice, student attendance is determined not simply by admis-sions policies, but also by many other factors. Although some of these factors clearly cannot be attributed to state policies, many can be. Thus, even after a state dismantles its segregative . . . policy, there may still be state action that is traceable to the state prior *de jure* segregation and that continue to foster segregation" (*United States v. Fordice*, 1992, p. 10).

Responses to the Supreme Court decision in unsurprising ways illus-trate a context of strong race conflict in Mississippi. Though the court strongly ruled the existence of continuing race discrimination, many of the plaintiffs disagree with other details of the court decision. Many adopt a view of the states' civil rights problem different from that of the court. Focusing narrowly upon only a portion of the court's concern, active plaintiffs view as a transcendent issue unequal treatment by the College Board of the state's three traditionally African-American institutions.

Armstrong, the 1994 president of the Jackson City Council and one of the original plaintiffs, recalls, for example, his days as a student at Jackson State when the case got underway in the 1970s: students and others were upset about continuing disparities in funding and facilities between the white and African-American institutions and recognized the increasingly successful civil rights strategy of inaugurating court action to force more equal treatment, in this instance by the College Board and state govern-ment. Broadening the issue, Armstrong interprets the underlying civil rights problem in higher education as one of weak African-American community empowerment. Students at Jackson State were not interested in attending Mississippi State; they simply wanted new buildings and programs like the ones under construction at Mississippi State. The College Board provides fewer resources to those institutions "owned" and run by African-Americans for African-Americans.

Proponents of this view downplay the fact that the Court views racially identifiable institutions as a means or as an outcome of restricting African-American and white students' choices. From a nationalist perspective African-American universities, on the contrary, are institutional mechanisms for advancing African-American students' rights and opportunities and for obtaining equal wealth and privilege, an avenue developed through ownership by the African-American community against white opposition. In this regard, TBIs do a much better job than TWIs. Separate but equal higher education within a modern legal context constitutes the best avenue toward broader ownership, control, and exercise of legal rights. It is one of the few such avenues available within Mississippi. Within Mississippi society, African-American and white citizens remain distrustful of one another and, therefore, will not mix freely. Current separation reflects years of adjusting to absence of legal barriers, which has been characterized by continuing unwillingness by whites to share power and public resources. The goal for African-Americans involves controlling a set of universities that possess resources required to train and credential African-American youth (Armstrong, 1994). Legal scholars createsupport for interpretations like Armstrong's. According to Brown-Scott, for example,

Historically Black colleges continue to provide the best opportunity for many African-Americans to earn a college or graduate degree. Yet, as Derrick Bell noted, "(t)he fact that these schools are more educationally effective than ever before is deemed constitutionally irrelevant." *Fordice* has provided an opportunity to make educational effectiveness a compelling state interest because it constitutes a sound educational policy.

Black colleges are constitutionally effective not only because they provide liberal arts and science training. They also inculcate the concepts of group empowerment and positive cultural identity to counter the adverse consequences of the negative social constructs of African-Americans perpetrated and perpetuated by the dominant culture. They serve the liberating and redemptive role that educational institutions have played in the historical development of African-Americans. (Brown-Scott, 1994, pp. 59–60)

Whether such views are correct and whether they broadly characterize the thinking of regular citizens, they show clear race conflict and clear local perception of discrimination.

Interestingly, the College Board, in its plan for desegregation, many would argue, adopted a narrowly focused version of the civil rights problem endorsed by the court: the institutional structure of the system with eight separate institutions continues to separate African-Americans from whites. Consolidating institutions and eliminating duplicate institutional missions will require African-Americans and whites to attend the same universities. Responses against this approach were most widespread and vocal. The College Board plan most strongly conflicts with the strategy of more equal resources for African-American universities and appears unfair to African-American institutions, but it is not incompatible with the court's civil rights approach in its purest version. The problem with ordering the closure of African-American institutions is the unwillingness of African-Americans to accept this alternative, not that the court would not permit it. Although the court's civil rights approach cannot embrace the private plaintiffs' nationalist interpretation, the court's narrow focus upon removing vestiges does not rule out enhancing African-American colleges as a means of expanding whites' free choices. Most private plaintiffs clearly are not deeply concerned with increasing white enrollment at Alcorn State, Jackson State, and Mississippi State, and leaders of these institutions seem to pay lip service to such a policy, adopting a short-term strategic view that increasing white enrollment marginally without relinquishing control will result in increased resources and protection from the College Board by federal courts.

It also should be observed that the College Board's original desegregation plan and responses to it provide evidence of "race masking" also observable during earlier years in Georgia enforcement. The College Board plan, as earlier indicated, contained proposals for downsizing the system that had been proposed unsuccessfully to the state legislature in earlier years. Review of the plan reveals little acknowledgment of segregation problems that are only indirectly discussed. Although the former Mississippi commissioner claims he led the board in the direction of adopting a systemwide restructuring approach to desegregation after he and the board considered other alternatives, his leadership perhaps did not go far enough toward acknowledging and identifying problems the plan was supposed to remedy.

Recognizing this weakness in the College Board's plan raises the important issue of reaching a final order to desegregate. Armed with the new *Fordice* interpretation, the district court judge, on remand from the Supreme Court, considered evidence of continuing discrimination, assessed the soundness of proposed remedies and arguments against them, and produced an order. Chapter 4 describes and analyzes the Mississippi plan in greater detail, discerning response patterns and drawing comparisons with Alabama, Louisiana, and other states involved in earlier times. Further analysis of the events described thus far, characterizing the early stages of policy formulation and planning in Mississippi, provide insight into the broader issue of continuing race discrimination and the need for federal civil rights policymaking. Is it correct to interpret what has taken place in Mississippi as evidence of race conflict reflective of continued discrimination? Or does the conflict suggest persuasive evidence of uncontrollable factors unrelated to past segregation?

More briefly at this point, the Mississippi remedy emphasizes enhancing Alcorn State, Jackson State, and Mississippi Valley State toward the goal of increased white enrollment. The order places notably little emphasis upon enrolling more African-Americans at white institutions. Five of the seven vestiges the district court did not approve focused upon African-American access to white institutions. One of the eight dismissed, unequal funding for maintenance, suggests enhancement of African-American institutions. However, participation in segregated athletic conferences, the last of the eight dismissed, neither strongly enhances African-American institutions nor promises increased African-American participation at white institutions. Six of the vestiges found by the district court deal with African-American university enhancement. The seventh, systemwide admissions policies, the Supreme Court clearly identified in *Fordice* as requiring attention on remand. The seventh approved vestige also is consistent with the College Board's continuing attempt to downsize the state's university system, not to desegregate it. The plan sidesteps the issue of merging or closing TBIs, providing a compromise of limited scope involving enhancement of TBIs. From the perspective of conservative whites, limited compromises are acceptable because they postpone sharing power. Even many progressive whites harbor strong doubts that members of their race soon will attend traditionally African-American institutions because, in their race mates' strong widespread view, TBIs are too unsafe, too unclean, and prejudiced against whites.

The risk involved in the district court compromise emerges clearly from the *Fordice* case. In *United States v. Fordice* (1992), the court concluded that: "Though certainly closure of one or more institutions would decrease the discriminatory effects of the present system . . . based upon the present record we are unable to say whether such action is constitutionally required." The justices responded specifically to private plaintiffs' request for an order to upgrade Mississippi's three African-American universities: "If we understand private petitioners to press us to order the upgrading of Jackson State, Alcorn State, and Mississippi Valley solely so that they may be publicly financed, exclusively black enclaves by private choice, we reject that request" (*United States v. Fordice*, 1992, p. 23).

Sidestepping renewed controversy, Biggers ordered a study of the feasibility of merging Mississippi Valley State and Delta State instead of a finding for merger. Alcorn State remains independent. The report developed inconclusively the absence of a sound educational justification and added expense involved in merging Delta State and Fort Valley State (Kronley, Butts, & Washington, 1996). The trend that African-American stakeholders rely upon continues.

Relying upon federal civil rights enforcement through the court system, which for 25 years has been twisted to suit a more limited purpose, African-American college stakeholders do not fear that historical white hegemony will, today, spread too far. Though regresssive changes in civil rights law are taking place, U.S. political culture still unwillingly tolerates clear examples of race discrimination, exemplified by closing Fort Valley State and merging Alcorn State. African-American stakeholders also rely upon expansion of their state and local political power, exemplified by more than 30 African-American state legislators currently holding office. For their part, whites interpret broad conservative changes within the nation's political culture as steadily diminishing federal civil rights enforcement, despite the *Fordice* ruling. They rely upon retaining power through reaching compromises favorable to them with African-Americans who, absent federal enforcement, still possess comparatively few political resources. They continue to affirm their own high political authority, diminished as it might be.

It is worth noting, though, that not all African-American stakeholders in Mississippi disinterestedly regard remedies aimed at desegregating white institutions. Judged by enrollment patterns, many African-American youth and parents would like to see increased opportunities for African-Americans to attend the state's previously segregated colleges and universities. At the other end of the state spectrum, African-American stakeholders on the board of the Northern Mississippi Legal Services Corporation fired the lawyer for the plaintiffs, demonstrating disapproval of expending limited public resources in the direction of increasing opportunities to attend college anywhere. Many of Mississippi's large population of disproportionately poor African-American stakeholders may view other opportunities as more important.

The two most far-reaching remedies in the Mississippi plan involve establishing uniform, systemwide student admissions standards and providing financial resources to enhance African-American institutions. The new admissions standards potentially decrease the pool of African-American students aspiring and applying to college, particularly the TBIs. The new state plan anticipates that some high-school graduates, at least in the beginning years, will not meet minimum admissions requirements as specified in the College Board's 1995–1996 policy and will make provisions for summer enrichment programs.

Opponents of the new standards, many of them African-American college stakeholders, question whether is it likely that GPAs and test scores will increase sufficiently over the course of a single summer. They fear a decline in the number and percentage of African-American high-school graduates applying and declines in African-American enrollment at both TWIs and, especially, TBIs. These issues were raised during the most recent district court trial and will be raised again during the appeals court litigation. In the district court's view, such risks are less important than making sure that patterns of choice to attend a TBI or a TWI, restricted by prior standards, are no longer constrained. The court's view gets interpreted by critics to make it acceptable to restrict aspirations to enroll in the first place, even though African-Americans' high-school opportunities, the major determinant of GPA and standardized test scores, are, in Mississippi, deficient in comparison with those of whites. The court, agreeing with the College Board, embraces the strategy of compelling increased high-school preparation and student commitment by raising college admissions standards; having access to required high-school courses — and many African-American students in Mississippi do not — is equally as important as being motivated to enroll in them. According to enrollment data reported in the news media, African-American enrollment in higher education in Mississippi declined last fall when the new admissions requirements were applied (Healy, 1996, p. 21).

TBI enhancement in the court order involves adding new programs at Jackson State and Alcorn State, spending $5 million for educational enhancements and race diversity programs at Jackson State and Alcorn State; spending $20 million on a matching basis at Alcorn State and $15 million at Jackson State for physical facilities; and conducting four program duplication studies, including the proposal to merge Fort Valley State and Delta State. The scope of each of these proposals is difficult to assess because they are not presented in great detail. No specific goals or problems are associated with the expenditures proposed. Presumably, the court decided to allow the College Board and the colleges to plan and spend the money as they deemed appropriate. Little information about how the court determined each amount is provided in the order. Other elements are clearer, such as the development strategy of requiring the two colleges to raise matching funds and addressing the ultimate goal of increasing white enrollment. As described, the court-ordered report regarding merger of Delta State and Mississippi Valley State adopts a program and physical facilities enhancement approach similar to early enforcement and similar to that previously applied to Jackson State and Alcorn State.

Disagreement among parties to the Mississippi litigation, centered upon these two important issues, clearly illustrates the extent to which race conflict continues to characterize public policymaking, at least in areas of the nation like Mississippi. Failure to negotiate a Title VI remedy despite several attempts over the years, legislative activism pitting organized African-Americans against planned desegregation remedies, organized African-American protest against desegregation proposals by the court and the College Board, the plaintiffs' overall litigation strategy of not proposing remedies assuring that local courts and government officials will not assess them fairly, and the College Board convening segregated meetings with white college presidents, and unabashed assertions by white and African-American public officials of mistrust between the races — all illustrate considerable evidence of modern race strife in Mississippi.

Sustained and substantial race conflict gained support from indisputable district and Supreme Court findings in Mississippi that current higher education policies prohibit African-Americans' civil rights. Many such findings went uncontested by the state during trial. Reflecting broader race conflict in society at large, defendants focused upon preventing expansive remedies, serving the point of view that, even though past discrimination existed, current beneficiaries must not be made to pay deep penalties for it. Court scenarios illustrating conflict directed along these lines could not be clearer than in Mississippi in recent years.

Civil rights enforcement constitutes a form of regulatory policymaking aimed at accomplishing redistributive goals. Federal government under Title VI threatens the sanction of withdrawing federal funding of higher education, and the federal court, in the final analysis, threatens to remove or punish state officials unless compliance with the law is achieved. Broadly speaking, the clear policy goal in Mississippi, Alabama, Louisiana, and other states involves redistributing and reassigning seats in college classrooms from whites to African-Americans. Redistribution is generally accomplished by keeping the same number of places and allowing African-Americans to replace whites, or a higher percentage of African-Americans can occupy new places created through expansion.

Disingenuously, in Mississippi the College Board proposed downsizing the system as a strategy for redistributing college resources. Regardless of the strategy used, the long-run expectation is that more college degrees will increase private wealth among African-Americans as a race-defined group.

Redistributive regulatory policies are difficult to implement because they attract greater public attention and create substantially more conflict — always between the races in Mississippi — than milder forms of policymaking. More than any other civil rights remedy, merging or closing African-American institutions arouses active, organized political conflict. Organized protests over proposed or actual mergers or closings in Tennessee, Virginia, Florida, Georgia, and, most recently, Mississippi illustrate this phenomenon. What has sustained and increased African-Americans' attention and conflict in Mississippi is concern for Fort Valley State, Jackson State, and Alcorn State. Alumni, current students, faculty, administrators, and other elements of the state's African-American college community were demonstrably upset by College Board plans to merge or close all three institutions. However, concern has spread because of the issue of fairness involved. The president of the national branch of the NAACP and leaders of other national civil rights organizations at one time or another over the past four years have visited Mississippi, protesting plans to close Mississippi Valley State and to merge Alcorn State. Even Associate Justice Clarence Thomas agrees that African-American institutions should not perversely bear the burden of removing vestiges of prior segregation. Proposals along this line seem to violate widely held and deeply felt "fairness norms" within communities where they emerge and within the nation as a whole.

Conflict over the fairness of closing Mississippi's TBIs contributes to and illustrates the state's broader continuing race-relations problems. Observably, Mississippi litigants and other higher education stakeholders do not deeply trust one another. Perhaps in Mississippi it is naive to expect otherwise. However, whites and African-Americans do not expect each other to play by the nation's common norms and rules of local, state, and federal politics. Such circumstances, personalities aside, also demonstrate mutual disrespect. In African-American stakeholders' view, the Supreme Court, conservative as it may be, more likely would present a fairer and more reliable remedy than state courts and state officials. Moreover, Supreme Court authority would be needed to force implementation, compelling state officials to meet their commitments.

The risks of adopting this strategy are clear. For example, the district court judge ruled that insufficient evidence of problems of junior-senior college articulation was presented during the trial. The court issued no ruling of whether lower African-American rates of progression from two-year to four-year institutions constitute a vestige, instead ordering a study of this issue. Plaintiffs' decision not to expect much from the Mississippi district court may have resulted in failure to capitalize upon important opportunities to bring about change.

Clearly, defendents became fed up with lack of cooperation and good faith proposals from the plaintiffs. Recent public conservatism, perhaps reflected in an increasingly Republican and more conservative state legislature and state house over the past several years, facilitated approval of a widely unpopular proposal, one that promised to reduce state spending for higher education over the expected disapproval of the state's public higher education community.

The correct interpretation of Title VI enforcement involves recognition of continuing race discrimination not only through evidence arrived at in applying the Supreme Court's ruling. Evidence of racism and race conflict underlying the currently unfolding policymaking process also leads to the same conclusion. Assistant Secretary Brad Reynolds during the mid-1980s interpreted race conflict of the kind later observable in Mississippi as uncontrollable and justifiable reaction against overly zealous federal regulation (Reynolds, 1983). In view of evidence in Mississippi, such interpretations ring empty, suggesting disingenuous and purposefully misleading constructions of social and political reality intended to evoke public fear and partisan conservative policy decision making.

REFERENCES

American Association of University Professors. 1995. "Historically Black Colleges and Universities: A Future in the Balance." *Academe*, January–February 1995, pp. 49–58.

Applebome, Peter. 1996. "Equal Admissions Standards Leave Mississippi's Black Universities Wary." *New York Times*, April 24, 1996, p. 21.

Armstrong, Louis. Interview. Jackson, Mississippi, October 14, 1994.

Ayers v. Allain, 914 F. 2d 676 (CAS 1990 at 678); 674 F. Supp. 1523, 11562 (N.D. Miss. 1987).

Ayers v. Fordice, Civil Action No. GC75-9-B-O, Defendant Board of Trustees of State Institutions of Higher Learning's Proposed Remedies, October 22, 1992. Mimeographed.

Ayers v. Fordice, U.S. District Court for Northern Mississippi (1994).

"Ayers Wrinkle." *Clarion-Ledger*, February 23, 1994, p. 17.

Barton, Paul. 1992. "Lawmaker Urges Call for Session to Solve Ayers Case." *Commercial Appeal*, October 27, 1992, p. B1.

Bazemore v. Friday, 478 U.S. 385 (1986).

"Bd Member Wants Panel to Keep MUW Open." *Northeast Mississippi Daily Journal*, November 10, 1992, p. 5A.

"Black Lawmakers Want to Increase College Funding." *Sun Herald*, November 13, 1992, pp. B1, B4.

Brown-Scott, Wendy. 1994. "Race Consciousness in Higher Education: Does 'Sound Education Policy' Support the Continued Existence of Historically Black Colleges?" *Emory Law Journal*, Winter 1994, pp. 1–81.

Brown v. Board of Education, 347 U.S. 483 (1954).

Cleer, W. R. Interview. Jackson, Mississippi, October 14, 1994.

Editorial. *Commercial Appeal*, September 25, 1994, p. 17.

Green v. New Kent County Board, 391 U.S. 430 (1968).

Guernsey, Lisa, and Healy, Patrick. 1996. "Federal Court Orders Mississippi's Historically Black Colleges to Raise Their Admissions Standards." *Chronicle of Higher Education*, March 29, 1996, p. A48.

Healy, Patrick. 1996. "Mississippi Governor Proposes New Slate of Trustees." *Chronicle of Higher Education*, October 4, 1996, p. A32.

Healy, Patrick. 1996. "Black Enrollment Falls Sharply at Mississippi Public Colleges." *Chronicle of Higher Education*, September 27, 1996, p. 21.

Healy, Patrick. 1995a. "U.S. Officials Try Less Confrontational Approach to Gaining College Desegregation." *Chronicle of Higher Education*, September 22, 1995, p. A42.

Healy, Patrick. 1995b. "Black Lawmakers in Mississippi Block Remedial Program Funds." *Chronicle of Higher Education*, April 7, 1995, p. A17.

Healy, Patrick. 1993. "20-Year-Old Campaign to End Segregation at Mississippi's Colleges Goes Back to Federal Court." *Chronicle of Higher Education*, June 30, 1993, p. 17.

Jackson Advocate, January 27, 1994, p. 1.

Jackson Advocate, April 22, 1994, p. 12A.

Jaschik, Scott. 1995. "Ruling in Mississippi." *Chronicle of Higher Education*, March 17, 1995, p. A24.

Kronley, Robert A., Butts, William A., and Washington, Walter. 1996. "Transformation Through Collaboration — Desegregating Higher Education in the Mississippi Delta: A Report to the Mississippi Institutions of Higher Education." Unpublished. March 1996. Mimeographed.

Leggett, Mark. 1992. "Legislators Say Ayers Plan Hits All Universities." *Northeast Mississippi Daily Journal*, October 21, 1992, p. 11.

"Member Questions Vote to Close-Merge Universities." *Northeast Mississippi Daily Journal*, November 12, 1992, p. 4B.

Mercer, Joye. 1994. "Marching to Save Black Colleges." *Chronicle of Higher Education*, May 11, 1994, p. A28.

Mercer, Joye. 1992. "Plan to Desegregate Higher Education in Mississippi Unites State's Colleges, Black and White Alike." *Chronicle of Higher Education*, November 4, 1992, p. A23.

Mississippi Board of Trustees of State Institutions of Higher Learning. undated. *Ayers Decision*, vol. I. Mimeographed

"Mississippi Lawmakers Resist College Desegregation Funding." *Atlanta Journal-Constitution*, March 12, 1995, p. A3.

"NAACP Wants Members of College Board Ousted." *Sun Herald*, October 27, 1992, p. C2.

"Our Views — Ayers." *Clarion-Ledger*, July 27, 1992, p. 27.

Rado, Diane. 1994. "A Black and White Issue." *St. Petersburg Times*, July 6, 1994, p. 1A, 4.

Reynolds, William B. 1983. "The Administration's Approach to Desegregation of Public Higher Education." *American Education*, 19 (July 1983): 7–11.

Robinson, Jackie. Interview. Jackson, Mississippi, October 14, 1994.

"Save the W." *The Wall Street Journal*, May 6, 1994, p. 1.

Silverman, Charles. 1964. *Crisis in Black and White*. New York: Random House.

Smothers, Ronald. 1995. "Mississippi Mellows on Campus Bias Case." *New York Times*, March 10, 1995, p. 23.

Southern Education Foundation. 1995. *Redeeming the Promise: Report of the Panel on Educational Opportunity and Postsecondary Desegregation*. Atlanta, Ga.: Southern Education Foundation.

Sutton, William. Interview. Jackson, Mississippi, October 15, 1994.

Tisdale, Charles. 1994. "UMC Paper Bad Mouths Jackson State." *Jackson Advocate*, January 27, 1994, p. 1; April 22, 1994, p. 12A.

United States v. Fordice, 112 S. Ct. 2727 (1992).

U.S. Justice Department. 1993. "Practicable Alternative to Remnants that State Contends are Justified — Submitted by the United States in *Ayres v. Fordice*." Unpublished, p. 1. Mimeographed.

Winter, William. Interview. Jackson, Mississippi, October 14, 1994.

4

Civil Rights Enforcement in the 1990s: Alabama, Mississippi, and Louisiana Desegregation Remedies

Although the Office for Civil Rights (OCR) began monitoring Mississippi, Alabama, and Louisiana in the late 1960s, federal court litigation actually produced, several years later, a response to noncompliance. Mississippi and Louisiana were among the first group of states OCR monitored and notified of violations in the late 1960s. The office notifed Alabama in 1981. However, in Alabama, similar to Mississippi, the U.S. Justice Department eventually joined federal district court litigation established by private plaintiffs. Dissimilarly, in Louisiana, the Justice Department alone over the years introduced and sustained slow-paced litigation after the state failed to respond to OCR notifications. Federal district and circuit courts reached several decisions in *Knight v. Alabama* (1992) and *United States v. Louisiana* (1989) prior to *United States v. Fordice* (1992), but their work had to be reviewed and renewed after the 1992 Supreme Court ruling. Even though OCR has ruled several state systems in compliance with Title VI after years of planning and implementing desegregation remedies, as Norma Cantu, the current OCR director announced, each one is now subject to new scrutiny (*Federal Register*, 1994). In a real sense, then, another stage of civil rights enforcement may have gotten underway in 1992, exemplified by renewed enforcement in Mississippi, Alabama, and Louisiana.

Continuing the nation's civil rights enforcement saga, this chapter introduces the new stage of enforcement in the 1990s, describing and analyzing Mississippi court order in greater detail, along with the recent Alabama and Louisiana remedies. Adopting the approach used in earlier chapters, this chapter views described remedies as court-ordered state responses, at this point to requirements established in *Fordice*. Formal responses in the court remedies collectively involve interpreting race equity problems and remedy requirements and establishing remedial policy formulation and problem solving.

THE MISSISSIPPI COURT ORDER

What resulted from *Fordice* has been referred to as the "Fordice analysis." Three separate steps comprise this analysis: First, the plaintiffs must show that a specific policy or practice is both discriminatory and traceable to the state's former de jure system of segregation, "thus rendering it a vestige." Second, if the policy or practice is proven to be a "vestige," then defendant state officials must prove either that the policy, "though traceable to segregation, is not constitutionally objectionable because it does not today have segregative effects" or that eliminating the challenged policy or practice is not "educationally sound or practicable." If the state is able to prove either of these, then it is relieved of its duty to remedy the vestigial policy or practice. Justice Sandra Day O'Connor, in her concurring opinion, places limits upon such occurrences: "The circumstances in which a State may maintain a policy or practice traceable to *de jure* segregation that has segregative effects are narrow. . . . If the state shows that maintenance of certain remnants of its prior system is essential to accomplish its legitimate goals, then it still must prove that it has counteracted and minimized the segregative impact of such policies."

The third "step" mandates the state, if it is unable to show either absence of current segregative effects or absence of practicable alternatives, to devise remedies for the challenged policy or practice. "The onus is not on the plaintiffs to propose the remedy options to be considered": without devising remedies, the state "remains in violation of the Fourteenth Amendment," having failed to satisfy "its burden of proving that it has dismantled its prior [*de jure*] system [of segregated higher education]" (*United States v. Fordice*, 1992, pp. 1–2).

Following these instructions, plaintiffs identified, at the beginning of the trial, 14 vestiges of prior racial segregation that persist within the Mississippi university system. The court ruled that seven alleged vestiges were, indeed, traceable to prior de jure segregation, but seven were not. In the court's view, the following problems are not vestiges: unequal graduate student admissions rates, unequal allocations for physical facility maintenance and repair, lower African-American employment rates at the university campuses, inhospitable traditionally white institution (TWI) campus climates, unequal rates of employment at the College Board offices and unequal membership on the board, participation in racially defined athletic conferences, and unequal rates of appointment of students to graduate councils.

The court dispensed with the accusation that Mississippi universities participate in racially defined athletic conferences on the basis of lack of evidence: none of the evidence provided by any of the parties indicated either the feasibility or the desirability of modifying this practice. Furthermore, the court could not conclude that participating in these conferences promotes a segregated higher education system or that ending participation constitutes a sound educational practice. Unequal student membership on the graduate council the court judged to constitute a past problem, plaintiffs presenting no satisfactory evidence of continuing practice of discrimination.

In a similar manner, the court also asserted no sign of a current practice of preventing or impeding representation of African-Americans on the College Board or of arbitrarily limiting the authority and actions of administrators of traditionally black institutions (TBIs) in a way that impedes their ability to protect the rights of their students. The court indicated that African-Americans have actively participated on the board for more than 20 years.

Concerning low employment rates at university campuses, graduate student admissions, and inhospitable TWI campus climate, in the court's view, the state has implemented adequate corrective measures and, in some instances, made progress. The state's catalog revisions, following suggestions from the Educational Testing Service and involving use of Graduate Record Examination scores in the admissions process, are sufficient: no additional remedies are necessary. The court acknowledged that the administration and tenured faculty of TWIs remain racially identifiable and, to some extent, this problem constitutes a remnant of de jure segregation. As a result, however, of uncovering no current discriminatory practice or policy related to campus level employment, no remedy is offered. The court held, instead, that the TWIs are making a sincere and serious effort to attract and retain African-American faculty and administrators.

The court also found no convincing evidence of continuing negative campus climate policies and practices at TWIs. On the contrary, all higher education institutions in the state had made considerable progress toward increased diversity and toward providing a welcoming campus climate. In support of this finding, the court indicated that, nationally, predominantly white institutions retain African-Americans at lower rates than TBIs, but in Mississippi, the TBIs exhibit a lower retention rate for African-Americans than the TWIs. The steady increase in African-American enrollment at TWIs constituted further evidence of progress.

The court identified no continuing pattern of unequal facility maintenance and repair funding by the College Board. The judge decided that TBIs and TWIs probably share similar maintenance and repair problems, despite the fact that he could observe, having made site visits, differences in the shape of some of the institutions' physical structures. In comparison with the TWIs, some of the TBIs were inferior, but the differences could, in part, be attributed to the institutions' relative management and control over funds appropriated. The main point is that there are no facility funding policies and practices traceable to de jure segregation. Furthermore, centrally controlling the universities' operations and maintenance budgets constitutes an educationally unsound remedy.

The seven alleged vestiges around which the court established its remedy include unequal undergraduate admissions policies, racially disparate institutional missions, duplicative program offerings between TBIs and TWIs, unequal land-grant program funding, unequal library resource allocations, and operation of a system structure consisting of eight universities. The court found that these problems are traceable to de jure segregation and continue to produce racial separation. A remedy is required where each is involved.

The undergraduate admissions problems were incompletely acknowledged by the judge as requiring a remedy. Considerations included failure to use exceptions to systemwide admissions standards to admit African-American students and use of the ACT scores as the sole criterion for determining admission to a university, acceptance into a degree program, and scholarship awards. The court did not find sufficient evidence to support the plaintiffs' argument that the TWIs' limited use of the admissions exceptions to admit African-Americans constitutes a traceable vestige, but the judge agreed with the Supreme Court that "the admissions standards that existed at the time of the trial in 1987, although racially neutral on their face, are discriminatory when viewed under the legal standard established in *Fordice* and should be altered" (*United States v. Fordice*, 1992, p. 13). The *Fordice* decision reflects the widespread practice among colleges and universities of rarely using standardized test scores as the sole criterion for undergraduate admissions decisions. Instead, such scores get combined with other measures of merit, such as high-school grade point average and class rank, in this way providing a more comprehensive and accurate predictor of college academic performance. However, the district court argued that awarding alumni scholarships based on ACT scores does not constitute a violation of the law. The use of ACT scores for giving scholarships, the judge argued, is a common practice throughout the country.

The remedy next responds to a court finding that the state promoted segregation by limiting the mission and programs of the three TBIs. In response to plaintiffs' claims, the court finding and remedy simultaneously address program duplication, accreditation, and mission designation. The limited mission designations of the TBIs, in relationship to the TWIs, are, indeed, vestiges of the past, supported in a variety of ways by the state's past educational policies and practices. The court refers to the state's 1981 mission statement, concluding that it produces "the effect of maintaining the status quo with respect to programmatic offerings . . . and is consistent with the development of institutions during the de jure period. Existing program duplication constitutes a remnant of the old dual system of higher education which developed out of the 'separate but equal' doctrine."

Pointing out that program duplication is not uncommon in large higher education systems, the question for the court was whether existing duplication promotes a racial choice of institutions. It concluded that, combined with different admissions standards between TBIs and TWIs, existing duplication does promote segregation. Interestingly, defendents and plaintiffs agreed that maintaining eight universities constitutes a vestige with continuing segregative effects and without sound educational justification.

Plaintiffs also argued that state funding of TBIs created a barrier to their successful desegregation. The court found that the funding policies and practices were traceable to prior de jure segregation, but only to the extent that they followed the mission designations. At one time, funding was based primarily on the mission designation of a particular institution, with comprehensive universities, for example, receiving more funding than regional ones. However, in 1987, the state changed its funding formula so that each institution gets treated the same. Consequently, the current funding policies and practices are not unlawful and, therefore, do not need to be altered.

The court ruled that, concerning other state funding policies, beyond the formula for basic expenses and general expenses, inequities between the TBIs and the TWIs could not be addressed in a practical and educationally sound manner. Specific policies and practices allocating library funds and other resources follow mission designations and, like the funding formula, are traceable to de jure segregation. However, no additional remedies are needed, the court ruled, because adequate expansion of library facilities at TBIs is already underway.

Finally, the court found that differences in land-grant program approval and funding — differences in size and scope between Mississippi State University and Alcorn State University's land-grant operations — are traceable to the state's de jure past and 1981 assigned mission designations for these two institutions. However, the judge ruled that no current policy or set of practices today prevents or discourages African-American or white students from enrolling in either institution: current policies already are educationally sound.

In ordering remedies, the court's strategy consisted of:

simply determining whether existing state remedies, independently initiated in response to the 1992 Supreme Court case, are sufficient and endorsing those that were (as in the case of undergraduate and graduate admissions);

avoiding any remedy on the basis that either there was no educationally sound alternative (as in the case of land-grant inequities between Alcorn State and Mississippi State) or that more research was necessary (as in the case of the proposed merger of Delta State and Mississippi Valley);

devising original remedies after rejecting others submitted by plaintiffs and defendents (as in the instance of funding enhancements at Alcorn State and Jackson State).

More specifically, the judge first endorsed the 1995 admissions standard developed by the College Board for incoming freshmen, effective for the 1995–1996 academic year. The board already had published its new standards and required universities to meet them by this deadline. In the judge's view, the new standards will eliminate prior segregative effects of previous admissions standards differentiated by the universities' past racial identities. The new standards include using ACT scores in combination with a prescribed high-school grade point average, and systemwide intensive summer programs for students in need of remediation.

In keeping with the court's earlier reported findings, the remaining court-ordered remedies aim at resolving the mission designation inequity. The court accepted the College Board's proposal not to revise the mission designations of the various institutions but, instead, to enhance the programmatic offerings at two of the state's three TBIs — Jackson State and Alcorn State.

At Jackson State the court ordered, for the 1995–1996 academic year, new undergraduate degree programs in allied health, social work, and urban planning. A new doctoral program in business also should be added as soon as existing programs in this field receive accreditation. The court ordered an on-site institutional study of Jackson State to identify the strengths and weaknesses of existing programs; to plan the nature and direction of the new degree programs ordered; and to establish the feasibility of establishing an engineering school, a law school, and a pharmacy degree program. At Alcorn State, the court ordered a new master of business administration program starting not later than the 1996–1997 academic year.

The court next endorsed the College Board's proposal to provide, over a period of no more than five years, "up to fifteen million dollars" of state funding for property acquisition and campus improvements, including increased security, at Jackson State. State funding of an additional $5 million must be made over a five-year period in the form of an endowment for "educational enhancement and racial diversity" at both Jackson State and Alcorn State. The court instructed the state to provide special funds — which must be matched by the institution — of "up to four million each year" over a five-year period for the Small Farm Development Center at Alcorn State.

Finally, the court authorized appointment (by the court) of a committee, "composed of three disinterested individuals with experience in the field of higher education," to monitor implementation of its order and prescribed remedies. In addition to monitoring implementation of remedies already ordered by the court, the committee will assist the judge in resolving issues unresolved during the trial. To this end, the College Board must provide several reports to this committee, involving the following: nature and extent of program duplication between Jackson State and other institutions in the system, consolidation of Delta State University and Mississippi Valley State University offered by the College Board in light of no other educationally sound alternative, review of all the graduate school catalogs that outline admissions requirements, feasibility study of developing statewide coordination of the community colleges in Mississippi, and articulation between Jackson State and surrounding community colleges to promote racial diversity at Jackson State.

ENFORCEMENT IN ALABAMA

Knight, et al. v. Alabama (1991) combines separate suits by private plaintiffs and the U.S. Department of Justice brought before the U.S. District Court of the Northern District of Alabama, Southern Division, alleging that Alabama continued to operate a dual system. The first trial took place between July 1 and August 2, 1985. Substantial legal maneuvering preceeded and followed the litigation, including Auburn University's motion to disqualify presiding Judge U. W. Clemon, an African-American civil rights lawyer who successfully litigated school desegregation cases in Alabama prior to being appointed to the district court bench. On August 6, 1987, the Eleventh Circuit Court overturned Clemon's rulings, requiring plaintiffs and defendants to resubmit court documents for a new trial. A new trial took place October 29, 1990, to April 16, 1991, with Judge Harold Murphy of the Northern District of Georgia presiding. Clemon's dismissal by the Eleventh Circuit Court cast doubt upon other Alabama district court judges' suitability to try the current case.

Murphy dismissed portions of the plaintiffs' claims and reaffirmed several consent decrees between individual Alabama institutions and the U.S. Department of Justice that Clemons had ratified earlier. This action disposed of claims contained in the decrees against the University of South Alabama, University of Montevallo, Jacksonville University, Livingston University, Troy State University, Athens State, and Calhoun Community College. These institutions remained party to the 1990–1991 trial only where new claims were introduced, though the court retained jursidiction over implementation of the consent agreements.

Murphy found vestigial practices and policies in five areas. Specifically, Alabama's severe shortage of African-American faculty and administrators constituted a problem: the court directed Auburn, University of North Alabama, University of Alabama, University of Alabama-Huntsville, and Jacksonville State University to devise plans and programs within 90 days to address this problem and show progress after three years.

Murphy next found that the state's higher education funding formula "unfairly restricts the funding of institutions providing higher education opportunities to the less well prepared and poorer segments of Alabama's undergraduate population, who are primarily black, and the formula thus has a disparate impact upon African Americans seeking a post-secondary school education in Alabama's four year colleges and universities" (*Knight v. Alabama*, 1991, p. 831).

He ordered the Alabama Commission on Higher Education to modify the provision of the formula that uses average statewide tuition to calculate institutions' income prior to making a state appropriation: "After determining the average rate charged each full-time student for tuition and fees, per semester hour, . . . no more than ninety (90) percent of the rate charged by ASU and AAMU, respectively, shall be applied to the average of un-weighted on-campus semester credit hours . . . to obtain the amount of tuition and fee revenue to be deducted pursuant to the funding formula at Alabama State University and Alabama A&M University" (*Knight v. Alabama*, 1991, pp. 831–832). He further directed the Alabama Commission to modify its funding formula, increasing funds for remedial courses.

Next, the court found inequitable physical facilities at the historically African-American institutions to represent a vestige. He ordered defendents within 120 days to present a plan for remedy, implementation to begin by the start of the next fiscal year. The court retained the right to approve proposed expenditures for improved facilities by the two African-American institutions.

The court also found that current admissions policies at Auburn University exert "a disproportionate impact on black applicants" and ordered a modified admissions policy in place by the 1993–1994 school year.

The court ruled that academic program duplication between African-American and white institutions constitutes a vestige. As indicated, the Alabama Commission, the State Board of Education, and Calhoun State Community College entered into a consent decree with the U.S. Department of Justice that was reaffirmed by Murphy. As a result of the trial, the judge found unnecessary program duplication between Calhoun State's satellite campus in Huntsville and Alabama A&M, a TBI in the same location. The judge asked the Consent Decree Monitoring Committee, created by the settlement, to recommend steps to eliminate duplication in business education curricula within 90 days.

The court also found program duplication between Alabama State University and Auburn in Montgomery "in the area of business and education [sic]." The judge's remedial order includes a mandate to establish a Committee on Cooperation, composed of representatives from Alabama State's Board of Trustees, Auburn's board, the executive secretary of the Alabama Commission, and the governor or his representative. The committee should submit recommendations to the court within 90 days. Also, to address program duplication in Huntsville, Alabama A&M should receive preference for new teacher education programs in the Huntsville area, and both Alabama A&M and Alabama State should be given preference in establishing new high-demand academic programs in both Montgomery and Huntsville. All new academic programs planned by the commission must be approved by the court to assure that unnecessary duplication does not continue and impede desegregation.

The court found that low enrollment of white students at A&M and Alabama State constitutes a vestige and requested a plan to recruit white students at both institutions over a three-year period. The court ordered a statewide monitoring committee to develop and provide to the court annual reports describing compliance with the court's order. Monitoring committees established to oversee the earlier approved consent decrees were directed to report to the new statewide monitoring committee composed of representatives of all parties to the case.

Portions of the 1991 findings and remedies were appealed successfully, and in 1994, the U.S. Eleventh Circuit Court of Appeals remanded the case to the original district court. At a trial that began in early 1995, the district court, responding to instructions from the Eleventh Circuit Court, attempted to resolve three issues, largely regarding Alabama State and A&M and contested by the plaintiffs: first, more prestigious roles for the TBIs within Alabama's system of public higher education; next, a more equitable distribution of the land-grant and agricultural extension service resources between predominantly white Auburn and predominantly African-American A&M; finally, the creation of African-American studies departments throughout the Alabama system.

As the brief states, the district court was asked to formulate a decision regarding each of these issues, basing its decision upon the "massive" record that had accumulated after three earlier trials, including the most recent appeal to the Eleventh Circuit Court. Thankfully, the Supreme Court's 1992 *Fordice* opinion would provide some guidance.

Alabama State University and A&M's Roles and Programs

As reported in Chapter 3, *Fordice* requires lower courts to consider the idea of "free student choice" in their deliberations. The Court of the Northern District of Alabama in both the 1991 and 1995 decisions in *Knight* appears preoccupied with it. In attempting to identify factors that affect student choice — and, therefore, a student's ability to choose freely — the district court listed the following: tuition, costs, financial aid, academic reputation, location, size, social atmosphere, and special academic programs. With these factors in mind, the district court's goal, in this case, is not merely to make "ASU and A & M more desirable places to go" but to "expand student choice in the system as a whole."

The district court's focus upon this notion closely follows the language of the Supreme Court: "In a system based on choice, student attendance is determined not simply by admissions policies, but also by many other factors" (*United States v. Fordice*, 1992, p. 12). The court's list of factors follows this statement. However, though influential, these factors are of secondary importance when considered with respect to a college's or university's mission statement and role assignment. The Supreme Court feels that the fact "that different missions are assigned to the universities surely limits . . . an entering student's choice as to which university to seek admittance" (*United States v. Fordice*, 1992, p. 15). An applicant seeking admission to one of Alabama's public postsecondary schools would discover that Alabama State and A&M are relegated to Category II (master's level state universities) but TWIs like Auburn and the University of Alabama rank in the top Category I of Alabama's "role matrices" as "Comprehensive Universities." Such classifications, reflecting widely used Carnegie classifications categories, have the effect of severely limiting the types of programs that TBIs are able to develop, programs that could attract a diverse pool of students. The Supreme Court, concurring with the circuit court decision, states that, "the mission designations [have] the effect of maintaining the more limited program scope at the historically black universities." The *Fordice* opinion builds on this fact: "it is likely that the mission designations interfere with student choice and tend to perpetuate the segregated system" (*United States v. Fordice*, 1992, p. 12). A lack of oversight and accountable authority characterized Alabama's treatment of its Category II schools, especially Alabama State and A&M.

The 1991 district court finding and remedy, involving assignment of new programs to TBIs and elimination of duplication but no new mission, may not go far enough in the direction later embraced by the Supreme Court. The new remedies to this situation are examined later. However, it is important to note, at this point, the Supreme Court's defining criteria for remedial actions: "the State in dismantling [a segregative] system must take the necessary steps to ensure that [student] choice now is truly free" (*United States v. Fordice*, 1992, p. 8). It is the missions and roles of Alabama State and A&M, assigned by the state, that emerge under district court scrutiny. It seems the question the district court is trying to answer is, "What are the factors that are preventing white students from enrolling at these two institutions?" Both courts' answers are complex but, at times, unclearly delineated.

Unlike the Mississippi court case structured closely to follow the steps outlined in the "*Fordice* analysis," the 1995 Alabama district court's narrative (*Knight v. Alabama*, 1995) is, occasionally, disjointed. Working in "reverse order" (that is, by presenting first the court's findings and then the evidence), the judge's reasoning becomes more apparent. Simply stated, the court found that A&M's and Alabama State's proximity to TWIs in Huntsville and Montgomery, respectively, compromises students' ability to choose freely. One of the court's appointed "neutral expert witnesses," General Becton, testified that, "there will be some students who will not go to A & M. I believe there will be other students who will attend A & M. And I think that once the state gets serious about the business of demonstrating to A & M it is a quality institution, . . . that it will no longer be a concern of being a, quote, 'black institution,' but a quality institution" (*Knight v. Alabama*, 1995, p. 80). The court finds that Alabama practiced a sort of benign neglect of these two universities. Indeed, "The Court finds that although the State has funded ASU (Alabama State University) and AAMU (Alabama Agricultural and Mechanical University) better than the other state universities for at least the last twenty-five years, such funding has not yet put these institutions in the place they would have been but for their black heritage and the *de jure* system" (*Knight v. Alabama*, 1995, p. 80; italics added).

As a result, "The *underdevelopment* hinders the HBI in overcoming white students' and white parents' resistance to attending, or sending a child to, either ASU or A & M, especially when a high quality [HWI] exists in the same locale" (*Knight v. Alabama*, 1995, p. 81). Translating this into the language of *Fordice*, the district court concludes that the current relatively meager role of Alabama State and A&M within Alabama's system of higher education constitutes a vestige of earlier de jure segregation and, therefore, a violation of the Fourteenth Amendment. The situations of the respective universities in Huntsville and Montgomery illuminate this finding.

The Huntsville Situation

The evidence presented in the court's decision indicates the state's benign neglect of A&M: Alabama provided neither the guidance nor the resources necessary to make A&M programmatically competitive with its historically white neighbor, University of Alabama–Huntsville. Court evidence presents an interesting portrait of University of Alabama–Huntsville's history, compared with that of A&M.

University of Alabama–Huntsville is classified as a Category I-C institution: Urban Universities with Specialized Graduate and Professional Roles. Never lavishly funded to match its broad mission, University of Alabama–Huntsville has, nonetheless, managed to expand its programs and to thrive. Arguably, its broad mission provides the cover for high-paced development and innovation. Lacking sufficient state support to meet its broad mission, University of Alabama–Huntsville has evolved into the highest-cost insititution in Alabama's public system. Acquisition of significant financial debt also accompanied expansion. University of Alabama–Huntsville has tied closely the servicing of this debt to its ability to maintain enrollments. To guarantee enrollment, "UA-H made long-term financial commitments for the purpose of developing facilities needed for its instructional and research programs" (*Knight v. Alabama*, 1995, p. 36). Illustrative of its ability to maneuver within its broad mission assignment, University of Alabama–Huntsville issued a 13-year commitment to having its business program nationally accredited. The American Association of Collegiate Schools of Business (AACSB) "is the premier accreditation agency for business programs." In order to receive AACSB accreditation, University of Alabama–Huntsville painfully restructured its business and management programs and after 13 years of "concerted" effort achieved accreditation. Accomplishing this objective pays important dividends: "Accreditation helps to assure students and their parents of the program's high quality; gives the graduate an edge in the job market; . . . and *generally brings more prestige and respect to the institution*" (*Knight v. Alabama*, 1995, p. 37, italics added).

Through the lens of *Fordice*, this accreditation plays an important part in defining a university's mission and, therefore, influencing student choice. The court pays cursory attention to University of Alabama–Huntsville's education and nursing programs but clearly notes that these programs are strong and important to University of Alabama–Huntsville's mission. Examining these three programs, the court emphasizes that University of Alabama–Huntsville has been successful in attracting African-American students and that these programs have been an important aspect of accomplishing this outcome. The judge views University of Alabama–Huntsville's ability to attract African-American students not as the outcome of a concerted recruitment effort but as a result of creating high-quality programs. The court attempts in its finding to demonstrate that University of Alabama–Huntsville has several programs that are perceived as highly prestigious and that these programs are successful at influencing African-American and white students' decisions to enroll.

Alabama A&M University presents a very different situation. The court identifies only one prestigious program facilitating desegregation — teacher education — with graduating classes since the late 1970s being 50 percent white. The court's main body of evidence regarding A&M focuses upon the university's governance problems. Two examples clearly demonstrate the court's apparent preoccupation: first, the judge emphasizes, time and again, that A&M had six presidents between 1984 and

1995; second, he, at considerable length, highlights the "irresponsibility" of A&M's newly proposed bond issue. "On March 30, 1995 [A&M]'s Board of Trustees approved the issuance of Revenue Bonds worth $46,240,000. The stated use for these bond revenues included: (1) approximately $19 million to construct, furnish and equip a new dormitory (referred to as a 'living/learning complex'), which includes cafeteria and banquet hall; (2) approximately $11.6 million to construct, furnish and equip a new stadium . . . (3) approximately $4.7 million to construct . . . *a new business school*" (*Knight v. Alabama*, 1995, p. 49, italics added). The court's lamentations persist throughout its presentation of the evidence, but at one point, the judge issues an apparent outburst: "The Court finds that the bond issue clearly demonstrates [A&M]'s skewed priorities in light of this litigation, and shows an apparent unwillingness to assist the Court or the state in remedying the current effects of segregation. To spend almost twenty million on a single new dorm . . . while asking this Court to require the state to pay millions of dollars to create an engineering program is arrogant and irresponsible" (*Knight v. Alabama*, 1995, p. 49).

Although not explicitly stated, the court's impassioned discourse regarding A&M's lack of visionary leadership somehow demonstrates, as required by *Fordice*, that A&M's current situation is traceable to Alabama's de jure system of segregation. In fact, the court spends little time using the clear language of *Fordice*, suggesting ways in which the evidence can be interpreted to suggest traceability and continued segregation.

The court's ruling in regard to University of Alabama–Huntsville and A&M's situation favors the plaintiffs. This means that the court was satisfied that A&M's lack of prestigious programs and its subsequent inability to attract white students constitute a vestige of its history as a teacher-training college for African-Americans (A&M was founded as Huntsville Normal School for Blacks). Alabama's attempt to limit A&M's mission under de jure segregation as a teacher-training college can be linked to A&M's current designation as a Category II institution. The fact that the state in recent years funded A&M at a higher level than University of Alabama–Huntsville is insufficient. A&M needs a mission statement as broad as that of University of Alabama–Huntsville in order to expand and develop new programs that will attract white students. Failing to demonstrate that A&M's mission was not traceable or that it is educationally unsound or impractical to modify it, the state, in the court's judgment, needed to provide remedies.

One remedy along this line was immediately apparent. Alabama A&M, enjoying what amounted to a dual role of both defendant and plaintiff in the case, had earlier asked the state to fund a comprehensive engineering program on its campus. Because A&M is part of the Alabama state system, it technically is considered a defendant in this case. Therefore, its remedial solution is not contrary to the third step of the *Fordice* analysis. Its proposal now took on the mantle of an official state proffered remedy. Currently, A&M offers only a degree in engineering technology and a "stand alone" program in civil engineering. The court explicitly states that these limited offerings "in a state which has several schools of engineering is directly traceable to prior segregation." In ordering Alabama to fund A&M's proposal, the court cites several positive outcomes. The first is "A quality engineering program at an HBI successfully attracts white students . . . even when there is a high quality, proximate [HWI]." Also, the addition of an engineering program will expand student choice: "Engineering is one program that a student chooses ahead of the institution itself." Interestingly, the court notes that there is a need for more "minority engineers" in the Huntsville area, and the new A&M program will train them. Last, and most significantly in the court's view, "the addition of a quality program begins to change the perception that [A&M] is an inferior institution because it is historically black" (*Knight v. Alabama*, 1995, p. 83). That is, without actually doing so, the court hopes to change A&M's mission assignment.

The Montgomery Situation

Although not explicitly stated, the court also scrutinizes Alabama State's mission designation. The court never directly attacks the state's categorization of Alabama State as a Category II institution; the closest it comes to such a statement is, "White students' perceptions of the inferiority of black institutions are traceable to the *de jure* history of Alabama." The question that follows such a statement is, "How has this perception of inferiority been perpetuated?" The court's answer to this question focuses almost exclusively upon poor leadership at Alabama State. In the case of Alabama State, the court seems to be suggesting that ineffectual and incompetent leadership of Alabama State has contributed to perceptions of inferiority. In order to alter white students' negative perceptions, it is necessary to address this leadership situation. It is not necessarily the mission assigned to Alabama State that constitutes the problem. Instead, Alabama State has not responded effectively to advantages granted the state (like preferential funding) in recent history.

The court's attitude toward the Alabama State leadership is quite clear. A 1991 consent decree between the U.S. Justice Department and Troy State requires cooperative programming between Alabama State and Troy State University–Montgomery. Efforts along these lines failed "because ASU had an Interim President and the future leadership was uncertain . . . , ASU would take no action with regard to cooperative programs above the level of Academic Vice President." The court notes that an interim president ran Alabama State for an extended period, from 1991 to 1994. Absence of a permanent president explains why no innovative programs were undertaken at Alabama State University, according to the court opinion. The court's dour attitude is not inconsistent with the vice president's remarks regarding censure of Alabama State by the American Association of University Professors: "ASU's chief academic officer earlier testified in this case that 'the administration of Alabama State University is not interested in whether or not our institution is on the censure list.' we may place them on our censure list. . . . No substantial action has been taken to have ASU removed from the censure list" (*Knight v. Alabama*, 1995, p. 71).

Iconoclastic and irreverent statements such as this one clearly irritate the court. The court acknowledges that Alabama State's mission statement has had "some effect" on its ability to attract other-race students. However, it is the "acts and omissions" of its leadership that constitute the primary reason for its perceived inferiority. From the court's brief, it seems clear that it has adopted an attitude originally suggested by a defense attorney: "I take the position that [ASU] has self inflicted wounds having nothing to do with race that have contributed both to the problems that it has, and to the difficulty that it has had in recruiting other-race students" (*Knight v. Alabama*, 1995, p. 68).

The court agrees, explaining that,

While limited missions have had some effect, ASU and its leaders through acts or omissions, have adversely affected that institution's ability to attract other race students. (*Knight v. Alabama*, 1995, p. 68)

Failure of the Boards of Trustees and alumni . . . to actively support the campus leadership's desegregation efforts will result in substantially more limited range of, and considerably more draconian, remedies. (*Knight v. Alabama*, 1995, p. 68)

With responsibility shifted from mission assignment to TBI leadership, the court presents examples that illustrate Alabama State's inability to offer innovative programs aimed at attracting "nontraditional" students.

As noted earlier, the 1991 consent decree attempted to address the relationship between Alabama State and Troy State University–Montgomery. One provision of this decree ordered Troy State University–Montgomery to eliminate 23 degree programs (these programs averaged 464 students) in the hope that Alabama State would begin offering similar programs to attract students currently enrolled at Troy State University–Montgomery. The decree failed: "The record strongly indicates that [a local private institution], and not ASU, was the primary beneficiary of the Consent Decree." The court attributes this failure to poor Alabama State leadership: "ASU's president . . . believes that 'there is nothing unique about students who have jobs . . . and go to school.' ASU failed to demonstrate *any* desire until the Summer of 1994 to attract non-traditional students" (*Knight v. Alabama*, 1995, p. 63). Troy State University–Montgomery had been attracting so-called nontraditional students for many years. Indeed, Troy State University–Montgomery did not, at the time, actively recruit high-school students. Because Troy State University–Montgomery had been so successful in serving adult populations and Alabama State has been negligent in this area, the court ruled that it would be educationally unsound and impractical to transfer the programs to Alabama State University.

The only point of contention between Auburn University–Montgomery and Alabama State addressed during the 1995 trial involved their respective business programs. Similar to the Huntsville situation, Auburn University–Montgomery has a nationally accredited business program. Alabama State has a much less prestigious business degree: "The respective faculties demonstrate the differences in the emphasis of the ASU and AUM business programs. Almost all AUM faculty have terminal degrees and are heavily engaged in research and publication as well as teaching, while ASU's business faculty are less likely to have terminal degrees and place a significantly less emphasis on research and publication" (*Knight v. Alabama*, 1995, p. 76). Work and credentials of the faculty are key to gaining AACSB accreditation; research activities are preeminent. The court notes significant efforts by Auburn University–Montgomery to gain accreditation and rules that it is educationally unsound and impractical to transfer them to Alabama State. As an alternative, the court restricts Auburn University–Montgomery from offering "a Master's in Accountancy degree for five years, and ASU shall have sole authority to offer such a degree in Montgomery during that period."

The court provides two additional remedial solutions in its ruling, and both apply to Alabama State and A&M. It requires that state officials and the individual institutions establish "other-race scholarships" and endowments. This remedy reflects the court's finding that negative perceptions of Alabama State and A&M in comparison with proximate TWIs constitute a vestige of Alabama's de jure system. The state must establish scholarship funds solely for "other-race" students: in the case of Alabama State and A&M, white students. The court notes that, "Financial aid is a powerful magnet in attracting white students to HBIs." Both Alabama State and A&M are to compete for nontraditional students in their respective localities. To this end, the court mandates that, "financial assistance programs should be carefully targeted and designed specifically to promote desegregation," that is, as the court makes implicitly clear, Alabama State and A&M should expend fewer resources on attracting out-of-state African-American students and more resources on attracting local, probably part-time adult white students. Using short-run scholarship funds to attract white students to their campuses will enable Alabama State and A&M in the long run to change "White students' perceptions of the inferiority of black institutions." Perceptions of inferiority will be overcome, it is asserted, when a "critical mass" of other-race students appears on the TBI campuses. After all, the court says, the only racism it can address is that within its "remedial powers," not the racism that permeates society.

Although it apparently entertained such a proposal, the court decided not to order a closing of Troy State University–Montgomery, nor will a merger between Troy State University–Montgomery and Alabama State take place:

The court concludes that it would be neither educationally sound nor practicable to close TSUM or merge TSUM with ASU, given TSUM's great productivity with limited resources. The Court also concludes that merging TSUM and ASU would do nothing to further the cause of desegregation for the following reason: If the Court transferred the immensely successful TSUM program serving non-traditional students to ASU . . . it would send the message that ASU was incapable of competing for such students, which in turn would hurt rather than help their image. (*Knight v. Alabama*, 1995, pp. 118–119)

The second general remedial decree of the court is the establishment of endowments for both Alabama State and A&M. Endowments, it is felt, are an essential component of "improving institutional performance." The fact that Alabama State and A&M have limited endowments is a result of de jure segregation: "Insignificant or non-existent endowments result from historical underfunding of the universities. . . . [I]n Alabama, black citizens were forced to go to the HBIs for an education, but did not do very well economically, and as a result the HBIs suffered." The court concludes that "the State of Alabama can travel a long way toward erasing the inadequacies caused by *de jure* segregation through the creation of Trusts for Educational Excellence at ASU and [A&M]. The trusts established by the Court also allow the alumni of these institutions to prove their pride and support for these institutions" (*Knight v. Alabama*, 1995, p. 122).

The Land-Grant Issue

Another litigation issue, completely separate from the Alabama State and A&M mission designation problem, is the role of A&M within the Alabama Cooperative Extension System (ACES). This system is almost completely dominated by Alabama's historically white land-grant Auburn University. Its mission is to "link [A&M], Auburn, and Tuskegee universities' knowledge base to the people and communities of Alabama." (The role of Tuskegee University within this system lies outside the purview of this case.) State and federal, mainly agricultural research, dollars go to these three universities in exchange for dissemination of knowledge they generate. Public land-grant funding to colleges and universities throughout the nation is widely acknowledged as a major contributory to the remarkably expansive and very successful food production industry in the United States.

However, at one level, ACES is not much of a cooperative system. As the court observes, "Alabama has a 'loose confederation of three Extension systems rather than a single, comprehensive system.'" A&M, Auburn, and Tuskegee compete for the same funds; they do not, as the ACES title implies, share responsibilities. It is this situation that is the plaintiffs' cause for action, having failed in the 1991 trial to obtain relief: "The alleged vestiges with segregative effects are that the allocation of funds perpetuate the perception of inferiority of [A&M], results in lower funding generally for [A&M], and excludes blacks from policy making" (*Knight v. Alabama*, 1995, p. 124).

As required by *Fordice*, the plaintiffs must demonstrate that the policy or practice — that is, the loosely confederated ACES — is a vestige of de jure segregation. To this end, the court cites several facts: that "[AU] is so dominate [*sic*] that for all practical purposes, the other two extension [A&M and Tuskegee] systems border on invisibility"; that Auburn receives 90 percent of ACES extension funding; that Auburn completely dominates ACES leadership; that A&M's small extension staff receives 50 percent of the salary that Auburn's staff receives;

that A&M's "research specialists" receive only 85 percent of what Auburn's staff receives; and finally, that only 30 percent of ACES staff is African-American. The court also notes instances in which ACES staff in the Huntsville area required a specialist from Auburn because they were unsure whether A&M, only six miles away, had the necessary expertise.

These facts support the district court and the Eleventh Circuit Court's holding that the current structure of ACES is a vestigial policy traceable to Alabama's history of de jure segregation. However, discrimination no longer exists, because "of the degree of black participation in landgrant policymaking, the possibility of discrimination is nil" (*Knight v. Alabama*, 1995, p. 143). Furthermore, evidence is unconvincing that increased participation by A&M will increase the number of black farmers in the state (*Knight v. Alabama*, 1995, p. 143). The remedies are, therefore, limited and straightforward: unify the system into a single whole, and place an associate director at A&M with responsibilities for urban and "nontraditional" programming. There exist certain subtleties to these remedies that deserve attention. First, the court draws an important distinction between A&M being a "full participant," as opposed to a "partner," with Auburn in ACES. The court states, "Partner implies an equality of power and funding that is just not practicable, educationally sound, or desegregative. To split the funding in half, or to freeze AU's funding, allowing two systems to exist, would, at the least, decimate the excellent Alabama land grant system and create a system of separate and (maybe) equal land grant systems impermissible under *Brown v. Board of Education*" (*Knight v. Alabama*, 1995, pp. 151–152).

Therefore, the court feels it is necessary to make A&M a full participant in ACES with Auburn, relying upon additional remedial solutions to ensure that Auburn shares fully with A&M. One of these "additional solutions" concerns the director of ACES. The director of ACES is to be appointed, as he or she has been in the past, by the president and trustees of Auburn, because it is not "educationally sound" to change the selection process. The director's office will remain at Auburn University because it is not educationally sound to relocate him or her. However, to ensure that Auburn does not "dictate to" A&M, "it is crucial that the Director spend time at A & M. To that end the court requires that A&M maintain an office for the director."

The Curriculum Issue

The last issue on remand being considered by the court during the 1995 trial concerns the plaintiffs' First Amendment claims regarding the lack of black studies departments within Alabama's public higher education system. The Eleventh Circuit Court stated the court's task clearly: "The court should determine whether the curricula at the different HWIs are indeed deficient in the degree to which they incorporate black thought, culture, and history. The court should then proceed to determine whether that marginalization, if any, is traceable to Alabama's past regime of segregation and discrimination" (*Knight v. Alabama*, 1991, p. 1553).

In 1995, the district court set out to determine whether a lack of "black thought, culture and history" exists within the curriculum of Alabama's TWIs and whether such absence can be traced to the past segregation policymaking. It found that the plaintiffs' claims of a lack of "black thought, culture and history" in Alabama's TWIs were unfounded. Indeed, it notes the inclusion of aspects of "black thought, culture, and history" in many of the courses offered as part of the TWIs' general curriculum. Furthermore, the court notes that Alabama's TBIs do not have black studies departments. Therefore, how can it be expected that the TWIs would have such departments? The court's reasoning is no more complex than illustrated above. Because the plaintiffs have failed to demonstrate a deficiency, this issue is easily laid to rest. Plaintiffs failed to meet the burden of traceability, they did not present evidence of segregation effect, and good academic and economic reasons exist for not including black studies (*Knight v. Alabama*, 1995, pp. 172–175). "In light of those multitudinous findings [from the two previous trials], the Court has imposed what it believes to be the most desegregative remedy. . . . If the Court has erred, it is not the result . . . of [a] lack of consideration by the Court. . . . This Court has done all it can do" (*Knight v. Alabama*, 1995, p. 2).

THE LOUISIANA REMEDY

The issue before the U.S. District Court for the Eastern District of Louisiana is rather straightforward. The court's sole task during the most recent proceedings was to determine whether the remedies proposed during earlier deliberations are consistent with the Supreme Court's reasoning as outlined in *United States v. Fordice* (1992). As will be emphasized below, the issue of whether Louisiana's system of higher education is segregated is undisputed; it is the proposed remedies that were being scrutinized here. As the court demonstrates, these remedies seem to be consistent with *Fordice* and, thus, with the Constitution.

The Louisiana litigation has a rather lengthy pre-*Fordice* history not all presented here. In 1988, the federal district court in *United States v. Louisiana* (1988) held that measures undertaken between 1981 and 1987 to "eradicate" Louisiana's de facto segregated system of higher education had failed: a new "consent decree" needed to be planned. In July 1989, the court expounded on its 1988 decision. The 1989 opinion and order found, among other things, that

De *facto* racial identifiablity has continued to the present. . . . The governing boards of these institutions are also racially identifiable; . . . the present scheme for governing education in Louisiana — three operating boards and one coordinating board — has perpetuated illegal segregation in Louisiana and almost guarantees a standoff between the two "systems" (LSU and Southern) and the rest of higher education. . . . There is more program duplication . . . than is desirable. (*United States v. Louisiana*, 1989, p. 504)

Based on these findings, the court released a series of remedial orders. In October 1990, these findings were brought to the court for further modification — to "modify overly ambitious deadlines." The *Ayers* decision recently had been handed down, and the Fifth Circuit Court of Appeals found it to be "both controlling and binding" in *United States v. Louisiana*. As a result, the 1988 decision was vacated. In 1992, the Supreme Court reached its decision in *Fordice*. Again, *United States v. Louisiana* needed to be heard on remand: "The Court of Appeals then remanded the case to this [District] Court 'for further consideration in light of the United States Supreme Court's decision in *United States vs. Fordice*' and not necessarily for further evidentiary hearings and findings" (*United States v. Louisiana*, 1992, p. 6). In short, the 1992 litigation seeks merely to make the record consistent with the mandates of *Fordice*.

The only significant point of contention in this litigation was how to remedy Louisiana's segregated system of higher education. In a sense, the court was acting as an arbiter between the two parties, that is, hearing remedial solutions and deciding which were the most practicable. The record states, "Throughout this litigation, the only real issue and bone of contention between the parties was and remains to this day, remedy. All concerned considered the issue of liability secondary — almost a forgone conclusion given the historic treatment of blacks in the state of Louisiana and the well-known racial imbalance among its state universities" (*United States v. Louisiana*, 1992, p. 8). Unlike similar cases, like *Knight v. Alabama*, the Louisiana court is *not* being asked to determine whether segregation exists. Its task is much more limited and straightforward: issue a series of orders that are intended to bring greater racial and financial equality to Louisiana's institutions of higher education.

However, in light of the *Fordice* decision, both parties wanted the court to hear new evidence. The United States, in this case, asked the court to bolster the record because it "lacked specific findings in all areas" to be consistent with the balancing test used in *Fordice*. This claim was rejected: "The Court finds that the current record is sufficient to support the determination herein and further delay would be superfluous." As will be shown later, the court broadly highlights the manner in which the record *is* consistent with *Fordice*. The plaintiff, the State of Louisiana, also claimed the court's record falls short. The court notes, "the state defendants [Louisiana] allege that the Court has not made findings relative to the question of: (1) whether admissions standards and institutional mission assignments within the Louisiana higher education system perpetuate the prior *de jure* segregation and (2) whether it would be practicable and consistent with sound educational policy to eliminate any discriminatory effects created by the admissions standards and institutional mission assignments" (*United States v. Louisiana*, 1992, pp. 9–10). The court rejects the state's claim by noting, "For the Court to have followed the state defendants suggested course would have resulted in vain and unnecessary re-litigation of this entire matter at great expense" (*United States v. Louisiana*, 1992, p. 10).

After noting the United States' and Louisiana's objections to the shortcomings of the record in light of *Fordice*, the court made two sequential points: the first involved identifying the relevant features of *Fordice*, and the second involved demonstrating how the record is consistent with these features. The two components of the *Fordice* standard, as interpreted by this court, are the need to establish "traceability" and "educational soundness": "First, the factual record must demonstrate that state action attributable to prior *de jure* segregative policies continues to restrict freedom of choice. . . . Secondly [*sic*], the factual record must also support the conclusion that the state failed to justify its policies with sound education principles" (*United States v. Louisiana*, 1992, p. 11). The court felt that the record demonstrates that Louisiana's system of higher education was replete with examples of policies traceable to its dual de jure system: "There is no question in the Court's mind that Louisiana's dual system perpetuated by duplicative programs, multiple boards . . . has not spontaneously disappeared." Furthermore, the court notes that these findings are present in its July 1989 opinion and order.

The court also notes that the educational *un*soundness of these practices has been noted in the record. First, from the record, "The evidence suggests Louisiana's arrangement has led to unnecessary and costly program duplication." Later, the court highlights findings that illustrate Louisiana's flawed approach to admissions policies: "Thus, with an open admissions system, students enter higher education . . . easily, but do not readily leave with degrees. Moreover the problem is particularly acute at institutions with large black population [*sic*]" (*United States v. Louisiana*, 1992, p. 15). In short, the court felt it had previously satisfied both parts of the *Fordice* balancing test: it had shown that Louisiana's system of higher education is replete with policies that are traceable to its de jure system and that these policies lack any educationally justifiable soundness:

When the record in this case is viewed as a whole, the analytic framework and requisite factual inquiries now required as articulated in Fordice were made by this Court long before it had the benefit of the Supreme Court's guidance. . . . [The record demonstrates that] (1) The state of Louisiana continues to act through its policies and practices in a manner that promotes segregation within its higher education system; (2) those policies and practices are traceable to Louisiana's long history and endorsement of segregation; and (3) Louisiana's policies and practices are without sound educational justification and can be practicably eliminated. (*United States v. Louisiana*, 1992, p. 17)

All of these things were demonstrated in the record, and the need for further litigation was averted. The only thing for the court to do, then, was to lay out its remedial decree.

The decree is based largely upon the court's 1989 findings as presented in its opinion and order. It calls for profound changes in the structure of Louisiana's system of higher education. Such changes seem wholly consistent with the court's contention that Louisiana's participation in the systems of slavery and segregation placed its population of African-Americans at a significant disadvantage — that is, only deep structural changes can be hoped to rectify the injustices of Louisiana's racist history. Having sufficiently demonstrated the soundness of its reasoning, the court then merely had to reinstate its 1989 opinion and order that detailed the steps that Louisiana needed to take to bring its system of higher education in line with the Constitution.

Summary of the 1989 Remedial Order

The court's earlier order contains nine separate, descriptively titled sections: single governing board, classification of state universities, comprehensive community college system, program transfer and enrollment management, Louisiana law schools, funding for implementation of the order, other-race recruitment and retention, monitoring committee, and supplemental provisions.

Single Governing Board

The state is to disband the four governing boards that had been overseeing public higher education in Louisiana. From these four, a single board was to be formed within 60 days of the implementation date, composed of 17 voting members and 1 student member. This new board is charged with duties ranging from selecting a full-time president to overseeing the implementation of the remedial order. Also, the new board is to select chancellors for each of Louisiana's public colleges, universities, and community colleges. For the first five years of the board's existence, the court retains the right to veto its composition.

Classification of State Universities

Louisiana State University is to be designated the flagship university of the state system. As such, it is to have the most selective admissions criteria and the largest number of graduate and research programs. Undergraduate admissions "shall be limited to the top echelon of graduating high school seniors." Remedial education is to be eliminated from its curriculum. There is to be an "intermediate level" of slightly less selective institutions. These universities are to offer "significant doctoral and other graduate programs." Originally, the institutions that were to comprise this "tier" were Louisiana Tech, Southern University–Baton Rouge, University of New Orleans, and University of Southwestern Louisiana. Finally, the remaining four-year institutions are to be designated "comprehensive universities." They are to have "very limited graduate/research missions and less selective or open admissions." Initially, these institutions are Grambling, Nicholls, Southern University–New Orleans, Louisiana State University–Shreveport, McNeese, Northeastern, Northwestern, and Southeastern. As a result of these new designations, graduate programs at the comprehensive institutions are to be evaluated for continuance within 180 days of the implemention date.

Selective Admissions Standards

Admissions standards consistent with the program designations outlined above are to be instituted within 120 days of the implementation date. These new standards shall be based upon a combination of "high school grades, high school class rank, high school course taken, personal recommendations, extracurricular activities, essays or personal statements, interviews and standardized test scores." The new standards are to be closely evaluated by the new board. The board is to develop programs for high schools, appropriately informing them of the course work required to gain admissions. Each state university shall set aside 15 percent of its entering class for other-race students.

Comprehensive Community College System

The two-year community colleges are to be organized into a single "comprehensive community college system for Louisiana." This new system is to be overseen by the new systemwide governance board. A vice president for community colleges is to be appointed by the board and will report to the president. The community colleges are to retain open admissions policies and their remedial course offerings. The feasibility of opening new community colleges "in areas of the state where none currently exist" is to be studied by the board.

Program Transfer and Enrollment Management

No institutions are to be closed under this order. The system president is to be assigned the mission of reviewing all course offerings to "address the problem of program duplication and accompanying waste of resources and segregation." The board is to "take appropriate action with respect to eliminating, consolidating and setting enrollment levels for academic programs. . . . The [Board] shall ensure that such action is sensitive to the desegregation goals of this plan."

Louisiana Law Schools

"The LSU Law Center shall undertake as soon as practicable, . . . vigorous efforts to recruit black and other minority students from inside and outside the state." These efforts are to include financial assistance, a 10 percent admissions exception for minority students, the appointment of a special admissions officer to recruit minority students, and the development of curricular and extracurricular activities to assist minority students with their adjustment to law school (*United States v. Louisiana*, 1989, p. 32).

Funding for Implementation of This Order

Budgets are to be created for the newly classified institutions from the funds "freed" from the elimination of duplicative programs. Particular attention is to be paid to "improving the quality of PBIs whenever fiscally possible" (*United States v. Louisiana*, 1989, p. 35).

Other-Race Recruitment and Retention

The board is to create programs for the "recruitment and retention of other race students, faculty, administrators, and staff" throughout the state system. These efforts are to include scholarships for other-race students, other-race admissions officers, equal opportunity statements, public information efforts, "developing relationships between high schools and colleges," and the establishment of "integration progress goals for each institution."

Monitoring Committee

Three persons are to be appointed by the court to "monitor progress towards desegregation." They are to verify the progress being made by the board and each institution toward compliance with this order. "The monitoring committee shall give the new board a period of five years to achieve substantial progress toward eliminating racial identifiability."

Supplemental Provisions

The board is to take necessary measures to desegregate the faculties and staffs of all public institutions. This is to be done through a variety of recruiting and hiring policies. Finally, the court's injunction is to remain in effect until "December 31 of the seventh year following the calender year of the Implementation Date."

SUMMARY AND ANALYSIS

The plans substantiate the existence of continuing race discrimination associated with apparent race conflict. Moreover, they outline each state's response to civil rights requirements and strategy for remedying discrimination. Comparing the three, the Mississippi court more narrowly focuses upon two vestiges — systemwide admissions standards and underdevelopment of TBIs. The 1991 and 1995 Alabama decrees, in contrast, deal with eight — program duplication, African-American staff and faculty underrepresentation, discriminatory admissions policies (at Auburn), TBI development inequities, land-grant program inequities, curriculum, TBI physical facilities, and systemwide expenses and general funding inequities. Most expansive is Louisiana's long list of problems — system governance structure segregation, inequitable mission designations, program duplication, staff and faculty underrepresentation, systemwide admissions policies, African-American and white student underrepresentation, and inequitable TBI development.

The reasoning involved in establishing vestiges not unexpectedly entails determining whether and in what ways students' choices to attend one institution or another are affected by their race or the "race" of institutions within the system. In Mississippi, state admissions standards specifying different minimum ACT scores channel African-American students into African-American institutions, and vice versa. Because the state assigned TBIs limited missions in comparison with white colleges in the state, African-American students end up disproportionately channeled in curricularly limited postsecondary communities. In Alabama, the state's two TBIs were founded to train teachers, and forcing the two colleges to continue a primary focus upon education constitutes placing limits upon their development as institutions. The limited profile of TBIs means that students will choose not to attend. In Louisiana, the different governance boards and locations of African-American and white institutions with duplicated curricula within the same geographical region constitute the result of policies clearly connected to past segregation.

Free choice constitutes a more advanced interpretation of the nation's civil rights problem that emerged from case law on K-12 desegregation. This doctrine is widely endorsed in the Alabama case, underlying discovery of vestiges and prescribed remedies. Application of the free choice interpretation does not permeate the Mississippi case in the same way, but thinking along this line clearly underlies certain aspects of it, like the systemwide admissions standards problem and remedy. Concerning the free choice goal of desegregation, TBIs constitute a nonculpable state vehicle for channeling students into segregated higher education communities, not a segregated subcommunity that has been discriminated against. Missing from the Alabama and Louisiana court orders is reasoning asserting that TBIs constitute an institution of the state's African-American community that, as such, has been a priori the victim of race discrimination. However, the student choice, the dual system, or the TBI discrimination view of the problem can justify TBI enhancement as a remedy, as opposed to a policy of closure or consolidation, which, at least currently, most stakeholders would like to avoid. All three plans avoid ordering closures or mergers, though, in all three states, such a proposal was entertained by the court.

At one level, Louisiana's remedy is more far-reaching in scope than Alabama's and Mississippi's. The Louisiana remedy promises to change substantially the governance structure and policymaking "environment" of public higher education by centralizing control over the system. However, an equally plausible reinterpretation is possible. Adopting a more substantial remedy is not inconsistent with the long list of vestige problems identified by the Louisiana district court, but it may simply be the case that Alabama and Mississippi higher education policymakers earlier than leaders of Louisiana did away with racially separate central governance structures in an attempt to avoid federal sanctions and intervention. In this view, the Louisiana remedy may, indeed, be more expansive, but it is also less progressive, expressing the state's more dogmatic, longer perpetuated effort to maintain segregation. This interpretation also may project a more limited effect of the Louisiana plan. If consolidating governance structures took place earlier in Alabama and Mississippi and civil rights problems persisted in these two states, then Louisiana's governance restructuring plan holds potential for being implemented, similar to Alabama and Mississippi, in ways that foster continued segregation. Centralized or decentralized governance structures may characterize segregated as well as desegregated systems of higher education. As a remedy, decentralization or centralization may serve civil rights goals. In Louisiana, centralization clearly is associated with changes aimed at increased race equity.

It also may be the case that centralized governance is required for the first time in Louisiana as a prerequisite for improving the quality of the system. Increased race equity and policies of open admissions, voluntarily undertaken in many states, are widely associated, though not necessarily connected through evidence, with a decline in the quality of higher education over the past two and one-half decades. It is interesting that higher education officials at one time or another in Alabama and Mississippi advanced plans that simultaneously, though surreptitiously, embraced goals of increased efficiency, quality, and desegregation. The strategy for accomplishing all three involved increased centralized governance and downsizing.

The Mississippi College Board plan, which involved consolidating several of the state's eight universities, argued that freer student choice would emerge in a newly configured system. It is also the case that the board previously had introduced this same plan for consolidation, arguing efficiency and quality goals. In Alabama, the state's weakly chartered central higher education agency at one time developed a desegregation plan that also involved mergers, closures, and downsizing. It argued for increasing the central system's authority to order restructuring and approve new programs. Though then-Governor George Wallace disagreed with specific provisions of the central office's desegregation plan, the plan he developed also involved centralization as a means of reducing costs.

Increased centralization as a remedy for segregation, low quality, and poor efficiency is not inconsistent with the Reagan administration's civil rights interpretation. As indicated in Chapter 1, Assistant Secretary William Bradford Reynolds in 1983 interpreted the Justice Department's Title VI enforcement goals in Louisiana to involve accomplishing "quality education in a desegregated environment" (Reynolds, 1983).

Centralization proposals in Alabama and Mississippi met with disapproval by the courts, but the court-ordered Louisiana plan adopts this strategy. Because the Justice Department was the sole plaintiff in Louisiana, adopting this strategy may come as no surprise. It exemplifies the approach Reynolds and his colleagues inaugurated in the 1980s.

Contrasting the tones of the court decisions, the Alabama and Louisiana judges exhibit considerable impatience and frustration. Clearly, these two judges have, for a longer period, adjudicated difficult higher education civil rights litigation. Like the federal district court judge in Washington during the 1970s and early 1980s, their frustration reportedly reflects the fact that stakeholders in the cases engage in less than religious conformity with the orders issued by the court. The Louisiana judge, for his part, viewed both plaintiffs' and defendants' attempts to prolong litigation as a delaying tactic. In Alabama, the judge focused his displeasure upon the leaders of the state's TBIs, denouncing their failure to implement court-ordered remedies that he thought favored them. This judge's repeatedly stated opinion was that TBI leaders demonstrated poor leadership, failing to inaugurate new programs aimed at attracting adult, white, nontraditional students.

The Alabama case demonstrates that many African-American college leaders, reflecting the wishes of their most immediate constituencies, purposely may resist court-ordered actions that increase white enrollment. For others, difficulty in balancing internal resistance to white enrollment increases from African-American college stakeholders with court mandates, because increased white enrollment may result in limited presidential tenure. Building a dormitory and student center suggests a strategy of continuing to attract full-time undergraduate African-American students from the state of Alabama and southern region of the nation, as opposed to local, part-time adult white students the court ordered enrolled. This approach is obstinate but not mindlessly ill-considered.

No account of state and local responses to the Alabama and Louisiana court orders is presented at this time. It is certain, however, that informal responses of the negative kind associated with implementation in Georgia and Mississsippi will emerge, if they have not already. Obvious from the court record, neither plaintiffs nor defendants were pleased by the court's decision to turn over governance of the entire system to a single board. Assuming appropriate control will be difficult for new board members and will take time. At the campus level, one also should not expect smooth sailing to characterize implementation of the desegregation order. William "Bud" Davis, the chancellor of the state's flagship institution, Louisiana State University, resigned in late October 1996, admitting that he had failed to properly administer the institution's minority scholarship program. The student newspaper uncovered the fact that he and his assistant, David "Sonny" DeVillier, over two years awarded most of the 54 minority scholarships to white students (*Atlanta Journal–Constitution*, 1996). In Alabama, Murphy reviewed progress in September 1996 and ordered additional remedy measures because he felt unjustifiably slow and inadequate efforts and results were apparent (Healy, 1996, p. A27).

NOTES

I gratefully acknowledge the assistance of Mark Meyerrose and Frank Tuitt, graduate students at the Harvard Graduate School of Education, in preparing this chapter.

REFERENCES

Healy, Richard. 1996. "Judge Demands Progress in Desegregation of Alabama Colleges." *Chronicle of Higher Education*, September 20, 1996, p. A27.

Knight, et. al. v. Alabama, 787 F. Supp. 1030 (N.D. Ala. 1991); *modified*, 801 F. Supp. 577 (N.D. Alabama 1992).

Knight v. Alabama, Civil Action No. 83-M-1676, August 12, 1995, "Findings of Fact, Conclusions of Law, and Remedial Decree."

"LSU Scandal Spurs Resignation." *Atlanta Journal–Constitution*, November 2, 1996, p. C2.

"Notice of Application of Supreme Court Decision." *Federal Register*, 59, no. 20, (1994): 4272.

Reynolds, William Bradford. 1983. "The Administration's Approach to Desegregation of Public Higher Education." *American Education*, 19 (1983): 9–11.

United States v. Louisiana, 718 F. Supp. 499 (E.D. La. 1989); 811 F. Supp. (E.D. La. 1992); Civ. A. No. 80-3300, August 2, 1988.

United States v. Fordice, 112 S. CT. 2727 (1992).

5

Findings, Conclusions, and Recommendations

Federal civil rights enforcement in higher education today gets interpreted in two contradictory ways:

systemwide Title VI enforcement overextended reasonable bounds of government intervention under circumstances of declining race discrimination, failing to reflect uncontrollable factors that limit rationally planned outcomes and, instead, produce unacceptable, unintended consequences, or

enforcement produced poor results because remedies were weakly designed and poorly implemented.

Through close review of evidence used to reach both interpretations, which seems most accurate and inclusive? Does evidence of race discrimination characterize official documents describing past and current enforcement? What form does evidence of limited effort adopt? Is there evidence of producing unintended consequences? Are there aspects of enforcement that compel a different interpretation from the two mentioned? These are questions addressed in the prior chapters.

Federal responses at one level contributed a context for state action. Chapter 1 illustrates two federal enforcement contextual response patterns, one centered upon interpreting legal requirements and the other upon approving and monitoring remedies. First, Office for Civil Rights (OCR) and Department of Education interpretations of Title VI requirements changed from time to time between 1969 and 1988. Federal officials began in 1969 with a dual system approach, moved perhaps in a stronger direction in adopting a racial balance strategy, later adopted a weakened direction toward accomplishing "quality education in a desegregated environment," and most recently moved toward achieving "free student choice" in the 1992 Supreme Court case and subsequent court litigation. In addition to official federal interpretations, members of the African-American college community, most visibly in Mississippi, offer a slightly different fourth interpretation, a dual system view, putting aside the long-accepted edict from *Brown* (1954) that separate is inherently unequal, insisting instead that separate can be made equal in today's race relations context.

Among these alternatives, no single interpretation thoroughly characterized enforcement for a substantially long period of time. It is more likely that competing interpretations have always been and continue to be used by different stakeholders in identifying discrimination problems and in designing, implementing, and assessing remedies. Because evolving and competing civil rights requirements do not fall into the category of strong enforcement, it is impossible to clearly associate one type of remedy with one interpretation more than another. Stakeholders make little effort to rationalize adopting one remedial strategy over another with adequate understanding of their system's segregation problems, in this way providing at least the impression of producing fragmented and incomplete remedies and of insincere effort.

The strength of federal enforcement reflects not only the content of policy interpretations but also their legitimacy — capacity to compel agreement among reasonably large groups of stakeholders. Where systemwide Title VI enforcement has taken place, even among African-Americans as a class of potential beneficiaries, legal interpretations and remedies observed in earlier chapters are not strongly and consistently endorsed. Past interpretations, including the recent Supreme Court free choice doctrine, seem, in the final analysis, to satisfy few stakeholders of either race. Failure to invent a view of enforcement that a sufficiently diverse group of stakeholders can buy into provides increased insight into widely perceived weak implementation and poor outcomes of enforcement during the period 1964–1990.

Illustrating the problem of limited enthusiasm, strong support for the 1978 guidelines, OCR's most substantial legal interpretation, remains conditionally weak even among the most avid Title VI supporters. In the manner of primary- and secondary-school desegregation case law, the guidelines present racial balance as a prescription for or interpretation of dismantling dual systems. However, it should be remembered that race imbalance proved to be an increasingly unpopular school desegregation doctrine. Liberal critics of this interpretation within the K–12 arena argue that this prescription does not extend far enough, aiming only at structural or schematic changes, rather than changes in important, more deeply embedded educational operations and functions. Mixing African-American and white students constitutes only a first step toward true compliance. Conservative criticism is similar, on the one hand agreeing that race mixing is insufficient but on the other asserting that more substantial desegregation approaches are too risky and potentially intrusive, compromising students' and parents' right to choose where to attend school and local education agencies' right to choose what to teach and how to run schools. Once expanded K–12 school desegregation policies got perceived as too risky, progress stopped. Arguably, new civil rights interpretations somehow must neutralize the risks that conservative higher education critics identify if progress is to be made.

The second pattern of federal response displayed in Chapter 1 involved asking for desegregation plans, ruling weak state plans and the compliance activities as adequate, issuing new orders ostensibly requiring expanded enforcement when ordered to do so by the federal court, and repeating earlier judgments of the adequacy of weak stategies and incomplete designs. By the end of the 1980s, official disagreement between the executive branch civil rights officials and the federal district court ended, leaving unresolved the dilemma that had been created. Other responses, for example, referring states to the Justice Department for litigation, were available but largely went unused by OCR. Moreover, when OCR referred states to Justice for litigation, Justice officials moved slowly. The Louisiana and Mississippi cases illustrate this trend.

Another alternate strategy might have involved providing federal funds for higher education desegregation planning and implementation. States requested funds for desegregation planning and implementation, but they were never provided by Washington. A more diverse response strategy of both promising sanctions and providing incentives came to characterize public K–12 desegregation, and such approaches were, in principle, available to OCR, concerning higher education. Some supporters of civil rights enforcement downplay such approaches, arguing that states should provide the funds needed to correct civil rights problems they created. However, federal government, at least through inaction, also created civil rights problems. Also, proponents of the uncontrollable factors interpretation of enforcement judge such alternatives as politically impossible during the late 1980s. Moreover, such strategies penalize citizens who never contributed to race discrimination. However, many among this group are politicians who create and control federal priority setting, making passage of federal funding for colleges and universities undergoing enforcement possible, if not risky.

Unofficial responses undermining enforcement seem to stem from the context established by indecisive and weak federal interpretations. Increasingly, state officials got the message that engaging in good faith responses was the nation's most appropriate civil rights enforcement effort. In an effort to further understand the unresolved standoff of the 1980s and to suggest the correct interpretation of Title VI enforcement in public higher education, Chapter 2 presents official documents describing enforcement in the state of Georgia for what seemed the most active early period — 1978–1989. Chapter 2 describes and analyzes state officials' responses to federal enforcement. Within the official record, the most compelling evidence for an interpretation of poor state effort consists of unofficial aspects of state response. Clear official responses provide evidence of poor design and poor implementation of weak remedies, as the federal courts repeatedly ruled. However, not widely acknowledged, state officials, with the approval of federal monitors, established subtle, unofficial, noncompliant responses of many different forms, including misinterpreting requirements and overestimating goal achievements, denying the existence of civil rights problems and failing to diagnose them adequately, falsely reifying state policies and population demographics, obfuscating limited enforcement, implementing remedies in ways that contradict enforcement goals, and presenting plans for downsizing and centralizing higher education as desegregation remedies.

Correct interpretation of enforcement relies not only upon formal responses like plans and implementation strategies but also upon unofficial, at times intangible and subtle, responses like the ones observed. Unofficial response elements are, in many instances, more determinant of outcomes than official ones, particularly poorly designed official plans and poorly implemented actions.

Chapter 2 does not purposefully overlook evidence of unintended negative outcomes. If strong evidence of unintended negative consequences of enforcement and diminished discrimination exists, states, not unreasonably, would have included it in desegregation plans and compliance reports. However, it simply does not exist in official documents. Former Assistant Secretary William Bradford Reynolds inferred that closing traditionally black institutions (TBIs) might suggest overstepping the boundaries of proper government action, resulting in unintended compromise of local citizens' needs and priorities. His claim concerns the

Louisiana judge's impending plan to order closure of the traditionally African-American Southern University law school. However, Reynolds' interpretation appears empty, because attempts to merge or close TBIs have emerged repeatedly and been defeated throughout the extended period of Title VI enforcement. Plans along this line consistently meet with substantial public resistance. Such plans, therefore, constitute weak evidence of government overstepping its bounds. In fact, when Title VI enforcement began, federal government moved quickly to eliminate the impression that such strategies would be widely approved. The 1978 guidelines postpone requiring TBIs to set white student enrollment goals, because the African-American college and university lobby in Washington successfully pressured OCR to temper its apparent approval of such strategies. Enhancing TBIs constitutes a longstanding compromise of varying interpretations of Title VI, as illustrated in Chapter 1.

Evidence in official documents suggests changes in race inequity problems within higher education but no definitive and consistent progress. In fact, the state of Georgia, by its own admission, never reached its enrollment and employment goals. The fact that litigation consistently and with little ambiguity has resulted in repeated court findings of continued race discrimination also undermines claims that discrimination, at least in public higher education in previous de jure segregated states, has declined. Reasonably, recent litigation would most clearly establish evidence of race progress, but the Alabama, Louisiana, and Mississipi rulings do not follow this prediction. In fact, many claims of discrimination in these three states were not even challenged by defendants.

Chapter 3 presents evidence of continuation of the same policymaking context and response patterns established during the 1970s and 1980s, with some of the same federal and state enforcement problems in the 1990s in Mississippi. Similar to what took place in other states and in Washington between 1964 and 1989, more than one interpretation of Title VI requirements compete for wide acceptance and actualization, in this instance, local stakeholder groups involved in implementation of the 1992 Supreme Court *Fordice* decision competing with the federal courts. The court's free choice emphasis contrasts with many important local stakeholders' strongly asserted dual system view that involves independent development of TBIs within a 1990s race relations context. Similarly as well, state officials' responses reveal some of the unofficial character of earlier enforcement, including presenting plans for downsizing as desegregation plans, excluding African-American college presidents from important policy forums, reifying outside factors, and obfuscating effort and outcomes. The Mississippi episode also provides convincing evidence of strong race conflict during the observed early mobilization phase of enforcement. Such evidence suggests continuing race discord, which the conservative interpretation of civil rights compliance assumes out of existence.

The desegregation plans summarized in Chapter 4 contain the varying outline of current enforcement brought about by recent court rulings and monitoring. Different from the earlier period of OCR-initiated enforcement, the recent plans emphasize free choice interpretations contained in the 1992 Supreme Court ruling. The 1993 Louisiana plan uniquely features restructuring central control of the entire public higher education system and includes potentially more comprehensive remedies. The Mississippi and Alabama remedies seem more narrowly focused upon enhancing TBIs as a means of inceasing their white enrollment, in this way applying the *Fordice* free choice standard. Relatively high undergraduate African-American enrollment rates at traditionally white institutions (TWIs) in Mississippi were interpreted by plaintiffs' lawyers to rule out making a case for continuing vestiges. Similarly, in Alabama, prior to *Fordice*, enrollment agreements were reached with many TWIs within the state system. The most recent *Knight* (1995) litigation focused narrowly upon a handful of vestige issues, not including African-American TWI enrollment. Private plaintiffs instead argued that segregated curriculum — absence of African-American studies programs — constitutes a vestige. Adopting this approach seemed appropriate, because, even though African-American student access has increased at TWIs, the campus community and academic environment of recently desegregated institutions constituted a vestigial barrier to African-American student retention and performance.

REINTERPRETING TITLE VI ENFORCEMENT: INADEQUATELY INTERPRETING POLICY, ESTABLISHING WEAK REMEDIES AND IMPLEMENTATION, AND "MASKING"

The documents described and analyzed in this study clearly support neither of the two previous interpretations of enforcement. Very little evidence supports the conservative version: race discrimination remains a problem within the public higher education communities of previously segregated states, no government policies have intrusively compromised local prerogatives and choices, and no grossly intractable obstacles are apparent. Systematic attempts to present evidence supporting these assertions might, to some extent, prove otherwise. The compelling conclusion of this study is current lack of supporting data.

Evidence supports the familiar, liberal view of limited remedies and weak implementation but also illustrates the limitations of this interpretation of enforcement. Remedies were weak, and implementation did not fully occur, but this problem is distinct from a federal interpretation of civil rights requirements progressively growing weaker as time passed, in this way establishing a context for poor remedy design and partial implementation. For purposes of more complete understanding, it also is informative to differentiate unofficial response elements that did not facilitate enforcement. Extending liberal understanding of what took place, unofficial responses, and federal government establishing a context facilitated weak state remedies and limited implementation.

INADEQUATE FEDERAL POLICY INTERPRETATIONS: ESTABLISHING POLITICAL CONTEXT

As illustrated, federal policy interpretations moved in an increasingly benign direction during the 1980s, in the end, justifying rulings of compliance based upon good faith effort. Currently in the Alabama, Louisiana, and Mississippi plans, establishing free choice among students (the Supreme Court's most definitive interpretation of Title VI) may or may not sustain policy resource intensity needed for strong enforcement. Judged by the Alabama, Louisiana, and Mississippi court orders, the Supreme Court's new standard is not compelling in the sense of promoting sufficient agreement among important stakeholders or subsequently setting a standard for remedy development and implementation. The student choice diadem weighed heavy upon the countenance of the Alabama judge but wielded no regal influence in Mississippi and Louisiana. Most legal experts agree that further attention by the court will occur.

Factors emerging from student choice research also may be used to justify slow progress. Prior to *Fordice*, Georgia public officials used research identifying student-defined barriers to student choice as a rationalization for failing to achieve planned civil rights goals. Supplemented by a 1987 review of research on student choice, the Georgia chancellor claimed that independent factors, beyond the reach of state policy, caused a decline in first-year African-American enrollment within the Georgia system. This claim complements the speculative opinions of researchers like Q. Whitfield Ayres that "student choice is affected by so many factors that are not easily manipulated by federal and state officials" (Ayres, 1984, p. 128) and can easily justify doing nothing. However, in fact, more broadly defined choice research demonstrates the positive effect of government policies upon student choice — for example, federal financial aid grants as opposed to loans increase and redistribute minority student enrollment and foster persistence (St. John, 1989, 1996).

Producing further disagreement, free choice, as an interpretation of federal civil rights law within the higher education community, can be associated with incentive-based federal policymaking aimed at goals unrelated to the Supreme Court's interpretation of the Constitution and Title VI. Though student financial aid programs are widely viewed as a federal strategy for increasing the enrollment of low-income students, such policies also represent a strategy for reorganizing colleges and universities into a marketplace, as opposed to their current public bureau-cratic system. Reorganization serves the controversial purpose of increased efficiency within U.S. higher education. The nation's advancing conservative federal leadership has strongly endorsed increased efficiency and other cost-cutting policies toward higher education in an effort to reduce overall federal budgets. Many within this group also believe that increased opportunity to attend college, whatever form it takes, will increase college costs and inefficient use of limited federal resources.

College and university costs, it has been strongly illustrated, have increased for years at rates substantially higher than rates of important economic indicators. Over the past 14 years, for example, public four-year college tuition increased at three times the rate of inflation and three times the rate of household income — by 234 percent between 1980–1981 and 1994–1995 (U.S. General Accounting Office, 1996, p. 5). Higher educa-tion leaders have not provided satisfactory explanations for this trend, leaving an open playing field for state and federal fiscal current conserva-tive policymakers.

Seizing the initiative, neoconservative politicians and policymakers argue, in addition to poor cost management, that benefits of college atten-dance accrue disproportionately to individual college degree recipients, not to society at large. Increasing benefits to individuals does not consti-tute a sound economic basis for federally funding students. Growth of the economy depends upon availability of a workforce that possesses technical skills that only a small portion of college students obtain through obtaining a degree. The fact that colleges graduate so few of the students they enroll proves their inefficiency, and the fact that colleges graduate so few students with work skills enabling them immediately to fill emerging, technically situated service industry jobs illustrates their limited contribution of public, external benefits. If the benefits of college attendance accrue to individuals, not to society as a whole, then expanding access and college opportunity is less essential. If expanding opportunity to race minority youth as a justification for past discrimination can be eliminated, then overall college expansion will decrease and costs will decline, including the federal student budget.

Reflecting this trend, the 1996 South Carolina legislature passed a law allocating funds to the state's higher education system entirely on performance criteria. According to the new law, funding would be based on 37 performance criteria instead of student enrollments and capital needs. Explaining the new law, Austin Gilbert, chairman of the state commission on higher education, commented that,

"We are faced with a crisis in credibility." If South Carolina's 33 public colleges want more state money, he said, they must submit to high-stakes performance evaluations and demonstrate that they have improved. . . . He pointed to a graph illustrating how the administrative costs at public colleges have soared at a time when, he said, that institutions' quality has improved little. South Carolinians have come to doubt that public colleges are using their tax dollars wisely, . . . and this has made lawmakers reluctant to spend more on higher education. (Schmidt, 1997)

Political struggle over control of higher education expansion establishes a negative policy context for systemwide Title VI enforcement. Title VI enforcement at bottom involves expanding African-American and Latino enrollment in higher education. Emphasizing this point, the federal OCR guidelines require increased total African-American enrollment, increased first-time-in-college enrollment, and increased enrollment of African-American high-school graduates. From a liberal civil rights perspective, making such increases benefits U.S. society in a number of ways: with additional African-American and Latino college graduates entering the workforce, total wealth of society expands; aggregate socioeconomic status of the nation's African-American and Latino communities increases; untapped talents, expanded and enhanced through college attendance, positively affect schools, industry, government, and other institutional sectors; and the social, political, and monetary costs of government policymaking decline as larger percentages of African-American and Latino families move out of poverty.

However, does evidence exist to support such assertions? Is it likely that increased enrollment, characterized by meeting race minority students' unique needs, can be accomplished without increasing college costs? In what ways can expanded, more racially diverse, but more efficient colleges and universities actually increase the social and economic status of race minority communities? The civil rights dialogue accompanying Title VI enforcement displays weakness by failing to engage such issues and by failing in other ways to confront more broadly focused "increasing inefficiency" and "decreasing external benefits" policy struggles.

Instead of confronting such arguments, many leaders of the higher education community, for their part, enthusiastically endorse federal student aid as a means of expanding low-income and race minority student enrollment and quietly resist policies that, at bottom, follow the prescription of reorganizing higher education into a free marketplace. Through the years, an accommodation between federal policymakers and college leaders evolved in which higher education has slowly moved in the direction of marketplace organization, accepting huge amounts of federal student aid dollars delivered in ways that prevent rapid reorganization. At the state level, central administrators, backed by cost-cutting legislators in the 1990s, have substantially reduced state budgets, in part by introducing policies not incompatible with marketplace development. Still, many changes that are neccessary for total reorganization into a marketplace — for example, equal transfer of academic credit from one state system to another, and full rationalization of the relationship between tuition and costs within state systems — are not yet fully accomplished (McPherson & Schapiro, 1991, pp. 187–216).

Many college leaders believe that expanding student choice to increase low-income student access or to cure vestiges of past racial segregation, in the manner of creating a marketplace, will disrupt highly valued aspects of the organization, governance, and culture of higher education systems. Continued skepticism stems from the fact that many important dynamics of the nation's higher education community and of individual colleges and universities do not mimic those of business and industry. Moreover, free market systems are widely known, despite good intentions, to increase, not decrease, inequities among students and employee groups. Barring deliberate challenges, expanding student choice as a remedy for past race discrimination likely will be viewed with skepticism by college leaders, a broad sector of civil rights enforcement stakeholders.

The Supreme Court's free student choice interpretation of civil rights enforcement also may eventually undermine a longstanding consensus upon enhancing TBIs as a civil rights remedy. Through the years, concern over enhancing, closing, or merging African-American institutions has contributed a great deal of civil rights discourse. Official responses to this controversial issue traditionally adopt the form of compromise. Illustrative of this trend, even superconservative Supreme Court Justice Clarence Thomas prepared a concurring opinion in *Fordice*, arguing that dismantling TBIs in Mississippi in order to accomplish desegregation constitutes perversely unjust treatment. His opinion duplicates that of liberal TBI community stakeholders, though the arguments advanced by the two groups are different.

As a strategy, enhancing TBIs fits accommodatingly into more than one policy perspective. Many liberal, racial balance stakeholders argue that TBIs perform a special function within current state systems, more successfully than TWIs graduating African-American students. In keeping with this interpretation, the 1978 guidelines, responding to pressure from the TBI Washington lobby, ended up postponing required increases in white enrollment at TBIs. The guidelines instead embrace what was viewed as a less risky approach of first eliminating segregation at TWIs, in this way avoiding placing burdens upon African-American stakeholders. Furthermore, enhancing TBIs, it was argued, would attract white students. In these two ways, racial imbalance would be corrected. Responsible, modern, conservative, dual-system stakeholders, including the Supreme Court justices, view TBIs as part of a system of institutions that all students should have free choice to attend. It may make no sense to close either the historically white or historically African-American subsector, because both contain educational resources that all students can profit from encountering. TBI enhancement is needed to eliminate unequal choices that all students currently are forced to make. The quality education approach arrives at TBI enhancement as a means of avoiding government compromises of local community needs. More than consensus arrived at in different ways, what continues to preserve agreement about the fate of TBIs is the sad image, widely portrayed for fund-raising through national news and entertainment media, of a TBI closing its doors to poor African-American students who otherwise would not receive a college education. The message provided by such images is, at this time, incontrovertible with evidence of TWIs' poor accomplishments in educating race minority youth.

However, several factors challenge the time-honored consensus on TBI enhancement in Mississippi and Alabama in particular. Most notably, enhancement is not required in a manner that promises true success. Neither plan establishes a sufficient context for planning and implementing a necessarily complicated process of developing TBIs. No sufficiently sophisticated TBI development plan is included in the court orders, though the Mississippi one does make provision for planning substantial academic program expansion at Jackson State. Similarly, new resources for TBIs seem small and insufficient as well as unplanned. Moreover, substantial resistance to expansion of public higher education systems, within Mississippi state government in particular, places unacknowledged constraints upon successfully implementing a sufficiently sophisticated institutional development strategy. Similar to Mississippi, the Alabama judge seems to have underestimated what it will take realistically to assess needs and expand the TBIs' curricula. The Louisiana court places confidence in the new central board's commitment and capacity to undertake almost all undetailed aspects of enforcement in the court order, including TBI enhancement. Other important factors, particularly in Alabama, are TBIs' resistance to enhancements that facilitate increased white enrollment and the judge's impatience with such responses to his order. If failure this time around to enhance TBIs emerges, closure and merger emerge once again as viable alternatives. Moreover, if legal appeals fail to change existing state admissions requirements in Mississippi, lowered TBI enrollment presents the opportunity for implementing alternate solutions.

Expanding the Poor Remedy–Weak Implementation Perception

Continued disagreement over TBI enhancement goals, like in the state of Alabama, coupled with the perception of continued failure despite generous effort, in addition to the Supreme Court's free choice emphasis, challenge TBIs. Stakeholders in Alabama seem to disagree over continuing to emphasize the traditional mission of educating full-time, 18–25-year-old African-Americans from the local region, conducting enhancements that facilitate such goals, or undertaking enhancements that attract adult, part-time, nonresidential, white students from a more local area. Some TBIs, like Kentucky State and Savannah State, have enhanced themselves, at least in the short run, by pursuing both missions simultaneously, but the decision to do so was not easily reached, and serious unresolved conflict seems to accompany such efforts.

Failure to incorporate an overall development plan for TBIs and to establish funding according to such a plan illustrates one aspect of weak remedy making that is widely acknowledged to have negatively affected past civil rights enforcement in higher education. Together, weaknesses of this kind illustrate a broader problem of failing to establish an organizational context for enforcement. Desegregation is, at one level, a planned organizational change process. Planned organizational change comes about voluntarily and involuntarily through government civil rights regulation. Planned change within formal college organizations can be viewed as voluntarily responding to changing conditions within an institution's local or other relevant environment. Because of a variety of factors, most colleges over the past 30 years have voluntarily adapted in small ways to enrollment of larger numbers of race minority students. Changes in the demographic character of the 18–25-year-old student pool and changes in civil rights laws required such a response. Most campus adaptation features routine transactional responses involving rule changes, new policies and procedures, and reassigning responsibility for dealing with unique race minority students' needs from one unit to another. Incorporating such strategies, desegregation can be viewed in this way as a routine transactional institutional change process.

Sometimes, colleges and universities do not voluntarily and adequately respond to race-defined changes in student enrollment and staff employment pools. Court- and OCR-ordered desegregation in higher education takes on an additional dimension of government civil rights officials drawing attention to race underenrollment and employment brought about through a change in environment (a new civil rights law making African-Americans eligible to attend for the first time) and monitoring institutional responses to it. To what to respond, how to respond, and how much is enough constitute decisions reasonably and responsibly associated with desegregating a college campus, shared with outsiders in the case of systemwide Title VI enforcement. Most colleges and universities that have voluntarily or involuntarily opened their doors to race minority students and staff over the past 30 years have faced these issues, though the issues themselves may have been formulated only after the process of desegregation was underway.

Sometimes, colleges and universities respond inadequately within the framework of civil rights law to needs brought about by including or increasing race minority students and staff. Understanding ways in which colleges and universities normally respond to changes in their organizational environment and judging whether normal responses are adequate for purposes of the law provide a context for undertaking civil rights enforcement. However, state and federal enforcement does not always incorporate important aspects of organizational context as a basis for policymaking. For example, in a recent public forum, a former OCR director expressed the view that OCR officials ought to formulate a model of successful programs for the recruitment and retention of race minority students. Such a model (or models) should then be disseminated to state and local campus officials to assist them in formulating remedies and to make clear the federal expectations of their performance. More than he perhaps realized, the former director articulated an unmodified view of organizational change widely incorporated into government policy toward education until recent years.

Establishing a more modern organization change perspective has emerged as a widely acknowledged policymaking task for purposes of improving K–12 school systems. "Restructuring" school districts "from top to bottom" today involves more than describing and disseminating model instructional programs on the assumption that school stakeholders will diligently apply them. The 25-year history of accomplishing Title VI compliance (assuming 1988–1989 OCR compliance findings constitute a fraud) mirrors an early period of top-down decision making that failed to improve the quality of K–12 schooling. Viewed as a system reform parallel to the K–12 experience, Title VI enforcement requires adopting a different character.

Stated differently, aggresssive Title VI policies do not incorporate an acceptable view of how modern universities operate and of how change regularly takes place within them. Organizational change concepts underlying the enforcement approach articulated by the former OCR director constitute an important element of policy context. Absence of adequate concepts results in widely observed failure of Title VI enforcement. Remedies were not designed adequately, implementation was undertaken inadequately, and monitoring occurred unsuccessfully, to some extent because organizational context was missing. If more modern organizational change approaches that involve transforming campus community or challenging race-biased canons of knowledge were incorporated, in what ways would Title VI enforcement get interpreted and be judged? The nation's civil rights dialogue, unlike the K–12 school improvement discourse, does not debate the most appropriate organizational change strategy to incorporate in enforcing Title VI. It does not even acknowledge the need for identifying the best strategy. However, evidence of the need for adopting a more total perspective and for choosing the right one is persuasive.

The following example illustrates (but does not prescribe) how a widely accepted, decidedly conservative theory of how colleges work and, by implication, how they change in response to changes in their external and internal environment can be used to establish a more functional and appropriately aggressive civil rights enforcement strategy. It involves adapting and applying Robert Birnbaum's concept of *How Colleges Work* (Birnbaum, 1988). By implication, his model suggests that enforcement ought to require not only increased other-race enrollment and employment but also a planned change process that entails relatively independent subsystems and subunits of the university:

establishing new norms of organizational culture,

searching for appropriate responses to increase African-American enrollment and employment,

searching for new operations to replace old ones that do not facilitate changes brought about by increasing African-American participants,

providing support strategies by leaders, and

getting units of the campus community operating on a compatible range of race-relations issues.

These concepts provide a more process-defined and comprehensive road map for planning and implementing desegregation than the traditional program modeling approach. It requires application of widely accepted, more modern organizational change principles. Adaptation of its principles, if not its content, for purposes of civil rights enforcement most importantly establishes a new mind-set about enforcement among stakeholders. Elements of the proper new mind-set include incorporating wide participation in identifying vestiges, in planning and implementing remedies, in establishing the importance and scope of tasks involved, and in legitimizing attention to enforcement; stressing the importance of structuring opportunities for leaders to provide symbolic public and other forms of support; and viewing college and university communities as "loosely coupled" environments consisting of semiautonomous units that establish semi-independent, culture-prescribed operating routines and constitute the most important setting in which change may occur. Concerning establishing a new mind-set, enforcement is viewed as involving unique operational requirements affecting each college unit dissimilarly. New norms are to be developed within each unit that, through content and methodology, convey the urgency of searching for and finding a different set of operations not incompatible with need established through increased race diversity. Both the organization and the new students display new needs when desegregation takes place. Vestiges of past segregation may take the form of organizational norms that do not facilitate transactional changes within an institution, or they may involve important units failing in their own way to engage in action of the five kinds identifiable from Birnbaum's book. Beyond enrolling and hiring an increased number of "other race" students and faculty, remedies should establish norms that facilitate appropriate changes in operation.

Unofficial Responses — "Masking" Race Relations

Taking into account or placing civil rights enforcement into an organizational change context expands widely held interpretations of poorly designed and implemented civil rights enforcement. Interpreting obfuscating enforcement aspects produces similarly expanded insight. Claiming to have produced programs that were never undertaken, reifying social phenomena to justify taking no further action, presenting limited budget requests as accomplished outcomes — these are factors largely undetailed and overlooked as contributing to failure.

However, unofficial responses of this kind are not easy to interpret, particularly obfuscation, in the halfhearted, very amateurish character it adopts in desegregation plans and reports. No experienced higher education or civil rights leader, manager, or researcher would fail to observe the examples earlier presented in this study, but why does amateurish unofficial obfuscation characterize civil rights enforcement? Are desegregation planners and report writers inexperienced bureaucrats, exercising poor judgment under circumstances of weak supervision? Perhaps, top federal and state officials, mildly devoted to compliance, allow staff to engage in the sport of obfuscation because, if they win, the civil rights problem disappears and, if they lose and draw criticism, it is possible to disavow responsibility for uninformed plans and reports. If the game gets played long enough, stakeholders may grow tired and allow the problem to disappear. Perhaps, amateur obfuscation signals disdain, a form of arrogant dismissal of the problem without directly confronting stakeholders who stand to gain; stakeholders who stand to benefit simply possess too little influence.

At one level, obfuscating state and local enforcement is best interpreted as evidence of what Lindblom refers to as "People struggling with each other over terms of their cooperation" (Lindblom, 1980, p. 17), or what Mazmanian and Sabatier identify as "interaction of stakeholders involving both competition for power and efforts to develop more effective ways of addressing [civil rights policy] implementation" (Mazmanian & Sabatier, 1983, p. 21). Civil rights enforcement inevitably involves race- or gender-identifiable stakeholder groups interacting with one another and struggling for power. Setting the stage for such contests, the reviewed documents present increasingly apparent agreement that Title VI enforcement would not be taken seriously. However, why was such an agreement necessary? Were federal and state stakeholders involved in reaching it — most likely domestic policy leaders in Washington and state governors and higher education chancellors and system board members — concerned about destroying higher education? Were they concerned about improperly extending the reach of government? Were they concerned with inappropriately expanding budgets? Were they concerned with relinquishing power? Were they concerned about fueling uncontrollable race conflict? Raising expectations among African-American stakeholders and offending white stakeholders are well-known potential outcomes of past civil rights enforcement. Such outcomes are to be avoided, because ensuing race conflict will easily expand and become uncontrollable, once again challenging the nation's socioeconomic stability. U.S. society remains uncertain of its capacity to resolve race conflict, which has played a major role in its history, and certainly OCR, state higher education officials, and local campus leaders can affect the problem only in minor ways through expanded college and university opportunity. Such an interpretation of the obfuscation game involved in Title VI enforcement undercuts attempts to persuade the public that race conflict has declined to the point of no longer requiring government action. If this were the case, there would be little need to engage in obfuscation of enforcement failures, because few persons would view such failures with great concern.

Stated plainly, race conflict remains a dominant social issue. Interpreting civil rights enforcement outcomes and implementation as required effort, interpreting positive but brief and narrowly focused demographic trends in enrollment and employment as evidence of the elimination of race discrimination, failing constructively to acknowledge continuing race discrimination in desegregation plans, declining engagement of race discrimination as an important public issue, and claiming that repeal of segregation laws alone constitutes a sufficient remedy all constitute active strategies for the denial of civil rights. Such strategies provide undeniable evidence of serious race conflict and in this way undercut their own message. Such strategies and other obfuscations of enforcement may be interpreted as a modern version of an old-fashioned political phenomenon widely referred to in 1960s' race relations discourse as "masking." Masking typically describes interpersonal relations between individual whites and African-Americans, but descriptions of the phenomenon have been extended to describe the interaction of white and African-American bureaucrats, policymakers, and other stakeholders.

Ralph Ellison (1966, pp. 70–71) provides an applicable explanation:

America is a land of masking jokers. We wear the mask for purposes of aggression as well as for defense; when we are projecting the future and preserving the past. In short the motives hidden behind the mask are as numerous as the ambiguities the mask conceals.

(Masking) is a role which Negroes share with other Americans, and it might be more "Yankee" than anything else. It is a strategy common to the culture, and it is reinforced by our anti-intellectualism, by our tendency toward conformity and the related desire of the individual to be left alone; often simply by the desire to put more money in the bank. But basically the strategy grows out of our awareness of the joke at the center of the American identity. . . . The white American has charged the Negro American with being without past or tradition . . . just as he himself has been so charged by Europeans . . . ; and the Negro knows that both were "mammy-made" right here at home. What's more each secretly believes that he alone knows what is valid in the American experience, and that the other knows he knows but will not admit it, and each suspects the other of being at bottom a phony.

The white man's half-conscious awareness that his image of the Negro is false makes him suspect the Negro of always seeking to take him in, and assume his motives are anger and fear — which very often they are. On his side of the joke the Negro looks at the white man and finds it difficult to believe that . . . (whites) can be so absurdly self-deluded over the true interrelatedness of blackness and whiteness. To him the white man seems a hypocrite who boasts of a pure identity while standing with his humanity exposed to the world.

A visit tomorrow to Alabama, Georgia, Louisiana, Mississippi, or Washington, D.C., to discuss civil rights enforcement in higher education with major stakeholders would constitute one of the truest and most compelling "masking" experiences that Ellison insightfully could have imagined. The obfuscation responses in Title VI compliance reports mask ambiguities and aim aggressively and defensively at projecting the future and preserving the past. Underlying the experience of enforcement are feelings of hypocrisy on both sides: whites fear being taken in by African-American stakeholders' insistence upon continued race discrimination, and African-Americans interpret whites' token desegregation responses as disengenously unreflective of continuing racial injustice, which white consciousness must inevitably, at some level, acknowledge. At stake in Mississippi, Georgia, Alabama, and Louisiana is prescribing what is good in and for U.S. society, and each party to the disagreement claims superior knowledge, unwilling to admit belief in the other's superiority. At the broadest level, what compels civil rights enforcement is exposure of modern claims of race equity up against increasing new evidence — race riots in Florida and Pennsylvania, approval of Proposition 603 in California, the Army sex scandal, the Texaco race discrimination settlement — of continued denial of civil rights.

Masking supports civil rights enforcement as a policy game aimed at preventing race conflict that gave rise to civil rights laws, the brand and intensity of conflict with which U.S. society as a whole has never dealt successfully. Operating as a ritual, it draws attention, through limitedly expanding higher education opportunity, to a profound problem with which many people remain deeply concerned, it evokes discussion, and it offers small responses that disagreeing stakeholders can, at least temporarily, accept. However, without support from similar enforcement in other institutional sectors, the game eventually loses its meaning. Declining societywide, public support for civil rights undermines little-known enforcement rituals and other power struggles and, in this way, raises the importance of civil rights upon the nation's public agenda. In this optimistic interpretation, neoconservative policymakers seem to have miscalculated their efforts, perversely producing increased civil rights discourse and concern. However, conservative assaults continue to expand.

In March 1997 a group of four African-American and seven white plaintiffs instigated legal action against the Georgia university system, claiming that prior race-based desegregation policies have perpetuated segregation within the state's public higher education. The plaintiff group is notably diverse. One of the African-American plaintiffs is a teacher who graduated from Georgia College and State University, a TWI; one is a white teacher who graduated from Fort Valley State, a TBI; one is a white faculty member at Fort Valley; two black plaintiffs are married and have a child who attended an unspecified institution within the Georgia system. Two of the white plaintiffs are students and claim they were denied admission to University of Georgia's undergraduate degree program because of race admission policies — lower scoring "minority" students gained admission instead.

Citing 1994 student enrollment and faculty employment data, plaintiffs argue that public institutions within the Georgia system remain racially identifiable. Plaintiffs claim that disproportionately larger numbers of developmental studies students have been enrolling at TBIs, contributing to segregation and perpetuating the TBIs' reputation of academic inferiority. In support of their claim that TBIs are academically inferior, the plaintiffs' brief cites comparatively low standardized test score data for TBI students, and argues that TBIs pursue recruitment policies and programs aimed at attracting "non-white" students, faculty, and administrators. Racial identifiability of TBIs contributes to segregation at white institutions within the system.

The plaintiffs continue their argument claiming that various actions contribute to racial segregation, including

failure to implement systemwide admissions, retention, and graduation policies aimed at ending the racial identifiability and academic inferiority of TBIs;

failure to implement systemwide faculty employment and promotion policies;

allowing local institutions to recruit, hire, and promote faculty;

duplication of programs at TWIs and TBIs; and

failure to adhere to unspecified prior desegregation commitments.

Plaintiffs also claim that race-conscious admissions programs exist to promote "an unspecified, subjective determination of diversity. Many of these students would not be considered socially, educationally, or economically disadvantaged or as increasing the 'diversity' of the institution except for their status as non-white applicants, and therefore are being granted admissions based on their race" (*Woodson, et al. v. Georgia Board of Regents*, 1997, p. 7).

Plaintiffs further claim that race-conscious admissions policies do not foster desegregation, are "over-inclusive and under-inclusive," and are not narrowly tailored to achieve a compelling state interest. Race-conscious admissions policies, instead, deflect attention from the need for "realistic" desegregation, "persuading influential black legislators and citizens to not seek a truly desegregated higher education system; and as a token effort designed to appease black citizens. . . . The use of race in admitting students at these institutions has denied members of the represented class equality of treatment without regard to race" (*Woodson, et al. v. Georgia Board of Regents*, 1997, p. 8).

Matthew Billips, one of three lawyers for the plaintiffs, reportedly remarked that, "The remedy they have now is obviously not effective. . . . All it does is discriminate against innocent applicants on the basis of race while having no effective consequence on eliminating segregation" (Healy, 1997, p. A25). A second lawyer for the plaintiffs, A. Lee Parks, gained national notoriety in 1995 in a Supreme Court case dismantling a majority African-American voting district.

This legal argument emerged shortly after the Georgia Board of Regents decided to continue its race-based scholarship and other affirmative action programs even though Michael Bowers, the state attorney general, ruled such programs illegal in light of *Texas v. Hopwood* (1996), suggested eliminating them, and indicated that he would not defend them in court. Apparently, lawyers for the plaintiffs plan the same legal argument that proved successful in the *Hopwood* case — that race-based admissions policies contradict the Supreme Court's *Adarand Constructors Inc v. Pena* (1995).

REFERENCES

Ayres, Q. Whitfield. 1984. "Racial Desegregation in Higher Education." In *Implementation of Civil Rights Policy*, edited by Charles S. Bullock and Charles M. Lamb, pp. 118-147. Monterey, Calif.: Brooks/Cole.

Bakke v. Regents of the University of California, 438 U.S. 265 (1998).

Birnbaum, Robert. 1988. *How Colleges Work*. San Francisco, Calif.: Jossey-Bass.

Brown v. Board of Education, 347 U.S. 483 (1954).

Ellison, Ralph. 1966. *Shadow and Act*. New York: New American Library.

Healy, Patrick. 1997b. "Lawsuit Attacks Race-Based Policies in University System of Georgia." *Chronicle of Higher Education*, March 4, 1997, p. A25.

Lindblom, Charles. 1980. *The Policymaking Process*. Englewood Cliffs, N.J.: Prentice-Hall.

Mazmanian, Daniel A. and Sabatier, Paul A. 1983. *Implementation of Public Policy*. Glenview, Ill.: Scott, Foresman.

McPherson, Michael and Schapiro, Morton. 1991. *Keeping College Affordable*. Washington, D.C.: Brookings Institution.

Schmidt, Peter. 1997. "Rancor and Confusion Greet Change in South Carolina Budgeting." *Chronicle of Higher Education*, April 4, 1997, p. A26.

St. John, Edward P. 1989. "The Influence of Student Aid on Persistence." *Journal of Student Financial Aid*, 19 (1989): 52–68.

St. John, Edward P., Paulsen, Michael B., and Starkey, Johnny B. 1996. "The Nexus Between College Choice and Persistence." *Research in Higher Education*, 37 (1996): 175–220.

Texas v. Hopwood, 78 F. 3rd 932 (1996).

United States v. Fordice, 112 S. Ct. 2727 (1992).

U.S. General Accounting Office. 1996. *Higher Education Tuition Increasing Faster Than Household Income and Public Colleges' Costs*. Washington, D.C.: U.S. Government Printing Office.

Woodson, et al. v. Georgia Board of Regents, Unnumbered Civil Action, Plaintiff Brief, February 26, 1997.

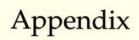

Appendix

TABLE A.1

Status of Minorities in Higher Education — Alabama Demographic Characteristics

Access to College — 1992

| | High School Graduates | | First-Time Freshmen | |
	Number	Percent	Number	Percent
White	24,446	63.0	23,036	67.0
Black	13,654	35.0	10,503	30.0
Hispanic	77	0.2	171	0.5

Full-Time Undergraduate Enrollment at TWIs and HBCUs

| | 1980 | | 1992 | | Percent Change, |
	Number	Percent	Number	Percent	1980–1992
Traditionally White Institutions					
Total	60,994	100	111,509	100	83
White	54,500	89	92,044	83	69
Black	5,320	9	15,643	14	194
Historically Black Colleges and Universities					
Total	8,587	100	12,841	100	50
White	277	3	974	8	252
Black	7,562	88	11,622	91	54

Bachelor's Degrees and Doctorates Awarded

| | 1979 | | 1991 | | Percent Change, |
	Number	Percent	Number	Percent	1979–1991
Bachelor's Degrees					
Total	16,345	100	18,308	100	12
White	13,217	81	15,126	83	14
Black	2,730	17	2,499	14	−8
Doctorates					
Total	267	100	396	100	48
White	222	83	277	70	25
Black	7	6	14	4	−18

Graduate and Professional Enrollment

| | 1980 | | 1992 | | Percent Change, |
	Number	Percent	Number	Percent	1980–1992
Graduate Enrollment					
Total	14,392	100	20,541	100	43
White	11,370	79	15,514	76	36
Black	1,862	13	2,490	12	34
First Professional Enrollment					
Total	3,281	100	3,389	100	3
White	2,995	91	2,945	87	−2
Black	168	5	288	9	71

188

Full-Time Faculty and Administrators — 1991

	Total	White		Black	
		Number	**Percent**	**Number**	**Percent**
Faculty	9,196	7,601	83	1,062	12
Administrators	556	477	86	75	13

Source: Southern Education Foundation. 1995. *Redeeming the Promise: Report of the Panel on Educational Opportunity and Postsecondary Desegregation* (p. A-7). Atlanta, Ga.: Southern Education Foundation.

TABLE A.2
Status of Minorities in Higher Education — Georgia Demographic Characteristics

Access to College — 1992

| | High School Graduates | | First-Time Freshmen | |
	Number	Percent	Number	Percent
White	35,284	64	22,916	73
Black	18,952	35	7,142	23
Hispanic	217	0	391	1

Full-Time Undergraduate Enrollment at TWIs and HBCUs

| | 1980 | | 1992 | | Percent Change, |
	Number	Percent	Number	Percent	1980–1992
Traditionally White Institutions					
Total	56,786	100	117,432	100	107
White	48,999	86	93,490	80	91
Black	5,985	11	17,799	15	197
Historically Black Colleges and Universities					
Total	4,586	100	6,688	100	46
White	86	8	235	4	−39
Black	4,030	88	6,359	95	58

Bachelor's Degrees and Doctorates Awarded

| | 1979 | | 1991 | | Percent Change, |
	Number	Percent	Number	Percent	1979–1991
Bachelor's Degrees					
Total	16,135	100	22,322	100	38
White	13,367	83	17,789	80	33
Black	2,397	15	3,367	15	40
Doctorates					
Total	530	100	827	100	56
White	417	79	528	64	27
Black	40	8	53	6	33

Graduate and Professional Enrollment

| | 1980 | | 1992 | | Percent Change, |
	Number	Percent	Number	Percent	1980–1992
Graduate Enrollment					
Total	22,193	100	32,935	100	48
White	17,462	79	24,744	75	42
Black	3,071	14	4,282	13	39
First Professional Enrollment					
Total	6,333	100	8,974	100	42
White	5,689	90	7,279	81	28
Black	481	8	986	111	5

Full-Time Faculty and Administrators — 1991

	Total	White		Black	
		Number	**Percent**	**Number**	**Percent**
Faculty	11,407	9,502	83	1,310	11
Administrators	1,163	1,088	87	137	12

Source: Southern Education Foundation. 1995. *Redeeming the Promise: Report of the Panel on Educational Opportunity and Postsecondary Desegregation* (p. A-15). Atlanta, Ga.: Southern Education Foundation.

TABLE A.3

Status of Minorities in Higher Education — Louisiana Demographic Characteristics

Access to College — 1992

	High School Graduates		First-Time Freshmen	
	Number	Percent	Number	Percent
White	19,198	60	14,364	63
Black	12,117	38	7,258	32
Hispanic	388	1	400	2

Full-Time Undergraduate Enrollment at TWIs and HBCUs

	1980		1992		Percent Change, 1980–1992
	Number	Percent	Number	Percent	
Traditionally White Institutions					
Total	73,521	100	93,824	100	28
White	60,167	82	74,688	80	24
Black	8,674	12	13,545	14	56
Historically Black Colleges and Universities					
Total	12,247	100	19,012	100	55
White	65	1	440	2	577
Black	11,679	95	18,310	96	57

Bachelor's Degrees and Doctorates Awarded

	1979		1991		Percent Change, 1979–1991
	Number	Percent	Number	Percent	
Bachelor's Degrees					
Total	14,765	100	16,309	100	10
White	11,171	76	11,906	73	7
Black	2,937	20	3,156	19	7
Doctorates					
Total	275	100	417	100	52
White	222	81	262	63	18
Black	11	4	11	3	0

Graduate and Professional Enrollment

	1980		1992		Percent Change, 1980–1992
	Number	Percent	Number	Percent	
Graduate Enrollment					
Total	17,401	100	24,599	100	41
White	13,178	76	17,259	70	31
Black	2,707	16	3,335	14	23
First Professional Enrollment					
Total	4,206	100	5,919	100	41
White	3,786	90	4,779	81	26
Black	280	7	575	10	105

Full-Time Faculty and Administrators — 1991

	Total	White		Black	
		Number	**Percent**	**Number**	**Percent**
Faculty	8,794	6,966	79	1,143	13
Administrators	726	599	83	101	14

Source: Southern Education Foundation. 1995. *Redeeming the Promise: Report of the Panel on Educational Opportunity and Postsecondary Desegregation* (p. A-23). Atlanta, Ga.: Southern Education Foundation.

TABLE A.4
Status of Minorities in Higher Education — Mississippi Demographic Characteristics

Access to College — 1992

| | High School Graduates | | First-Time Freshmen | |
	Number	Percent	Number	Percent
White	12,152	53.0	12,720	63.0
Black	10,495	46.0	7,040	35.0
Hispanic	50	0.2	74	0.4

Full-Time Undergraduate Enrollment at TWIs and HBCUs

| | 1980 | | 1992 | | Percent Change, 1980–1992 |
	Number	Percent	Number	Percent	
Traditionally White Institutions					
Total	26,937	100	67,683	100	151
White	24,920	93	52,335	77	110
Black	956	4	13,878	21	1,352
Historically Black Colleges and Universities					
Total	11,402	100	10,101	100	−11
White	130	1	106	1	−18
Black	11,076	97	9,911	98	−11

Bachelor's Degrees and Doctorates Awarded

| | 1979 | | 1991 | | Percent Change, 1979–1991 |
	Number	Percent	Number	Percent	
Bachelor's Degrees					
Total	8,682	100	9,106	100	5
White	6,307	73	7,017	77	11
Black	2,230	26	1,868	21	−16
Doctorates					
Total	216	100	340	100	57
White	187	87	249	73	33
Black	16	7	22	6	38

Graduate and Professional Enrollment

| | 1980 | | 1992 | | Percent Change, 1980–1992 |
	Number	Percent	Number	Percent	
Graduate Enrollment					
Total	8,236	100	10,444	100	27
White	5,616	68	7,142	68	27
Black	2,053	25	1,724	17	−16
First Professional Enrollment					
Total	1,642	100	1,800	100	3
White	1,540	94	1,630	91	−2
Black	81	5	112	6	71

Full-Time Faculty and Administrators — 1991

	Total	White		Black	
		Number	**Percent**	**Number**	**Percent**
Faculty	5,363	4,451	83	683	13
Administrators	238	203	85	33	14

Source: Southern Education Foundation. 1995. *Redeeming the Promise: Report of the Panel on Educational Opportunity and Postsecondary Desegregation* (p. A-31). Atlanta, Ga.: Southern Education Foundation.

Related Works

Social science researchers and policy analysts have failed to explore extensively the phenomenon of civil rights enforcement within the nation's higher education community. This observation does not overlook legal scholars' substantial analysis of case law attempting to formulate civil rights policies correctly.

The following works, drawn from a small volume of books, journal articles, and published reports, provide additional information about systemwide implementation of civil rights laws and policies within previously segregated public higher education communities.

Bullock, Charles S. and Charles M. Lamb, eds. 1984. *Implementation of Civil Rights Policy*. Monterey, Calif.: Brooks/Cole.

Dentler, Robert A., Catherine Baltzell, and Daniel Sullivan. 1983. *University on Trial*. Cambridge, Mass.: Abt Associates.

Halpern, Stephen C. 1995. *On the Limits of the Law*. Baltimore, Md.: Johns Hopkins University Press.

Orfield, Gary. 1990. *The Reagan Administration's Abandonment of Civil Rights Enforcement in Higher Education*. Washington, D.C.: Joint Center for Political and Economic Studies.

Southern Education Foundation. 1995. *Redeeming the Promise: Report of the Panel on Educational Opportunity and Postsecondary Desegregation*. Atlanta: Southern Education Foundation.

St. John, Edward P. forthcoming. "Higher Education Desegregation in the Post-*Fordice* Environment: An Historical Perspective." In *Readings on Equal Education*, edited by Richard Fossey. New York: AMS Press.

U.S. Commission on Civil Rights. 1981. *The Black/White Colleges: Dismantling the Dual System of Higher Education*, Clearinghouse Publication 66. Washington, D.C.: U.S. Commission on Civil Rights.

Wildman, Terry. 1976. "A Statistical Review of State Plans Submitted in Response to the *Pratt* Decision." In *Equality of Opportunity in Higher Education: Myth or Reality?*, edited by Paul Mohr, pp. 28–69. Lincoln, Neb.: Chicago-Southern Network.

Williams, John B., ed. 1988. *Desegregation of America's Colleges and Universities: Title VI Regulation of Higher Education*. New York: Teachers College Press.

The following list is a sampling of analyses of recent court cases addressing systemwide civil rights enforcement in previously segregated states.

Bunch, Kenyon D. and Grant B. Mindle. 1992. "Testing the Limits of Precedent: The Application of *Green* to the Desegregation of Higher Education." *Seton Hall Constitutional Law Journal*, 2 (1992): 541.

Days, Drew, III. 1984. "Minority Access to Higher Education in the Post-Bakke Era." *University of Colorado Law Review*, 55 (1984): 491.

Kujovich, Gil. 1987. "Equal Opportunity in Higher Education and the Black Public College: The Era of Separate but Equal." *Minnesota Law Review*, 72 (1987): 29.

Scott-Brown, Wendy. 1994. "Race Consciousness in Higher Education: Does 'Sound Education Policy' Support the Continued Existence of Historically Black Colleges?" *Emory Law Journal*, 43 (1994): 3.

Index

ABOUT THE AUTHOR

JOHN B. WILLIAMS is Professor of Education at the University of Alabama–Birmingham. He previously taught at Vanderbilt and Harvard. During several years at Harvard, he also served as Assistant to the President, as Assistant Dean of the Graduate School of Education, and as Interim Faculty Chairperson of the Urban Superintendents Program. For several years he served as founding director of an urban public school district–university collaborative, organizing and conducting community-based training programs aimed at improving schooling in New Jersey cities. He also has held a variety of positions in New Jersey state government and the federal government.

ISBN 0-275-95983-X

EAN

9 780275 959838

HARDCOVER BAR CODE

Riley